Contents

Introduction

In the early years of learning the knitting craft, I was eager to make something of "my own." It was more than finding just the right sweater or sock pattern. Despite spending hours browsing the pages of books, Ravelry, and magazines, I couldn't find the shape and the stitch patterning that best suited the yarn and gauge I was determined to use. I wanted a pullover, with a v-neck, set-in sleeves, and an all-over cable pattern that wasn't complex and was knit in DK-weight yarn with a gauge of about 6 stitches per inch (with the cables). It forced me down a rabbit hole of math, shape, and construction to make different stitch patterns fit into the silhouette I had envisioned. Only good came from that experience (a good that led to my knitwear design life), but I've seen many a knitter experience frustration at the thought of having to go through such intense effort.

You might just be one of those knitters, someone eager to broaden your skills and personalization without diving into the depths of learning a whole new trade. Perhaps you are eager to try new stitch patterns and techniques without committing to decisions about construction. Maybe it's simply about personal, interactive pattern-making to help you achieve your yarn's outcome. Whatever the reason, this blend of recipes plus dictionary offers a unique experience in the craft of knitting.

In chapter 1, we will go through how to use this book. From measurements to yarn selection, swatching, and finishing instructions, you'll learn everything about how to best "switch and knit" for the various patterns ahead.

The core of *Switch & Knit*, chapter 2, includes 12 design "recipes," with instructions for every applicable gauge. Choose your pattern recipe, such as a hat or shawl, select the gauge that most matches yours, and follow the table column for the specific numbered instructions in the desired size. I've tried to include a varied portfolio of projects to suit whatever you might be craving.

The beauty, though, is that every design recipe is based on a "4-stitch multiple" stitch pattern. Chapters 3 through 6 make up a dictionary of more than 80 written and charted stitch patterns. I've even made sure they are easy to read, whether you are knitting flat or in the round. Each stitch pattern is interchangeable with any recipe, offering a wealth of new fabrics for every personality.

It doesn't matter what your yarn, stitch gauge, or size is, because the instructions in these pages promise a beautiful, engaging experience from start to finish.

CHAPTER 1

HOW TO SWITCH AND KNIT

The formatting of these interactive patterns might look a little unusual, but I will walk you through the basic steps, from choosing yarn to reading the instructions, so you have a great experience from start to finish.

Step One: Pick the Perfect Yarn

The yarn is the star of the show! Understanding its weight and fiber makeup will have a big impact on the success of your final piece. That knowledge will also guide you in choosing an appropriate gauge and stitch pattern for a beautiful transformation into a final knitted piece.

YARN WEIGHT STANDARDS

First things first: Know the weight of your yarn. This ensures that it is appropriate for the pattern selection. For example, a bulky-weight yarn might not be the best choice for a summery tank top.

The Craft Yarn Council website has a booklet and downloadable symbol chart you can use to confirm your chosen yarn. The table below reflects the general guidelines.

FIBER CONTENT

After the weight of the yarn, look at the fibers used in the makeup. There are a wealth of amazing fibers and blends available, and they each offer their own distinct effect on the fabric you'll end up with. Here's a breakdown of the major fibers and materials you'll find:

- **Wool:** This sheep fiber has a "natural memory," which helps the stitches remember what to do with themselves. What that means for you is that the fabric wants to return to its natural shape, making it ideal for every level of knitter and a wide range of stitch patterns. Wool is lightweight, warm, and breathable.
- **Superwash wool:** Superwash wool has all the same properties of regular wool but with more smoothness. Because the scales have been removed or glued down, you

Standard Yarn Weight System

Categories of yarn, gauge ranges, and recommended needle and hook sizes

Yarn Weight Symbol & Category Names	0 LACE	1 SUPER FINE	2 FINE	3 LIGHT	4 MEDIUM	5 BULKY	6 SUPER BULKY	7 JUMBO
Type of Yarns in Category	Fingering, 10-Count Crochet Thread	Sock, Fingering, Baby	Sport, Baby	DK, Light Worsted	Worsted, Afghan, Aran	Chunky, Craft, Rug	Bulky, Roving	Jumbo, Roving
Knit Gauge Range in Stockinette Stitch to 4 inches*	33–40 sts**	27–32 sts	23–26 sts	21–24 st	16–20 sts	12–15 sts	7–11 sts	6 sts and fewer
Recommended Needle in Metric Size Range	1.5–2.25 mm	2.25–3.25 mm	3.25–3.75 mm	3.75–4.5 mm	4.5–5.5 mm	5.5–8 mm	8–12.75 mm	12.75 mm and larger
Recommended Needle in U.S. Size Range	000 to 1	1 to 3	3 to 5	5 to 7	7 to 9	9 to 11	11 to 17	17 and larger
Crochet Gauge Ranges in Single Crochet to 4 inches*	32–42 double crochets**	21–32 sts	16–20 sts	12–17 sts	11–14 sts	8–11 sts	7–9 sts	6 sts and fewer
Recommended Hook in Metric Size Range	Steel*** 1.6–1.4 mm Regular hook 2.25 mm	2.25–3.5 mm	3.5–4.5 mm	4.5–5.5 mm	5.5–6.5 mm	6.5–9 mm	9–15 mm	15 mm and larger
Recommended Hook in U.S. Size Range	Steel 6, 7, 8*** Regular hook B–1	B–1 to E–4	E–4 to 7	7 to I–9	I–9 to K–10½	K–10½ to M–13	M–13 to Q	Q and larger

* GUIDELINES ONLY: The above reflect the most commonly used gauges and needle or hook sizes for specific yarn categories.

** Lace weight yarns are usually knitted or crocheted on larger needles and hooks to create lacy, openwork patterns. Accordingly, a gauge range is difficult to determine. Always follow the gauge stated in your pattern.

*** Steel crochet hooks are sized differently from regular hooks—the higher the number, the smaller the hook, which is the reverse of regular hook sizing.

Source: Craft Yarn Council of America's **www.YarnStandards.com**

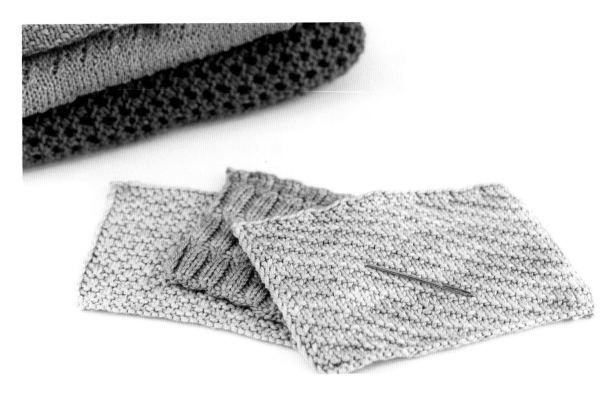

can agitate it a little more when washing without worrying about felting (i.e., it's easier to care for).

- **Alpaca:** This protein fiber is dense, warm, and often smooth, though it isn't elastic. That lack of elasticity means that it might droop, depending on your project and looseness of gauge, but it has a lovely drape that is addictive.
- **Mohair:** This angora goat fiber is soft and distinctive, though it can be rather slippery. The unique halo and elasticity are fascinating to work with, especially when blended with stronger fibers.
- **Luxury fibers:** Cashmere, bison, yak, and qiviut, to name a few, are down (or undercoat) hairs with unparalleled softness and insulation. The downside to them is how short and fine the fiber is; it means that they are better blended with something stronger and more elastic to compensate.
- **Silk:** Part animal, part plant, silk adds a delicious luster, as well as a luminous, smooth sheen to fabrics. It is quite inelastic and heavy on its own, so it is best used in a blend with something like wool.
- **Cotton:** Softness reigns supreme with this plant fiber, perfect for next-to-skin projects. On its own, it can be heavy (droopy) and inelastic, so choose your projects with this quality in mind. Blended with a breathable fiber, cotton provides a lovely drape and additional strength.

- **Linen and hemp:** Coming from the stalk of the plant, these fibers are super strong, lustrous, and light. They boast a stunning drape and a softness that gets better with each washing. They aren't warm or elastic, though, so they can overpower the stitch pattern you choose.
- **Cellulose fibers:** Bamboo, flax, and rayon (there are others) all come from a lengthy chemical process that breaks down a plant's cellulose. Smooth, strong, drapey, and silky are the major qualities they boast, but there's one significant reason to avoid them on their own: Their lack of surface texture means that the stitches can't hold on to each other, and so the fabric will stretch with gravity.
- **Synthetic fibers:** Each synthetic fiber (acrylic, nylon, Lycra) boasts its own individual qualities, the most common being softness and durability. They are usually an inexpensive option for knitters. Machine washable, they hold shape well, though they might not respond to blocking as hoped for (in fact, acrylic can melt from too much heat).

What do you do with this fiber content knowledge? Fine-tune your pattern selection. If you're aiming for a super lacy piece, you might prefer to find a yarn that holds its shape well, is lightweight, and has drape versus a heavy, dense yarn that is super warm and bulky.

Step Two: Above All Else, SWATCH

Years ago, I met a knitter working on a giant, mitered square jacket. It was glorious, with all the stripes and changing directions from the individual blocks. Nearly done and about to advance to the seaming stage, she approached me at the end of one of my gauge workshops. Despite being an advanced knitter for more than thirty years, she was dumbfounded when she overheard me talking to another knitter about the difference between finished (or blocked) gauge and unfinished (unblocked) gauge.

She grabbed my arm, panic clear on her face. "I didn't swatch because I am always close to gauge. You're telling me my jacket might not fit?"

"Well . . . I hope it does."

I ran into her a few days later at the local yarn store, her squares all spread out on a table. She was ripping out the yarn of a sleeve, winding the wrinkled yarn back into a ball.

"What's going on?" I asked.

Her sigh was as heavy as I'd ever heard from a fellow knitter. "You were right. I should have swatched. I went home after talking to you and washed a sleeve like I planned to wash the sweater and . . . and . . ."—she sighed again—"it would be two inches too small. All this work and I wouldn't even be able to wear it!"

"Gosh. I am so sorry!"

"It's OK. I will make a few more squares and size up the main body and just be able to reknit the sleeves for the next size up, too, since my gauge works with those measurements to fit better."

And sure enough, when I ran into her again a few months later, she was wearing her gorgeous new jacket with pride.

There's a moral to this story: Swatch, swatch, swatch before you move any further.

And here's how you do it.

Needle Sizes

Millimeter Range	U.S. Size Range
1.50 mm	000
1.75 mm	00
2 mm	0
2.25 mm	1
2.75 mm	2
3 mm	
3.125 mm	3
3.25 mm	3
3.50 mm	4
3.75 mm	5
4 mm	6
4.25 mm	6
4.50 mm	7
5 mm	8
5.25 mm	9
5.50 mm	9
5.75 mm	10
6 mm	10
6.50 mm	10 ½
7 mm	
8 mm	11
9 mm	13
10 mm	15
12.50 mm	17
12.75 mm	17
15 mm	19

HOW TO SWATCH

With the same needles you plan to use and the yarn you intend, make a best guess and cast on what you think will be six inches' worth. Yes, six inches. We want to ensure that we are far enough away from the edges for a flat measurement.

It doesn't matter whether you add a Garter edging or slipped stitches or whatever to the borders of your swatch. We're focusing on the stitch pattern itself on the inside center. My favorite way to swatch is to cast on two extra stitches and work like this: K1, work stitch pattern to last st, k1. It's just a Garter selvedge edge. Simple. Clean. Easy to follow.

Work six inches' worth of rows in the stitch pattern you plan to use. If you have more than one stitch pattern, repeat the swatching steps for each pattern.

FIRST MEASURE

Using your favorite measuring tool, measure four inches' worth of stitches and rows in the center of your swatch. Mark these as your UNFINISHED gauge, or what I call the "hot off the needles gauge." It's a handy reference for later when you need to get more specific on row length, in particular (see Row Lengths & Gauge, page 8), or make length adjustments (see Row Length Adjustments, page 8).

WASH AND BLOCK

Now, here's the trick: Wash and dry your swatch exactly as you plan to wash and dry the final garment. If you will hand wash and lay flat to dry your final sweater, do that. If you want to machine wash and low-heat dry, do that. If you will stretch lace out with pins after soaking, then you'll stretch out your swatch with pins after soaking. If you want to hit it with hot steam, then hit the swatch with hot steam (my favorite method for that first block).

SECOND MEASURE

Once your swatch is really (really) dry, take measurements just like before. Don't stretch or pin things down. Just lay it flat and count those stitches and rows over four inches. This is your FINISHED gauge and what you want to use for the pattern. Why? Because it is what determines the final size. (Side note: Use the finished, blocked gauge for every single pattern by every single designer anywhere in the world.)

TAKE IN EVERYTHING ELSE

But there's more to swatching than just gauge. This is your opportunity to see how the stitch pattern looks in the yarn, how the yarn handles, whether you need to make any color or needle adjustments. Does it look how you hoped? Is it the right yarn? Did the colors bleed and, if so, what will you need to do to mitigate that effect? Does it seem soft enough or will it pill? The swatch is like our crystal ball showing us the future of our hoped-for sample. We get to be like fortune-tellers, taking the vision to make wise choices for the finished product.

AN ADDENDUM

A single stitch can tip the scale. One row may be the difference between victory and defeat (my rip on the Emperor's quote in *Mulan*). OK, that might be a little dramatic, but I want to bring one point home: Gauge is a fickle, fickle mistress that promises nothing.

I can already hear your thoughts, "Geez, thanks a lot for making me do all that work for nothing." Wink. Let me clarify. . . . There are things that can affect your gauge: the time of day you knit, your emotions, changing the needles (which is why I stressed using the same needles to swatch), and even the weather. Compare your relaxed morning stitches to those you knit when you're mad at your partner for felting your favorite pair of handknit socks in the dryer (I'm still bitter). In knitting, there will be variation, inconsistency, and even dramatic change. Practice, of course, makes perfect. And then there's learning to make adjustments as you go with the flow. Practice, adjust, and practice some more. The point through it all, just as my friend learned with her jacket, is to not give up. Just keep swatching.

Step Three: Choose a Recipe

I wrote the pattern recipes in this book for a variety of sizes and gauges; as a result, there are certain segments left purposefully flexible for your preference. Let's start at the beginning to break down the areas you'll want to pay attention to when reading the patterns.

SKILL LEVEL

Every pattern in this book is suitable for the Advanced Beginner to Intermediate knitter. You should know about shaping, continuing a pattern as established, construction, and the bulk of foundational stitches (decreases, increases, etc.).

STITCH PATTERNS

Here I've indicated how many stitch patterns are used in the pattern recipe (most call for only one). I call them Fave Patterns, and you may select these from any of the stitch patterns in the dictionary section of the book. If you want to use more than one stitch pattern, though, go for it!

FINISHED MEASUREMENTS

For accurate sizing, use your final, blocked, finished gauge for every pattern recipe in the book. Because of the slight variations in gauge, the final measurements presented take the average of all the offered gauges and round them to the closest approximate. For garments, you'll find an additional chart of gauge-specific bust measurements for the sake of fit. Each pattern offers suggested ease, or variance, for selecting a size.

YARN REQUIREMENTS

Once you've swatched with your desired stitch patterns, you'll know what your stitch gauge is running. Use this number and your size to follow the table given in each pattern to determine the amount of yarn required.

NEEDLES & NOTIONS

This is rather self-explanatory. I offer suggestions on needle size based on the intended drape and fit of the pattern itself. You may have other notions to use depending on your stitch pattern, such as cable needles or stitch markers.

SAMPLE PROJECT

In every pattern, I will show what yarns, gauge, and stitch patterns were used in the pictured example.

PATTERN NOTES

These notes describe the basic construction of the piece and any special things to keep in mind. For example, for a garment that has seaming, it'll note that the pattern includes the selvedge stitch for seaming, so you don't have to worry about it.

PATTERN INSTRUCTIONS

Every instruction that is dependent on gauge/size will feature a "_____" (blank space symbol) followed by a table. The table will determine the number that fits in the _____ (blank space). The table presents the sizes along the top columns, with the smallest size on the left and the largest size on the right. In the rows to the left, you'll find the finished gauge list to work from.

In the pattern, locate your finished gauge and then the instruction based on your size to the right. Let's look at an example.

Using the Table

Cast on _____ sts:

Gauge	14³/₄" / 37.5cm	16" / 40.5cm	17¹/₂" / 44.5cm	19" / 48.5cm	20¹/₂" / 52cm	22¹/₄" / 56.5cm
3	44	48	52	56	60	68
4	60	64	72	76	84	88
5	72	80	88	96	104	112
6	88	96	104	116	124	132
7	100	112	124	132	144	156
8	116	128	140	152	164	176

If I were knitting this hat with a gauge of 5 sts per inch for a 16" / 40.5 cm circumference, I would look at the third row and second column to find the number 80. That means you must cast on 80 sts. Then move on to the next instruction.

Table Notes to Remember

1. If only ONE number is indicated, it is for all the gauges/sizes.
2. If a 0 is presented in the table, it means that there is nothing for your size/gauge to do, so ignore it and move on to the next instruction.
3. It might be helpful to circle all the numbers that pertain to your gauge/size for quick reference.

SCHEMATIC DRAWINGS

Each pattern recipe in the book includes a schematic. The measurements have taken all the listed gauges in the pattern and rounded them to an average. They are presented from smallest to largest, in both inches and centimeters.

I encourage you to reference the schematics throughout the knitting. Doing so will ensure that your shaping is looking as it is supposed to and guide you in areas where you can make personal length adjustments. These drawings are especially helpful during the blocking process.

ROW LENGTHS & GAUGE

Every pattern recipe is written to a specific length, but row gauge is the most fickle of areas to work with without a little math know-how.

When you read a line that says, "Work until piece measures xx" / xx cm," here's how to go about knowing how long that is:

1. To calculate how many rows that means to work, multiply the "Length Stated in Inches" by the "Finished Row Gauge" (see page 5) to get the number of rows to work. So let's say the pattern says to work for 10" / 25 cm. If your finished row gauge is 5 rows per inch, then you will work 50 rows (10 x 5 = 50).
2. Maybe you'd rather pull out your tape measure? Calculate the difference between your "Unfinished Row Gauge" and the "Finished Length." Divide "Number of Finished Rows" by your "Unfinished Row Gauge" to get the "Working Length." So 50 rows at a working, unfinished row gauge of 4.5 rows per inch means that your hot-off-the-needles length should measure 11.1" / 28 cm.

ROW LENGTH ADJUSTMENTS

You may find that you prefer to adjust the length to your own preferences. The easiest place to do that is within the "work even" sections (you'll notice these areas easily in the schematics). The second option is to adjust the rate of increasing or decreasing within shaping sections (such as a sleeve armhole).

1. First, how many rows? Check the schematic measurements, determine your difference, and calculate the number of rows based on your finished row gauge. For example, a

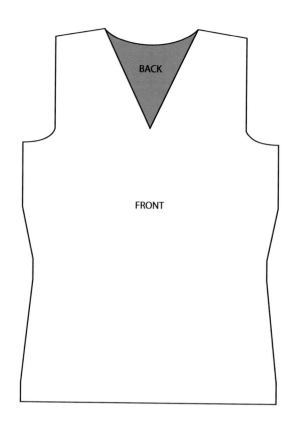

pattern calls for 10" / 25 cm, but you need 8" / 20 cm at a gauge of 5 sts per inch. That means you'll require 40 rows to decrease/increase over.

2. How many decreases/increases do you need? Take the largest number and subtract the smallest number. For example, in a sleep cap, we might need to decrease a total of 10 stitches over 50 rows, which turns out to be 5 stitches decreased on each side. 50 rows divided by 5 one-side decreases means that you'd decrease each side every 10 rows. So, remember that 5 (or 10 if you are only decreasing 1 stitch per row).
3. Calculate: 40 rows divided by 5 decreases = decrease every 8 rows.

Trickier Tapers

Say you have a non-whole-number result, like 42 rows divided by 5 = 8.4. That requires a wee bit more math:

1. Take the decimal and break it down into two numbers: the whole number before the decimal and the next higher even whole number, so 8 and 10.
2. Determine "First Rate": Take the "Higher Even Number" (10) and multiply it by the "Total Number of Decreases" (5). Example:

10 x 5 = 50. Then subtract the "Total Number of Rows" (50 - 42 = 8). And then divide that by 2 (8 divided by 2 = 4). This is your "First Rate" for your "Lowest Even Number": You'll decrease every 8 rows 4 times.

3. Determine "Second Rate": Now, subtract your answer from "First Rate" from the "Total Number of Decreases" (5 - 4 = 1). This is your "Second Rate" for your "Highest Even Number." You'll decrease every 10 rows 1 time.

Simplifying that result for your pattern looks like this: Work Dec Row every 8 rows 4 times and then every 10 rows 1 time.

Step Four: Select a Stitch

Chapters 3–6 are where you will find all of the wonderful stitch patterns to work with. "Knits and Purls," "Lace," "Cables," and "Texture" offer more than 80 different stitch patterns for fun variety. Each stitch pattern is written and charted in both flat and circular formats, so they are accessible to everyone.

Once you've selected your "Fave Pattern" for your recipe, you'll plug it in where stated in the instructions. For example, if the instruction reads:

K1, work Fave patt to last st, k1,

and you've selected K2p2 Rib (page 102) as your Fave Pattern, the row would be worked just like this:

K1, *k2, p2; rep from * to last st, k1.

Or, if you chose Wide Open (page 119), it would knit up like this:

K1, *ssk, yo twice, k2tog; rep from * to last st, k1.

Essentially, you'll take your chosen Fave Pattern and work it between the asterisk and the semicolon in the instructions.

Now you're ready to get started! Happy, happy exploration!

Reading Charts

Flat charts are read from right to left on right-side rows and left to right on wrong-side rows. It gets a little weird when reading wrong-side rows because you'll need to do the opposite of what the stitch symbol looks like. For example, a blank square indicates a knit on the right side, but on the wrong side, it would be a purl. The reason for this is so that the chart can be a visual representation of what the right side of your fabric looks like.

Circular charts are read from right to left on every row. Also, every stitch symbol is exactly what it says it is (i.e., a blank square means knit on every row it appears in).

Always consult the stitch key to understand what the symbols mean.

CHAPTER 2

PATTERN RECIPES

From socks or scarves to shawls or sweaters, you'll find a pattern recipe here to suit every personality or level. Simply choose your recipe, select the gauge that most matches yours, find a stitch pattern that suits the mood, and you're set to make a project uniquely yours.

COWL-NECK PULLOVER

Lush and cozy, this decadent pullover adds elegance and sophistication to any wardrobe. It features a reverse Stockinette stitch cowl neck, and, paired with your favorite stitch pattern, the look is endlessly addictive and flattering.

SKILL LEVEL
Intermediate

STITCH PATTERN
Choose one stitch pattern (the pattern recipe will refer to it as Fave patt) for the body. *The sample shown uses Oblique Rib (page 107).*

FINISHED MEASUREMENTS
Bust Circumference:

Gauge	32" / 81.5 cm	36½" / 92.5 cm	40" / 101.5 cm	44½" / 113 cm	48" / 122 cm	52½" / 133.5 cm	56" / 142 cm
3	32" / 81.5 cm	37.25" / 94.5 cm	40" / 101.5 cm	45.25" / 115 cm	48" / 122 cm	53.25" / 135.5 cm	56" / 142 cm
4	32" / 81.5 cm	36" / 91.5 cm	40" / 101.5 cm	44" / 112 cm	48" / 122 cm	52" / 132 cm	56" / 142 cm
5	32" / 81.5 cm	36.75" / 93.5 cm	40" / 101.5 cm	44.75" / 113.5 cm	48" / 122 cm	52.75" / 134 cm	56" / 142 cm
6	32" / 81.5 cm	36" / 91.5 cm	40" / 101.5 cm	44" / 112 cm	48" / 122 cm	52" / 132 cm	56" / 142 cm
7	32" / 81.5 cm	36.5" / 92.5 cm	40" / 101.5 cm	44.5" / 113 cm	48" / 122 cm	52.5" / 133.5 cm	56" / 142 cm
8	32" / 81.5 cm	36" / 91.5 cm	40" / 101.5 cm	44" / 112 cm	48" / 122 cm	52" / 132 cm	56" / 142 cm

The pattern will reference the averaged, seamed bust circumference measurements throughout the pattern charts and lengths: 32 (36½, 40, 44½, 48, 52½, 56)" / 81.5 (92.5, 101.5, 113, 122, 133.5, 142) cm.
Choose the size that is approx. 2–2¾" / 5–7 cm larger than your actual bust circumference.
Garment Length: 23¾ (24¾, 25¾, 26¾, 27¼, 27¾, 28¼)" / 60.5 (63, 65.5, 68, 69, 70.5, 72) cm
Sample size is 36¾" / 93.5 cm bust circumference.

YARN REQUIREMENTS

Gauge	32" / 81.5 cm	36½" / 92.5 cm	40" / 101.5 cm	44½" / 113 cm	48" / 122 cm	52½" / 133.5 cm	56" / 142 cm
3	650 yds / 594 m	735 yds / 672 m	815 yds / 745 m	925 yds / 846 m	1015 yds / 928 m	1120 yds / 1024 m	1215 yds / 1111 m
4	840 yds / 768 m	935 yds / 855 m	1030 yds / 942 m	1155 yds / 1056 m	1285 yds / 1175 m	1425 yds / 1303 m	1560 yds / 1426 m
5	1480 yds / 1353 m	1630 yds / 1490 m	1800 yds / 1646 m	2040 yds / 1865 m	2240 yds / 2048 m	2485 yds / 2272 m	2750 yds / 2515 m
6	1880 yds / 1719 m	2095 yds / 1916 m	2320 yds / 2121 m	2630 yds / 2405 m	2875 yds / 2629 m	3195 yds / 2922 m	3495 yds / 3196 m
7	2085 yds / 1907 m	2380 yds / 2176 m	2610 yds / 2387 m	2975 yds / 2720 m	3250 yds / 2972 m	3585 yds / 3278 m	3935 yds / 3598 m
8	2325 yds / 2126 m	2610 yds / 2387 m	2925 yds / 2675 m	3275 yds / 2995 m	3610 yds / 3301 m	4005 yds / 3662 m	4405 yds / 4028 m

NEEDLES & NOTIONS

Choose a needle size that is slightly larger than recommended for your yarn so as to achieve a relaxed drape.

- Set of needles (for the body) in the size necessary to obtain the desired gauge
- Circular needles (for the collar), 24" / 60 cm in length, in the same size as the body set
- Circular needles (for the collar), 24" / 60 cm in length, one size larger than the body set
- Stitch marker
- Yarn needle

SAMPLE PROJECT

The sample pullover shown is worked with 6 skeins Bernat Satin in Sultana (200 yards / 182 m per 3.5 oz / 100 g skein; 100% acrylic) with a finished gauge of 4 sts and 6 rows = 1" / 2.5 cm.

PATTERN NOTES

- The pullover is worked flat in pieces and then seamed. Because of the seaming, 2 sts have been added to the instructions, 1 on either side of your desired stitch pattern, that you'll knit on every row.
- The collar is worked in the round after seaming.
- Only work as instructed for your size. If the number for your size and gauge in the table is 0, omit those rows and/or stitches and move on to the next indicated stitch/ row instructions.

PATTERN Cowl-Neck Pullover

BACK

Hem

With smaller needles, CO ____ sts:

		32" / 81.5 cm	36½" / 92.5 cm	40" / 101.5 cm	44½" / 113 cm	48" / 122 cm	52½" / 133.5 cm	56" / 142 cm
Gauge	3	54	58	66	70	78	82	90
	4	70	78	86	94	102	110	118
	5	86	94	106	114	126	134	146
	6	102	114	126	138	150	162	174
	7	118	134	146	162	174	190	202
	8	138	154	170	186	202	218	234

Rib Row (RS): K1, *k2, p2; rep from * to last st, k1.
Rep Rib Row until back measures a finished length of approx. 1" / 2.5 cm from cast-on edge, ending with a WS row.

Body

Change to Fave patt for the body as follows:
Row 1 (RS): K1, work RS row of Fave patt to last st, k1.
Row 2 (WS): K1, work WS row of Fave patt to last st, k1.
Rep Rows 1–2, continuing the rows of Fave patt to the end and then repeating, until back measures a finished length of 2" / 5 cm from cast-on edge, ending with a WS row.

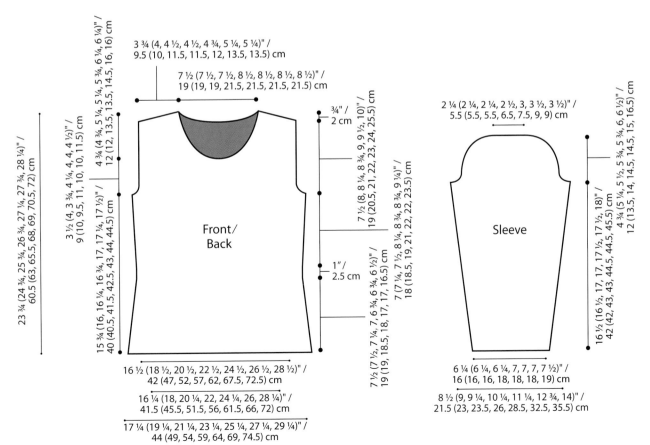

Shape Waist

Dec Row (RS): K1, ssk, maintain est Fave patt to last 3 sts, k2tog, k1. 2 sts dec'd.
Rep Dec Row every ____ rows:

Gauge	32" / 81.5 cm	36½" / 92.5 cm	40" / 101.5 cm	44½" / 113 cm	48" / 122 cm	52½" / 133.5 cm	56" / 142 cm
3	0	0	0	10	10	10	0
4	0	0	16	0	14	14	14
5	20	20	0	18	0	0	16
6	10	10	10	10	0	0	8
7	12	12	12	0	10	10	10
8	8	8	8	8	8	8	0

____ more time(s):

Gauge	32" / 81.5 cm	36½" / 92.5 cm	40" / 101.5 cm	44½" / 113 cm	48" / 122 cm	52½" / 133.5 cm	56" / 142 cm
3	0	0	0	1	1	1	0
4	0	0	1	0	1	1	1
5	1	1	0	1	0	0	1
6	1	1	2	3	0	0	1
7	2	2	3	0	1	1	2
8	1	1	3	4	5	5	0

Then rep Dec Row every ____ rows:

Gauge	32" / 81.5 cm	36½" / 92.5 cm	40" / 101.5 cm	44½" / 113 cm	48" / 122 cm	52½" / 133.5 cm	56" / 142 cm
3	12	12	12	0	0	0	10
4	18	18	0	16	0	0	0
5	0	0	20	0	18	18	0
6	12	12	12	0	10	10	10
7	14	14	0	12	12	12	12
8	10	10	10	10	0	0	8

____ more times:

Gauge	32" / 81.5 cm	36½" / 92.5 cm	40" / 101.5 cm	44½" / 113 cm	48" / 122 cm	52½" / 133.5 cm	56" / 142 cm
3	1	1	1	0	0	0	1
4	1	1	0	1	0	0	0
5	0	0	1	0	1	1	0
6	2	2	1	0	3	3	2
7	1	1	0	3	2	2	1
8	4	4	2	1	0	0	5

____ sts rem:

Gauge	32" / 81.5 cm	36½" / 92.5 cm	40" / 101.5 cm	44½" / 113 cm	48" / 122 cm	52½" / 133.5 cm	56" / 142 cm
3	50	54	62	66	74	78	86
4	66	74	82	90	98	106	114
5	82	90	102	110	122	130	142
6	94	106	118	130	142	154	166
7	110	126	138	154	166	182	194
8	126	142	158	174	190	206	222

Work even in est pattern until back measures a finished length of 8¾ (8¾, 8¾, 8¼, 8¼, 8½, 8¼)" / 22 (22, 22, 21, 21, 21.5, 21) cm from cast-on edge, ending with a WS row.
Inc Row (RS): K1, M1, maintain est patt to last st, M1, k1. 2 sts inc'd.
Rep Inc Row every __ rows:

Gauge	32" / 81.5 cm	36½" / 92.5 cm	40" / 101.5 cm	44½" / 113 cm	48" / 122 cm	52½" / 133.5 cm	56" / 142 cm
3	0	0	0	12	0	0	0
4	0	0	0	0	0	0	0
5	0	18	0	0	0	22	0
6	20	0	22	24	0	0	26
7	0	24	0	0	28	28	0
8	0	26	28	30	0	0	0

___ more time(s):

Gauge	32" / 81.5 cm	36½" / 92.5 cm	40" / 101.5 cm	44½" / 113 cm	48" / 122 cm	52½" / 133.5 cm	56" / 142 cm
3	0	0	0	1	0	0	0
4	0	0	0	0	0	0	0
5	0	1	0	0	0	1	0
6	1	0	1	1	0	0	1
7	0	1	0	0	1	1	0
8	0	1	1	1	0	0	0

Then rep Inc Row every ___ rows:

Gauge	32" / 81.5 cm	36½" / 92.5 cm	40" / 101.5 cm	44½" / 113 cm	48" / 122 cm	52½" / 133.5 cm	56" / 142 cm
3	0	12	0	0	0	14	0
4	0	0	0	0	0	0	0
5	0	0	0	22	0	0	0
6	0	22	0	0	26	26	0
7	24	0	26	28	0	0	30
8	26	0	0	0	32	32	34

___ more times:

Gauge	32" / 81.5 cm	36½" / 92.5 cm	40" / 101.5 cm	44½" / 113 cm	48" / 122 cm	52½" / 133.5 cm	56" / 142 cm
3	0	1	0	0	0	1	0
4	0	0	0	0	0	0	0
5	0	0	0	1	0	0	0
6	0	1	0	0	1	1	0
7	1	0	1	1	0	0	1
8	1	0	0	0	1	1	1

___ sts rem:

Gauge	32" / 81.5 cm	36½" / 92.5 cm	40" / 101.5 cm	44½" / 113 cm	48" / 122 cm	52½" / 133.5 cm	56" / 142 cm
3	50	58	62	70	74	82	86
4	66	74	82	90	98	106	114
5	82	94	102	114	122	134	142
6	98	110	122	134	146	158	170
7	114	130	142	158	170	186	198
8	130	146	162	178	194	210	226

Work even in est pattern until back measures a finished length of 15¾ (16, 16¼, 16¾, 17, 17¼, 17½)" / 40 (40.5, 41.5, 42.5, 43, 44, 44.5) cm from cast-on edge, ending with a WS row.

Armhole

BO ___ sts at beg of next 2 rows:

Gauge	32" / 81.5 cm	36½" / 92.5 cm	40" / 101.5 cm	44½" / 113 cm	48" / 122 cm	52½" / 133.5 cm	56" / 142 cm
3	1	3	3	4	5	6	7
4	2	3	4	5	6	8	10
5	2	4	5	7	8	10	12
6	3	4	6	7	10	12	15
7	3	6	7	9	11	14	17
8	3	6	8	10	13	16	20

___ sts rem:

Gauge	32" / 81.5 cm	36½" / 92.5 cm	40" / 101.5 cm	44½" / 113 cm	48" / 122 cm	52½" / 133.5 cm	56" / 142 cm
3	48	52	56	62	64	70	72
4	62	68	74	80	86	90	94
5	78	86	92	100	106	114	118
6	92	102	110	120	126	134	140
7	108	118	128	140	148	158	164
8	124	134	146	158	168	178	186

Dec Row (RS): K1, ssk, maintain est patt to last 3 sts, k2tog, k1. 2 sts dec'd.
Rep Dec Row every RS row ____ more times:

Gauge	32" / 81.5 cm	36½" / 92.5 cm	40" / 101.5 cm	44½" / 113 cm	48" / 122 cm	52½" / 133.5 cm	56" / 142 cm
3	0	2	2	3	4	5	6
4	1	2	3	4	5	7	9
5	1	3	4	6	7	9	11
6	2	3	5	6	9	11	14
7	2	5	6	8	10	13	16
8	2	5	7	9	12	15	19

____ sts rem:

Gauge	32" / 81.5 cm	36½" / 92.5 cm	40" / 101.5 cm	44½" / 113 cm	48" / 122 cm	52½" / 133.5 cm	56" / 142 cm
3	46	46	50	54	54	58	58
4	58	62	66	70	74	74	74
5	74	78	82	86	90	94	94
6	86	94	98	106	106	110	110
7	102	106	114	122	126	130	130
8	118	122	130	138	142	146	146

Work even in est Fave patt, knitting the first and last st of every row, until armhole measures a finished length of 6½ (7, 7¼, 7¾, 8, 8½, 9)" / 16.5 (18, 18.5, 19.5, 20.5, 21.5, 23) cm from bind-off edge, ending with a WS row.

Shape Back Neck

Row 1 (RS): K1, work in est Fave patt for ____ sts:

Gauge	32" / 81.5 cm	36½" / 92.5 cm	40" / 101.5 cm	44½" / 113 cm	48" / 122 cm	52½" / 133.5 cm	56" / 142 cm
3	17	17	19	20	20	22	22
4	21	23	25	26	28	28	28
5	27	29	31	32	34	36	36
6	31	35	37	40	40	42	42
7	38	40	44	46	48	50	50
8	44	46	50	52	54	56	56

Place center ____ sts onto stitch holder, join new ball of yarn on other side of neck, work in est Fave patt to last st, k1:

Gauge	32" / 81.5 cm	36½" / 92.5 cm	40" / 101.5 cm	44½" / 113 cm	48" / 122 cm	52½" / 133.5 cm	56" / 142 cm
3	12	12	12	14	14	14	14
4	16	16	16	18	18	18	18
5	20	20	20	22	22	22	22
6	24	24	24	26	26	26	26
7	26	26	26	30	30	30	30
8	30	30	30	34	34	34	34

Row 2 (WS): K1, work in est Fave patt to neck edge, drop yarn, change yarn for other side of neck (right shoulder), work in Fave patt as est to last st, k1.
Working both sides of the neck AT THE SAME TIME, BO ____ sts at EACH neck edge once:

Gauge	32" / 81.5 cm	36½" / 92.5 cm	40" / 101.5 cm	44½" / 113 cm	48" / 122 cm	52½" / 133.5 cm	56" / 142 cm
3	5	5	5	6	6	6	6
4	7	7	7	8	8	8	8
5	5	5	5	5	5	5	5
6	6	6	6	6	6	6	6
7	6	6	6	7	7	7	7
8	5	5	5	5	5	5	5

BO ___ sts at EACH neck edge once again:

Gauge	32" / 81.5 cm	36½" / 92.5 cm	40" / 101.5 cm	44½" / 113 cm	48" / 122 cm	52½" / 133.5 cm	56" / 142 cm
3	0	0	0	0	0	0	0
4	0	0	0	0	0	0	0
5	4	4	4	5	5	5	5
6	5	5	5	6	6	6	6
7	6	6	6	7	7	7	7
8	4	4	4	6	6	6	6

BO ___ sts at each neck edge once more:

Gauge	32" / 81.5 cm	36½" / 92.5 cm	40" / 101.5 cm	44½" / 113 cm	48" / 122 cm	52½" / 133.5 cm	56" / 142 cm
3	0	0	0	0	0	0	0
4	0	0	0	0	0	0	0
5	0	0	0	0	0	0	0
6	0	0	0	0	0	0	0
7	0	0	0	0	0	0	0
8	5	5	5	5	5	5	5

___ sts rem on each side of neck (each shoulder):

Gauge	32" / 81.5 cm	36½" / 92.5 cm	40" / 101.5 cm	44½" / 113 cm	48" / 122 cm	52½" / 133.5 cm	56" / 142 cm
3	12	12	14	14	14	16	16
4	14	16	18	18	20	20	20
5	18	20	22	22	24	26	26
6	20	24	26	28	28	30	30
7	26	28	32	32	34	36	36
8	30	32	36	36	38	40	40

Shape Shoulders
Maintaining est Fave patt, BO ____ sts at beg of next 2 rows:

Gauge	32" / 81.5 cm	36½" / 92.5 cm	40" / 101.5 cm	44½" / 113 cm	48" / 122 cm	52½" / 133.5 cm	56" / 142 cm
3	6	6	8	8	8	8	8
4	8	8	10	10	10	10	10
5	6	6	8	8	8	8	8
6	6	8	8	10	10	10	10
7	8	10	10	10	12	12	12
8	8	8	10	10	10	10	10

Maintaining est Fave patt, BO ____ sts at beg of next 2 rows:

Gauge	32" / 81.5 cm	36½" / 92.5 cm	40" / 101.5 cm	44½" / 113 cm	48" / 122 cm	52½" / 133.5 cm	56" / 142 cm
3	6	6	6	6	6	8	8
4	6	8	8	8	10	10	10
5	6	6	8	8	8	8	8
6	6	8	8	10	10	10	10
7	8	10	10	10	12	12	12
8	8	8	10	10	10	10	10

Maintaining est Fave patt, BO ____ sts at beg of next 2 rows:

Gauge	32" / 81.5 cm	36½" / 92.5 cm	40" / 101.5 cm	44½" / 113 cm	48" / 122 cm	52½" / 133.5 cm	56" / 142 cm
3	0	0	0	0	0	0	0
4	0	0	0	0	0	0	0
5	6	8	6	6	8	10	10
6	8	8	10	8	8	10	10
7	10	8	12	12	10	12	12
8	8	8	10	10	10	10	10

Maintaining est Fave patt, BO ____ sts at beg of next 2 rows:

Gauge	32" / 81.5 cm	36½" / 92.5 cm	40" / 101.5 cm	44½" / 113 cm	48" / 122 cm	52½" / 133.5 cm	56" / 142 cm
3	0	0	0	0	0	0	0
4	0	0	0	0	0	0	0
5	0	0	0	0	0	0	0
6	0	0	0	0	0	0	0
7	0	0	0	0	0	0	0
8	6	8	6	6	8	10	10

FRONT
Work as for Back to Armhole.

Armhole
BO ____ sts at beg of next 2 rows:

Gauge	32" / 81.5 cm	36½" / 92.5 cm	40" / 101.5 cm	44½" / 113 cm	48" / 122 cm	52½" / 133.5 cm	56" / 142 cm
3	1	3	3	4	5	6	7
4	2	3	4	5	6	8	10
5	2	4	5	7	8	10	12
6	3	4	6	7	10	12	15
7	3	6	7	9	11	14	17
8	3	6	8	10	13	16	20

___ sts rem:

Gauge	32" / 81.5 cm	36½" / 92.5 cm	40" / 101.5 cm	44½" / 113 cm	48" / 122 cm	52½" / 133.5 cm	56" / 142 cm
3	48	52	56	62	64	70	72
4	62	68	74	80	86	90	94
5	78	86	92	100	106	114	118
6	92	102	110	120	126	134	140
7	108	118	128	140	148	158	164
8	124	134	146	158	168	178	186

Dec Row (RS): K1, ssk, maintain est patt to last 3 sts, k2tog, k1. 2 sts dec'd.
Rep Dec Row every RS row ___ more times:

Gauge	32" / 81.5 cm	36½" / 92.5 cm	40" / 101.5 cm	44½" / 113 cm	48" / 122 cm	52½" / 133.5 cm	56" / 142 cm
3	0	2	2	3	4	5	6
4	1	2	3	4	5	7	9
5	1	3	4	6	7	9	11
6	2	3	5	6	9	11	14
7	2	5	6	8	10	13	16
8	2	5	7	9	12	15	19

___ sts rem:

Gauge	32" / 81.5 cm	36½" / 92.5 cm	40" / 101.5 cm	44½" / 113 cm	48" / 122 cm	52½" / 133.5 cm	56" / 142 cm
3	46	46	50	54	54	58	58
4	58	62	66	70	74	74	74
5	74	78	82	86	90	94	94
6	86	94	98	106	106	110	110
7	102	106	114	122	126	130	130
8	118	122	130	138	142	146	146

Work even in est Fave patt, knitting the first and last st of every row, until armhole measures a finished length of 3½ (4, 3¾, 4¼, 4, 4, 4½)" / 9 (10, 9.5, 11, 10, 10, 11.5) cm from bind-off edge, ending with a WS row.

Shape Front Neck

Row 1 (RS): K1, work in est Fave patt for ___ sts:

Gauge	32" / 81.5 cm	36½" / 92.5 cm	40" / 101.5 cm	44½" / 113 cm	48" / 122 cm	52½" / 133.5 cm	56" / 142 cm
3	17	17	19	20	20	22	22
4	21	23	25	26	28	28	28
5	27	29	31	32	34	36	36
6	31	35	37	40	40	42	42
7	38	40	44	46	48	50	50
8	44	46	50	52	54	56	56

Place center ___ sts onto stitch holder, join new ball of yarn on other side of neck, work in est Fave patt to last st, k1:

Gauge	32" / 81.5 cm	36½" / 92.5 cm	40" / 101.5 cm	44½" / 113 cm	48" / 122 cm	52½" / 133.5 cm	56" / 142 cm
3	12	12	12	14	14	14	14
4	16	16	16	18	18	18	18
5	20	20	20	22	22	22	22
6	24	24	24	26	26	26	26
7	26	26	26	30	30	30	30
8	30	30	30	34	34	34	34

Row 2 (WS): K1, work in est Fave patt to neck edge, drop yarn, change yarn for other side of neck (right shoulder), work in Fave patt as est to last st, k1.

Both sides of the neck will be worked AT THE SAME TIME as follows:

Neck Dec Row (RS): K1, work in est Fave patt until 3 sts before neck edge, k2tog, k1, change yarns to work right shoulder, k1, ssk, work in est Fave patt to last st, k1.

Rep Neck Dec Row every RS row ____ more times:

Gauge		32" / 81.5 cm	36¹/₂" / 92.5 cm	40" / 101.5 cm	44¹/₂" / 113 cm	48" / 122 cm	52¹/₂" / 133.5 cm	56" / 142 cm
	3	2	2	1	3	2	1	1
	4	2	2	0	2	1	7	7
	5	4	4	2	4	2	1	1
	6	6	6	4	6	4	2	2
	7	6	6	4	8	5	3	3
	8	8	8	5	9	7	4	4

Rep Neck Dec Row every OTHER RS row ____ times:

Gauge		32" / 81.5 cm	36¹/₂" / 92.5 cm	40" / 101.5 cm	44¹/₂" / 113 cm	48" / 122 cm	52¹/₂" / 133.5 cm	56" / 142 cm
	3	1	1	2	1	2	3	3
	4	3	3	5	4	5	-1	-1
	5	3	3	5	4	6	7	7
	6	3	3	5	4	6	8	8
	7	4	4	6	4	7	9	9
	8	4	4	7	5	7	10	10

____ sts rem on each shoulder:

Gauge		32" / 81.5 cm	36¹/₂" / 92.5 cm	40" / 101.5 cm	44¹/₂" / 113 cm	48" / 122 cm	52¹/₂" / 133.5 cm	56" / 142 cm
	3	12	12	14	14	14	16	16
	4	14	16	18	18	20	20	20
	5	18	20	22	22	24	26	26
	6	20	24	26	28	28	30	30
	7	26	28	32	32	34	36	36
	8	30	32	36	36	38	40	40

Shape Shoulders

Maintaining est Fave patt, BO ＿＿＿ sts at beg of next 2 rows:

Gauge	32" / 81.5 cm	36½" / 92.5 cm	40" / 101.5 cm	44½" / 113 cm	48" / 122 cm	52½" / 133.5 cm	56" / 142 cm
3	6	6	8	8	8	8	8
4	8	8	10	10	10	10	10
5	6	6	8	8	8	8	8
6	6	8	8	10	10	10	10
7	8	10	10	10	12	12	12
8	8	8	10	10	10	10	10

Maintaining est Fave patt, BO ＿＿＿ sts at beg of next 2 rows:

Gauge	32" / 81.5 cm	36½" / 92.5 cm	40" / 101.5 cm	44½" / 113 cm	48" / 122 cm	52½" / 133.5 cm	56" / 142 cm
3	6	6	6	6	6	8	8
4	6	8	8	8	10	10	10
5	6	6	6	8	8	8	8
6	6	8	8	10	10	10	10
7	8	10	10	10	12	12	12
8	8	8	10	10	10	10	10

Maintaining est Fave patt, BO ＿＿＿ sts at beg of next 2 rows:

Gauge	32" / 81.5 cm	36½" / 92.5 cm	40" / 101.5 cm	44½" / 113 cm	48" / 122 cm	52½" / 133.5 cm	56" / 142 cm
3	0	0	0	0	0	0	0
4	0	0	0	0	0	0	0
5	6	8	6	6	8	10	10
6	8	10	8	8	10	10	10
7	10	8	12	12	10	12	12
8	8	8	10	10	10	10	10

Maintaining est Fave patt, BO ＿＿＿ sts at beg of next 2 rows:

Gauge	32" / 81.5 cm	36½" / 92.5 cm	40" / 101.5 cm	44½" / 113 cm	48" / 122 cm	52½" / 133.5 cm	56" / 142 cm
3	0	0	0	0	0	0	0
4	0	0	0	0	0	0	0
5	0	0	0	0	0	0	0
6	0	0	0	0	0	0	0
7	0	0	0	0	0	0	0
8	6	8	6	6	8	10	10

SLEEVES (MAKE 2)

Cuff

With smaller needles, cast on ＿＿＿ sts:

Gauge	32" / 81.5 cm	36½" / 92.5 cm	40" / 101.5 cm	44½" / 113 cm	48" / 122 cm	52½" / 133.5 cm	56" / 142 cm
3	26	26	26	30	30	30	30
4	34	34	34	38	38	38	42
5	42	42	42	46	46	46	50
6	50	50	50	54	54	58	58
7	58	58	58	62	62	66	70
8	66	66	70	74	74	74	78

Rib Row (RS): K1, *k2, p2; rep from * to last st, k1.
Rep Rib Row until back measures a finished length of approx. 1" / 2.5 cm from cast-on edge, ending with a WS row.

Sleeve

Change to Fave patt for the body as follows:
Row 1 (RS): K1, work RS row of Fave patt to last st, k1.
Row 2 (WS): K1, work WS row of Fave patt to last st, k1.

Rep Rows 1–2, continuing the rows of Fave patt to the end and then repeating, until sleeve measures a finished length of 3" / 7.5 cm from cast-on edge, ending with a WS row.

Sleeve Shaping

Inc Row (RS): K1, M1, work in est Fave patt to last st, M1, k1. 2 sts inc'd.
Cont in est patt and rep Inc Row every ___ rows:

Gauge	32" / 81.5 cm	36½" / 92.5 cm	40" / 101.5 cm	44½" / 113 cm	48" / 122 cm	52½" / 133.5 cm	56" / 142 cm
3	0	0	8	8	6	4	2
4	0	8	8	8	6	4	4
5	10	10	8	6	6	4	4
6	8	8	8	6	4	4	4
7	12	8	0	6	4	4	0
8	10	8	6	6	4	0	2

___ more times:

Gauge	32" / 81.5 cm	36½" / 92.5 cm	40" / 101.5 cm	44½" / 113 cm	48" / 122 cm	52½" / 133.5 cm	56" / 142 cm
3	0	0	5	5	6	10	1
4	0	4	3	3	9	9	8
5	6	6	6	4	11	15	19
6	3	3	11	7	3	15	25
7	3	7	0	8	8	20	0
8	7	11	3	11	8	0	6

Then rep Inc Row every ___ rows:

Gauge	32" / 81.5 cm	36½" / 92.5 cm	40" / 101.5 cm	44½" / 113 cm	48" / 122 cm	52½" / 133.5 cm	56" / 142 cm
3	12	8	0	0	8	6	4
4	12	10	10	10	8	6	6
5	12	12	10	8	8	6	6
6	10	10	0	8	6	6	0
7	14	10	8	8	6	6	4
8	12	10	8	8	6	4	4

___ times:

Gauge	32" / 81.5 cm	36½" / 92.5 cm	40" / 101.5 cm	44½" / 113 cm	48" / 122 cm	52½" / 133.5 cm	56" / 142 cm
3	3	5	0	0	1	1	12
4	5	3	4	4	2	6	7
5	1	1	3	7	2	4	2
6	6	6	0	6	14	6	0
7	4	4	13	7	13	5	29
8	3	2	12	6	15	31	29

___ sts rem.

Gauge	32" / 81.5 cm	36½" / 92.5 cm	40" / 101.5 cm	44½" / 113 cm	48" / 122 cm	52½" / 133.5 cm	56" / 142 cm
3	34	38	38	42	46	54	58
4	46	50	50	54	62	70	74
5	58	58	62	70	74	86	94
6	70	70	74	82	90	102	110
7	74	82	86	94	106	118	130
8	88	94	102	110	122	138	150

Work even until sleeve measures a finished length of 16½ (16½, 17, 17, 17½, 17½, 18)" / 42 (42, 43, 43, 44.5, 44.5, 45.5) cm from cast-on edge, ending with a WS row.

Cap

BO ___ sts at beg of next 2 rows:

Gauge	32" / 81.5 cm	36½" / 92.5 cm	40" / 101.5 cm	44½" / 113 cm	48" / 122 cm	52½" / 133.5 cm	56" / 142 cm
3	1	3	3	4	5	6	7
4	2	3	4	5	6	8	10
5	2	4	5	7	8	10	12
6	3	4	6	7	10	12	15
7	3	6	7	9	11	14	17
8	3	6	8	10	13	16	20

___ sts rem:

Gauge	32" / 81.5 cm	36½" / 92.5 cm	40" / 101.5 cm	44½" / 113 cm	48" / 122 cm	52½" / 133.5 cm	56" / 142 cm
3	32	32	32	34	36	42	44
4	42	44	42	44	50	54	54
5	54	50	52	56	58	66	70
6	64	62	62	68	70	78	80
7	68	70	72	76	84	90	96
8	82	82	86	90	96	106	110

Dec Row 1 (RS): K1, ssk, work in est Fave patt to last 3 sts, k2tog, k1. 2 sts dec'd.
Maintain est Fave patt and rep Dec Row every RS row ___ more times:

Gauge	32" / 81.5 cm	36½" / 92.5 cm	40" / 101.5 cm	44½" / 113 cm	48" / 122 cm	52½" / 133.5 cm	56" / 142 cm
3	6	5	5	6	4	8	9
4	8	8	5	7	9	12	10
5	13	8	9	8	10	13	15
6	15	13	12	13	15	18	18
7	17	14	15	18	22	23	25
8	20	16	18	21	23	26	25

Then rep Dec Row every OTHER RS row ___ times:

Gauge	32" / 81.5 cm	36½" / 92.5 cm	40" / 101.5 cm	44½" / 113 cm	48" / 122 cm	52½" / 133.5 cm	56" / 142 cm
3	0	1	1	1	2	0	0
4	1	2	4	3	2	1	3
5	0	3	3	4	3	2	2
6	0	2	3	3	2	1	2
7	0	3	3	2	0	0	0
8	0	3	3	2	1	0	2

___ sts rem:

Gauge	32" / 81.5 cm	36½" / 92.5 cm	40" / 101.5 cm	44½" / 113 cm	48" / 122 cm	52½" / 133.5 cm	56" / 142 cm
3	18	18	18	18	22	24	24
4	22	22	22	22	26	26	26
5	26	26	26	30	30	34	34
6	32	30	30	34	34	38	38
7	32	34	34	34	38	42	44
8	40	42	42	42	46	52	54

BO ___ sts at the beg of the next 4 rows:

Gauge	32" / 81.5 cm	36½" / 92.5 cm	40" / 101.5 cm	44½" / 113 cm	48" / 122 cm	52½" / 133.5 cm	56" / 142 cm
3	2	2	2	2	2	2	2
4	2	2	2	2	2	2	3
5	3	3	3	3	3	3	3
6	3	3	3	3	3	3	3
7	3	3	3	3	3	3	3
8	4	4	4	4	4	4	4

BO the remaining ___ sts on the next RS row.

Gauge	32" / 81.5 cm	36½" / 92.5 cm	40" / 101.5 cm	44½" / 113 cm	48" / 122 cm	52½" / 133.5 cm	56" / 142 cm
3	28	28	28	30	32	38	40
4	38	40	38	40	46	50	50
5	48	44	46	50	52	60	64
6	58	56	56	62	64	72	74
7	62	64	66	70	78	84	90
8	74	74	78	82	88	98	102

FINISHING

Block pieces to measurements. Sew shoulder seams. Sew sleeve caps into armholes. Sew side and sleeve seams.

Cowl Neck Collar

With circular needle and WS facing, beg at right back shoulder pick up and knit ___ sts to back neck sts:

Gauge	32" / 81.5 cm	36½" / 92.5 cm	40" / 101.5 cm	44½" / 113 cm	48" / 122 cm	52½" / 133.5 cm	56" / 142 cm
3	5	5	5	6	6	6	6
4	7	7	7	8	8	8	8
5	9	9	9	10	10	10	10
6	11	11	11	12	12	12	12
7	12	12	12	14	14	14	14
8	14	14	14	16	16	16	16

Purl across ___ held back neck sts:

Gauge	32" / 81.5 cm	36½" / 92.5 cm	40" / 101.5 cm	44½" / 113 cm	48" / 122 cm	52½" / 133.5 cm	56" / 142 cm
3	12	12	12	14	14	14	14
4	16	16	16	18	18	18	18
5	20	20	20	22	22	22	22
6	24	24	24	26	26	26	26
7	26	26	26	30	30	30	30
8	30	30	30	34	34	34	34

Pick up and knit ___ sts to left shoulder:

Gauge	32" / 81.5 cm	36½" / 92.5 cm	40" / 101.5 cm	44½" / 113 cm	48" / 122 cm	52½" / 133.5 cm	56" / 142 cm
3	5	5	5	6	6	6	6
4	7	7	7	8	8	8	8
5	9	9	9	10	10	10	10
6	11	11	11	12	12	12	12
7	12	12	12	14	14	14	14
8	14	14	14	16	16	16	16

___ sts to front neck:

Gauge	32" / 81.5 cm	36½" / 92.5 cm	40" / 101.5 cm	44½" / 113 cm	48" / 122 cm	52½" / 133.5 cm	56" / 142 cm
3	11	11	11	12	12	16	16
4	15	15	19	20	20	24	24
5	19	19	23	24	24	28	28
6	23	23	23	24	28	32	32
7	24	24	28	28	32	36	36
8	28	28	32	32	36	40	40

Purl across the ____ held front neck sts:

Gauge	32" / 81.5 cm	36½" / 92.5 cm	40" / 101.5 cm	44½" / 113 cm	48" / 122 cm	52½" / 133.5 cm	56" / 142 cm
3	12	12	12	14	14	14	14
4	16	16	16	18	18	18	18
5	20	20	20	22	22	22	22
6	24	24	24	26	26	26	26
7	26	26	26	30	30	30	30
8	30	30	30	34	34	34	34

Pick up and knit ____ sts to right shoulder.

Gauge	32" / 81.5 cm	36½" / 92.5 cm	40" / 101.5 cm	44½" / 113 cm	48" / 122 cm	52½" / 133.5 cm	56" / 142 cm
3	11	11	11	12	12	16	16
4	15	15	19	20	20	24	24
5	19	19	23	24	24	28	28
6	23	23	23	24	28	32	32
7	24	24	28	28	32	36	36
8	28	28	32	32	36	40	40

____ sts.

Gauge	32" / 81.5 cm	36½" / 92.5 cm	40" / 101.5 cm	44½" / 113 cm	48" / 122 cm	52½" / 133.5 cm	56" / 142 cm
3	56	56	56	64	64	72	72
4	76	76	84	92	92	100	100
5	96	96	104	112	112	120	120
6	116	116	116	124	132	140	140
7	124	124	132	144	152	160	160
8	144	144	152	164	172	180	180

Pm and join for working in the round.
Rnd 1: Purl.
Rep Rnd 1 until the cowl measures 1″ / 2.5 cm from neck edge.
Inc Rnd: *P1, M1; rep from * to end of end.
____ sts.

Gauge	32" / 81.5 cm	36½" / 92.5 cm	40" / 101.5 cm	44½" / 113 cm	48" / 122 cm	52½" / 133.5 cm	56" / 142 cm
3	112	112	112	128	128	144	144
4	152	152	168	184	184	200	200
5	192	192	208	224	224	240	240
6	232	232	232	248	264	280	280
7	248	248	264	288	304	320	320
8	288	288	304	328	344	360	360

Rep Rnd 1 until cowl measures 5″ / 12.5 cm from neck edge.
Change to larger circular needles and Rep Rnd 1 until cowl measures 10″ / 25 cm from neck edge.
Rnd 2: Work K2P2 rib to end.
Rep Rnd 2 until the ribbing measures ¾″ / 2 cm.
BO loosely in patt.
Weave in ends.

SIMPLE SCARF

Long, lush, and utterly decadent, this simple scarf offers a wealth of textural opportunity. Whether lacy, textured, or cabled, every stitch becomes the highlight in this versatile accessory.

SKILL LEVEL
Advanced Beginner

STITCH PATTERN
Choose one stitch pattern (the pattern recipe will refer to it as Fave patt) for the body.
The sample shown uses Bee Stitch (page 164).

FINISHED MEASUREMENTS
Width: approx. 5 (7, 10¾)" / 12.5 (18, 27.5) cm
Length: approx. 50 (60, 70)" / 127 (152.5, 178) cm
Sample size is 10½" / 26.5 cm width.

YARN REQUIREMENTS

5 (7, 10¾)" / 12.5 (18, 27.5) cm

50 (60, 70)" / 127 (152.5, 178) cm

Gauge	5" / 12.5 cm	7" / 18 cm	10 ¾" / 27.5 cm
3	175 yds / 160 m	270 yds / 247 m	505 yds / 462 m
4	195 yds / 178 m	325 yds / 297 m	595 yds / 544 m
5	205 yds / 187 m	380 yds / 347 m	640 yds / 585 m
6	280 yds / 256 m	465 yds / 425 m	805 yds / 736 m
7	305 yds / 279 m	475 yds / 434 m	840 yds / 768 m
8	320 yds / 293 m	535 yds / 489 m	935 yds / 855 m

NEEDLES & NOTIONS
Choose a needle size that is larger than recommended for your yarn so as to achieve a moderate drape.
• Pair of needles in the size necessary to obtain the desired gauge
• Yarn needle

SAMPLE PROJECT
The sample scarf shown is worked with 2 skeins Premier Sweet Roll Yarn in Gelato Pop (245 yards / 224 m per 5 oz / 140 g skein; 100% acrylic) *with a finished gauge of* 3 sts and 4 rows = 1" / 2.5 cm.

PATTERN NOTES
• This scarf is worked flat from end to end. The side edges and borders feature Garter stitch edging.

*Measurements are an average of all the gauges listed.

PATTERN Simple Scarf

BORDER

Cast on ____ sts:

Gauge	5" / 12.5 cm	7" / 18 cm	10 ¾" / 27.5 cm
3	16	20	32
4	20	28	44
5	24	36	52
6	32	44	64
7	36	48	72
8	40	56	84

Setup Row (WS): Sl 1 wyif, knit to last st, sl 1 wyif.
Row 1 (RS): Knit.
Row 2 (WS): Sl 1 wyif, knit to last st, sl 1 wyif.
Rep Rows 1–2 once more.

BODY

Row 1 (RS): K4, work Fave patt Row 1 to last 4 sts, k4.
Row 2 (WS): Sl 1 wyif, k3, work Fave patt Row 2 to last 4 sts, k4.
Row 3: K4, work Fave patt Row 3 to last 4 sts, k4.
Row 4: Rep Row 2, continuing in Fave patt row as est.
Rep Rows 1–4, continuing through the remaining rows of Fave patt and then repeating, until scarf measures approx. 50 (60, 70)" / 127 (152.5, 178) cm from cast-on edge, ending with a WS row.

BORDER

Row 1 (RS): Knit.
Row 2 (WS): Sl 1 wyif, knit to last st, sl 1 wyif.
Rep Rows 1–2 once more.
Rep Row 1 once.
BO loosely.

FINISHING

Block to measurements. Weave in ends.

SLEEVELESS TUNIC

The simple construction of this pullover makes it wonderfully accessible for every level of knitter, but it also enhances the stitch options. Beautiful in lace or texture, it's a versatile garment for any day of the year.

SKILL LEVEL
Intermediate

STITCH PATTERN
Choose one stitch pattern (the pattern recipe will refer to it as Fave patt) for the body.
The sample shown uses Single Point Chevron (page 105).

FINISHED MEASUREMENTS
Bust Circumference:

Gauge		32" / 81.5cm	36½" / 92.5cm	40" / 101.5cm	44½" / 113cm	48" / 122cm	52½" / 133.5cm	56" / 142cm
	3	32" 81.5 cm	37.25" 94.5 cm	40" 101.5 cm	45.25" 115 cm	48" 122 cm	53.25" 135.5 cm	56" 142 cm
	4	32" 81.5 cm	36" 91.5 cm	40" 101.5 cm	44" 112 cm	48" 122 cm	52" 132 cm	56" 142 cm
	5	32" 81.5 cm	36.75" 93.5 cm	40" 101.5 cm	44.75" 113.5 cm	48" 122 cm	52.75" 134 cm	56" 142 cm
	6	32" 81.5 cm	36" 91.5 cm	40" 101.5 cm	44" 112 cm	48" 122 cm	52" 132 cm	56" 142 cm
	7	32" 81.5 cm	36.5" 92.5 cm	40" 101.5 cm	44.5" 113 cm	48" 122 cm	52.5" 133.5 cm	56" 142 cm
	8	32" 81.5 cm	36" 91.5 cm	40" 101.5 cm	44" 112 cm	48" 122 cm	52" 132 cm	56" 142 cm

The pattern will reference the averaged, seamed bust circumference measurements throughout the pattern charts and lengths: 32 (36½, 40, 44½, 48, 52½, 56)" / 81.5 (92.5, 101.5, 113, 122, 133.5, 142) cm.
Choose the size that is approx. 2–2¾" / 5–7 cm larger than your actual bust circumference.
Garment Length: 24¾ (25½, 26¼, 27¼, 28, 28¾, 29½)" / 63 (65, 66.5, 69, 71, 73, 75) cm
Sample size is 36½" / 92.5 cm bust circumference.

YARN REQUIREMENTS

Gauge		32" / 81.5cm	36½" / 92.5cm	40" / 101.5cm	44½" / 113cm	48" / 122cm	52½" / 133.5cm	56" / 142cm
	3	470 yds 430 m	535 yds 489 m	600 yds 549 m	700 yds 640 m	755 yds 690 m	860 yds 786 m	930 yds 850 m
	4	705 yds 645 m	790 yds 722 m	900 yds 823 m	1030 yds 942 m	1140 yds 1042 m	1270 yds 1161 m	1400 yds 1280 m
	5	850 yds 777 m	960 yds 878 m	1095 yds 1001 m	1250 yds 1143 m	1390 yds 1271 m	1545 yds 1413 m	1710 yds 1564 m
	6	1145 yds 1047 m	1290 yds 1180 m	1475 yds 1349 m	1690 yds 1545 m	1875 yds 1715 m	2085 yds 1907 m	2310 yds 2112 m
	7	1305 yds 1193 m	1460 yds 1335 m	1665 yds 1522 m	1915 yds 1751 m	2115 yds 1934 m	2365 yds 2163 m	2610 yds 2387 m
	8	1605 yds 1468 m	1800 yds 1646 m	2060 yds 1884 m	2355 yds 2153 m	2615 yds 2391 m	2910 yds 2661 m	3220 yds 2944 m

NEEDLES & NOTIONS
A looser gauge will provide nice drape, so choose a needle size that is the same or slightly larger than recommended for your yarn.
• Set of needles in the size necessary to obtain the desired gauge
• Circular needle, 16" / 40 cm in length, in the same size as Body needles
• Stitch markers (4)
• Yarn needle

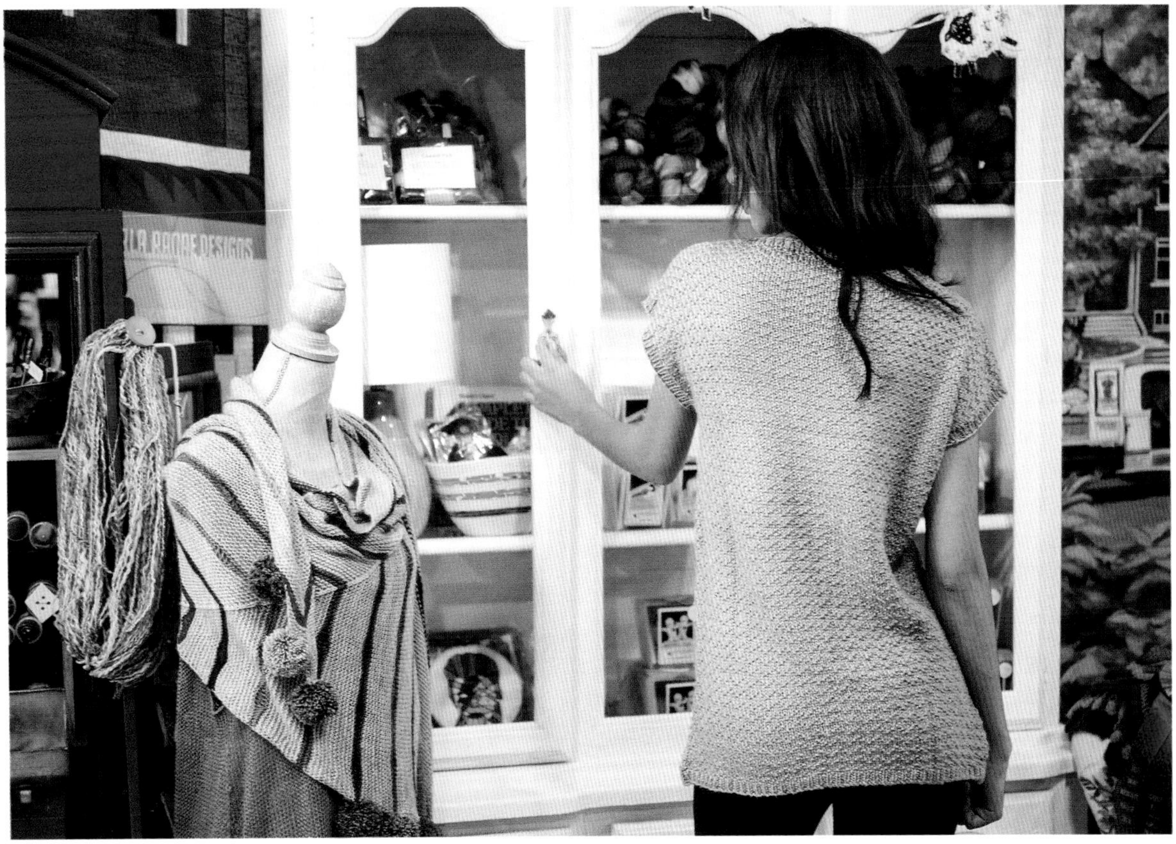

SAMPLE PROJECT

The sample pullover shown is worked with 7 skeins Knit Picks Gloss DK in Velveteen #25592 (123 yards / 112 m per 1.75 oz / 50 g skein; 70% merino wool, 30% silk) *with a finished gauge of* 4 sts and 6 rows = 1" / 2.5 cm.

PATTERN NOTES

- The pullover is worked flat in pieces and then seamed. Because of the seaming, 2 sts have been added to the instructions, 1 on either side of your desired stitch pattern, that you'll knit on every row.
- Only work as instructed for your size. If the number for your size and gauge in the table is 0, omit those rows and/or stitches and move on to the next indicated stitch/row instructions.

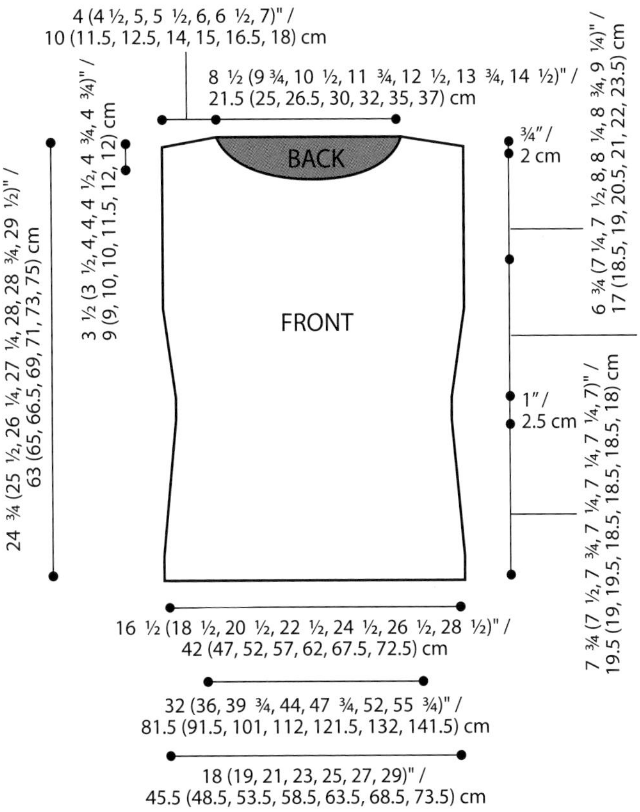
4 (4 ½, 5, 5 ½, 6, 6 ½, 7)" /
10 (11.5, 12.5, 14, 15, 16.5, 18) cm
8 ½ (9 ¾, 10 ½, 11 ¾, 12 ½, 13 ¾, 14 ½)" /
21.5 (25, 26.5, 30, 32, 35, 37) cm
BACK
FRONT
¾" /
2 cm
1" /
2.5 cm
24 ¾ (25 ½, 26 ¼, 27 ¼, 28, 28 ¾, 29 ½)" /
63 (65, 66.5, 69, 71, 73, 75) cm
3 ½ (3 ½, 4, 4, 4 ½, 4 ¾, 4 ¾)" /
9 (9, 10, 10, 11.5, 12, 12) cm
6 ¾ (7 ¼, 7 ½, 8, 8 ¼, 8 ¾, 9 ¼)" /
17 (18.5, 19, 20.5, 21, 22, 23.5) cm
7 (7 ¼, 7 ½, 8 ½, 8 ¾, 9, 9 ½)" /
18 (18.5, 19, 21.5, 22, 23, 24) cm
7 ¾ (7 ½, 7 ¾, 7 ¼, 7 ¼, 7 ¼, 7)" /
19.5 (19, 19.5, 18.5, 18.5, 18.5, 18) cm
16 ½ (18 ½, 20 ½, 22 ½, 24 ½, 26 ½, 28 ½)" /
42 (47, 52, 57, 62, 67.5, 72.5) cm
32 (36, 39 ¾, 44, 47 ¾, 52, 55 ¾)" /
81.5 (91.5, 101, 112, 121.5, 132, 141.5) cm
18 (19, 21, 23, 25, 27, 29)" /
45.5 (48.5, 53.5, 58.5, 63.5, 68.5, 73.5) cm

PATTERN Sleeveless Tunic

BACK

Hem
Cast on ___ sts:

Gauge	32" / 81.5cm	36½" / 92.5cm	40" / 101.5cm	44½" / 113cm	48" / 122cm	52½" / 133.5cm	56" / 142cm
3	54	58	62	70	74	82	86
4	74	78	86	94	102	110	118
5	90	94	106	114	126	134	146
6	106	114	126	138	150	162	174
7	126	130	146	158	174	186	202
8	142	150	166	182	198	214	230

Rib Row (RS): K1, *k1, p1; rep from * to last st, k1.
Rep Rib Row until back measures a finished length of approx. 1″ / 2.5 cm from cast-on edge, ending with a WS row.

Body
Change to Fave patt for the body as follows:
Row 1 (RS): K1, work RS row of Fave patt to last st, k1.
Row 2 (WS): K1, work WS row of Fave patt to last st, k1.
Rep Rows 1–2, continuing the rows of Fave patt to the end and then repeating, until back measures a finished length of 2″ / 5 cm from cast-on edge, ending with a WS row.

Shape Waist
Dec Row (RS): K1, ssk, maintain est Fave patt to last 3 sts, k2tog, k1. 2 sts dec'd.
Rep Dec Row every ___ rows:

Gauge	32" / 81.5cm	36½" / 92.5cm	40" / 101.5cm	44½" / 113cm	48" / 122cm	52½" / 133.5cm	56" / 142cm
3	1	0	0	0	0	0	0
4	2	0	0	1	1	1	0
5	2	1	2	0	0	0	1
6	0	1	0	2	2	2	3
7	5	0	1	1	3	1	0
8	2	3	2	1	1	1	2

___ more time(s):

Gauge	32" / 81.5cm	36½" / 92.5cm	40" / 101.5cm	44½" / 113cm	48" / 122cm	52½" / 133.5cm	56" / 142cm
3	0	12	0	12	0	12	0
4	10	18	18	0	0	0	16
5	8	0	12	20	10	20	10
6	8	12	12	12	12	12	0
7	8	26	14	0	0	0	12
8	8	0	16	14	14	14	14

Then rep Dec Row every ___ rows:

Gauge	32" / 81.5cm	36½" / 92.5cm	40" / 101.5cm	44½" / 113cm	48" / 122cm	52½" / 133.5cm	56" / 142cm
3	0	12	0	12	0	12	0
4	10	18	18	0	0	0	16
5	8	0	12	20	10	20	10
6	8	12	12	12	12	12	0
7	8	26	14	0	0	0	12
8	8	0	16	14	14	14	14

___ more times:

Gauge	32" / 81.5cm	36½" / 92.5cm	40" / 101.5cm	44½" / 113cm	48" / 122cm	52½" / 133.5cm	56" / 142cm
3	0	1	0	1	0	1	0
4	1	1	1	0	0	0	1
5	3	0	1	1	3	1	2
6	5	2	3	1	1	1	0
7	2	1	2	0	0	0	3
8	5	0	1	2	2	2	1

___ sts rem:

Gauge	32" / 81.5cm	36½" / 92.5cm	40" / 101.5cm	44½" / 113cm	48" / 122cm	52½" / 133.5cm	56" / 142cm
3	50	54	60	66	72	78	84
4	66	74	82	90	98	106	114
5	78	90	98	110	118	130	138
6	94	106	118	130	142	154	166
7	110	126	138	154	166	182	194
8	126	142	158	174	190	206	222

Work even in est pattern until back measures a finished length of 8¾ (8½, 8¾, 8¼, 8¼, 8¼, 8)" / 22 (21.5, 22, 21, 21, 21, 20.5) cm from cast-on edge, ending with a WS row.
Inc Row (RS): K1, M1, maintain est patt to last st, M1, k1. 2 sts inc'd.
Rep Inc Row every ___ rows:

Gauge	32" / 81.5cm	36½" / 92.5cm	40" / 101.5cm	44½" / 113cm	48" / 122cm	52½" / 133.5cm	56" / 142cm
3	0	0	0	12	0	0	0
4	0	0	0	0	0	0	0
5	18	18	0	0	22	22	0
6	20	0	22	24	0	0	26
7	0	24	0	0	28	28	0
8	0	26	28	30	0	0	0

___ more time(s):

Gauge	32" / 81.5cm	36½" / 92.5cm	40" / 101.5cm	44½" / 113cm	48" / 122cm	52½" / 133.5cm	56" / 142cm
3	0	0	0	1	0	0	0
4	0	0	0	0	0	0	0
5	1	1	0	0	1	1	0
6	1	0	1	1	0	0	1
7	0	1	0	0	1	1	0
8	0	1	1	1	0	0	0

Then rep Inc Row every ___ rows:

Gauge	32" / 81.5cm	36½" / 92.5cm	40" / 101.5cm	44½" / 113cm	48" / 122cm	52½" / 133.5cm	56" / 142cm
3	0	12	0	0	0	14	0
4	0	0	0	0	0	0	0
5	0	0	20	22	0	0	24
6	0	22	0	0	26	26	0
7	24	0	26	28	0	0	30
8	26	0	0	0	32	32	34

___ more times:

Gauge	32" / 81.5cm	36½" / 92.5cm	40" / 101.5cm	44½" / 113cm	48" / 122cm	52½" / 133.5cm	56" / 142cm
3	0	1	0	0	0	1	0
4	0	0	0	0	0	0	0
5	0	0	1	1	0	0	1
6	0	1	0	0	1	1	0
7	1	0	1	1	0	0	1
8	1	0	0	0	1	1	1

_____ sts rem:

Gauge	32" / 81.5cm	36½" / 92.5cm	40" / 101.5cm	44½" / 113cm	48" / 122cm	52½" / 133.5cm	56" / 142cm
3	50	58	62	70	74	82	86
4	66	74	82	90	98	106	114
5	82	94	102	114	122	134	142
6	98	110	122	134	146	158	170
7	114	130	142	158	170	186	198
8	130	146	162	178	194	210	226

Work even in est pattern until back measures a finished length of 16 (16, 16½, 17, 17¼, 17½, 17¾)" / 40.5 (40.5, 42, 43, 44, 44.5, 45) cm from cast-on edge, ending with a WS row.

Armhole
Place markers at beg and end of each row to mark beginning of armhole (for seaming).
Work even in est patt until armhole measures a finished length 6¾ (7¼, 7½, 8, 8¼, 8¾, 9¼)" / 17 (18.5, 19, 20.5, 21, 22, 23.5) cm from stitch markers, ending with a WS row.

Shape Shoulders
Maintaining est patt, BO _____ sts at beg of next 2 rows:

Gauge	32" / 81.5cm	36½" / 92.5cm	40" / 101.5cm	44½" / 113cm	48" / 122cm	52½" / 133.5cm	56" / 142cm
3	6	8	8	8	10	10	12
4	8	10	10	12	12	14	14
5	6	8	8	10	10	10	12
6	8	8	10	10	12	12	14
7	10	10	12	12	14	14	16
8	8	8	10	10	12	12	14

Then BO _____ sts at beg of next 2 rows:

Gauge	32" / 81.5cm	36½" / 92.5cm	40" / 101.5cm	44½" / 113cm	48" / 122cm	52½" / 133.5cm	56" / 142cm
3	7	6	8	9	9	10	10
4	8	8	10	10	12	12	14
5	6	8	8	10	10	10	12
6	8	8	10	10	12	12	14
7	10	10	12	12	14	14	16
8	8	8	10	10	12	12	14

BO _____ more sts at beg of next 2 rows:

Gauge	32" / 81.5cm	36½" / 92.5cm	40" / 101.5cm	44½" / 113cm	48" / 122cm	52½" / 133.5cm	56" / 142cm
3	0	0	0	0	0	0	0
4	0	0	0	0	0	0	0
5	8	6	9	7	10	12	11
6	7	10	9	12	11	14	13
7	7	10	10	13	13	16	16
8	8	8	10	10	12	12	14

BO _____ more sts at beg of next 2 rows:

Gauge	32" / 81.5cm	36½" / 92.5cm	40" / 101.5cm	44½" / 113cm	48" / 122cm	52½" / 133.5cm	56" / 142cm
3	0	0	0	0	0	0	0
4	0	0	0	0	0	0	0
5	0	0	0	0	0	0	0
6	0	0	0	0	0	0	0
7	0	0	0	0	0	0	0
8	6	10	8	12	10	14	12

Finally, BO ____ rem neck sts on next RS row:

Gauge	32" / 81.5cm	36½" / 92.5cm	40" / 101.5cm	44½" / 113cm	48" / 122cm	52½" / 133.5cm	56" / 142cm
3	24	30	30	36	36	42	42
4	34	38	42	46	50	54	58
5	42	50	52	60	62	70	72
6	52	58	64	70	76	82	88
7	60	70	74	84	88	98	102
8	70	78	86	94	102	110	118

FRONT

Work as for Back to Armhole.

Armhole

Place markers at beg and end of each row to mark beginning of armhole (for seaming). Work even in est patt until armhole measures a finished length 3¼ (3¾, 3½, 4, 3¾, 4, 4½)" / 8.5 (9.5, 9, 10, 9.5, 10, 11.5) cm from stitch markers, ending with a WS row.

Shape Front Neck

Row 1 (RS): Maintaining est patt, work ____ sts:

Gauge	32" / 81.5cm	36½" / 92.5cm	40" / 101.5cm	44½" / 113cm	48" / 122cm	52½" / 133.5cm	56" / 142cm
3	16	18	20	22	25	26	28
4	21	24	27	30	33	35	38
5	27	30	34	36	40	44	47
6	32	35	40	43	48	52	55
7	37	40	45	50	56	60	64
8	42	46	52	56	63	68	72

BO center ____ sts:

Gauge	32" / 81.5cm	36½" / 92.5cm	40" / 101.5cm	44½" / 113cm	48" / 122cm	52½" / 133.5cm	56" / 142cm
3	18	22	22	26	24	30	30
4	24	26	28	30	32	36	38
5	28	34	34	42	42	46	48
6	34	40	42	48	50	54	60
7	40	50	52	58	58	66	70
8	46	54	58	66	68	74	82

Continue in patt to end of row.

Row 2 (WS): K1, work in Fave patt as est to neck edge, join new ball of yarn on the other side of neck (left shoulder), work in patt to last st, k1.

Both sides of the neck will be worked AT THE SAME TIME as follows:

Neck Dec Row (RS): K1, work in Fave patt until 3 sts before neck edge, k2tog, k1, change yarns to work right shoulder, k1, ssk, work in Fave patt to last st, k1.

Rep Neck Dec Row every RS row ____ times:

Gauge	32" / 81.5cm	36½" / 92.5cm	40" / 101.5cm	44½" / 113cm	48" / 122cm	52½" / 133.5cm	56" / 142cm
3	0	2	1	3	4	4	4
4	2	4	4	6	7	6	8
5	4	6	7	7	7	10	10
6	7	7	9	9	11	12	12
7	8	8	7	11	13	14	14
8	10	10	12	12	15	16	16

Rep Neck Dec Row every OTHER RS row ___ times:

Gauge	32" / 81.5cm	36½" / 92.5cm	40" / 101.5cm	44½" / 113cm	48" / 122cm	52½" / 133.5cm	56" / 142cm
3	1	0	1	0	0	0	0
4	1	0	1	0	0	1	0
5	1	0	0	0	1	0	0
6	0	0	0	0	0	0	0
7	0	0	2	0	0	0	0
8	0	0	0	0	0	0	0

___ sts rem on each shoulder:

Gauge	32" / 81.5cm	36½" / 92.5cm	40" / 101.5cm	44½" / 113cm	48" / 122cm	52½" / 133.5cm	56" / 142cm
3	13	14	16	17	19	20	22
4	16	18	20	22	24	26	28
5	20	22	25	27	30	32	35
6	23	26	29	32	35	38	41
7	27	30	34	37	41	44	48
8	30	34	38	42	46	50	54

Shape Shoulders

Maintaining est patt and cont changing yarn at each neck edge, BO ___ sts at beg of next 2 rows:

Gauge	32" / 81.5cm	36½" / 92.5cm	40" / 101.5cm	44½" / 113cm	48" / 122cm	52½" / 133.5cm	56" / 142cm
3	6	8	8	8	10	10	12
4	8	10	10	12	12	14	14
5	6	8	8	10	10	10	12
6	8	8	10	10	12	12	14
7	10	10	12	12	14	14	16
8	8	8	10	10	12	12	14

Then BO ___ sts at beg of next 2 rows:

Gauge	32" / 81.5cm	36½" / 92.5cm	40" / 101.5cm	44½" / 113cm	48" / 122cm	52½" / 133.5cm	56" / 142cm
3	7	6	8	9	9	10	10
4	8	8	10	10	12	12	14
5	6	8	8	10	10	10	12
6	8	8	10	10	12	12	14
7	10	10	12	12	14	14	16
8	8	8	10	10	12	12	14

BO ___ more sts at beg of next 2 rows:

Gauge	32" / 81.5cm	36½" / 92.5cm	40" / 101.5cm	44½" / 113cm	48" / 122cm	52½" / 133.5cm	56" / 142cm
3	0	0	0	0	0	0	0
4	0	0	0	0	0	0	0
5	8	6	9	7	10	12	11
6	7	10	9	12	11	14	13
7	7	10	10	13	13	16	16
8	8	8	10	10	12	12	14

BO ___ more sts at beg of next 2 rows:

Gauge	32" / 81.5cm	36½" / 92.5cm	40" / 101.5cm	44½" / 113cm	48" / 122cm	52½" / 133.5cm	56" / 142cm
3	0	0	0	0	0	0	0
4	0	0	0	0	0	0	0
5	0	0	0	0	0	0	0
6	0	0	0	0	0	0	0
7	0	0	0	0	0	0	0
8	6	10	8	12	10	14	12

FINISHING

Block pieces to measurements. Sew shoulder seams. Sew side seams from hem to armhole marker.

Trim Armhole

With circular needle and RS facing, begin at underarm and pick up and knit an even number of sts around armhole. *Note: When working around, insert needle into 3 sts per 4 rows or into every BO stitch.* Pm and join for working in the rnd.

Rib Rnd: *K1, p1; rep from * to end of rnd.
Rep Rib Rnd until armhole measures 1" / 2.5 cm from sleeve edge.
Rep for other armhole.

Neckline Collar

With circular needle and RS facing, begin at right shoulder and pick up and knit an even number of sts around neckline. Pm and join for working in the rnd.

Rib Rnd: *K1, p1; rep from * to end of rnd.
Rep Rib Rnd until collar measures 1" / 2.5 cm from neck edge.
BO loosely.
Weave in ends.

CUFF-DOWN SOCKS

A good pair of socks goes a long way to making a knitter feel successful *and* comfortable! And it all starts with a beautiful pair of cuff-down socks, featuring a traditional heel flap and your favorite patterning.

SKILL LEVEL
Intermediate

STITCH PATTERN
Choose one stitch pattern (the pattern recipe will refer to it as Fave patt).
The sample shown uses Anchored Eyelets (page 132).

FINISHED MEASUREMENTS
Foot Circumference: approx. 4 (5¼, 6¼, 7¼, 8, 9)" / 10 (13.5, 16, 18.5, 20.5, 23) cm
Choose the size that is approx. 10% smaller than your actual foot circumference.
Foot Length is adjustable.
Sample size is 8" / 20.5 cm foot circumference.

YARN REQUIREMENTS

Gauge		4" / 10cm	5¼" / 13.5cm	6¼" / 16cm	7¼" / 18.5cm	8" / 20.5cm	9" / 23cm
	3	45 yds / 41 m	90 yds / 82 m	140 yds / 128 m	170 yds / 155 m	205 yds / 187 m	275 yds / 251 m
	4	50 yds / 46 m	115 yds / 105 m	175 yds / 160 m	205 yds / 187 m	235 yds / 215 m	310 yds / 283 m
	5	60 yds / 55 m	125 yds / 114 m	185 yds / 169 m	230 yds / 210 m	265 yds / 242 m	370 yds / 338 m
	6	75 yds / 69 m	150 yds / 137 m	235 yds / 215 m	295 yds / 270 m	325 yds / 297 m	455 yds / 416 m
	7	80 yds / 73 m	175 yds / 160 m	265 yds / 242 m	300 yds / 274 m	355 yds / 325 m	485 yds / 443 m
	8	85 yds / 78 m	180 yds / 165 m	280 yds / 256 m	325 yds / 297 m	385 yds / 352 m	525 yds / 480 m

NEEDLES & NOTIONS
A smaller gauge will provide good stability, so choose a needle size that is the same or slightly smaller than recommended for your yarn.
- Set of needles in the size necessary to obtain the desired gauge: set of 4 dpns; 32" / 80 cm circular for magic loop; or two 24" / 60 cm circulars for two-needle method
- 3 stitch markers (1 distinct for BOR)
- Yarn needle

SAMPLE PROJECT
The sample socks shown are worked with 1 skein Anzula Cloud in Peach (575 yards / 526 m per 3.5 oz / 100 g skein; 80% superwash merino, 10% cashmere, 10% nylon) *with a finished gauge of 8 sts and 11 rnds = 1" / 2.5 cm.*

PATTERN NOTES
- These socks are worked in the round from the cuff down. The heel is a standard heel flap, worked flat until after the heel turn, then rejoined in the round.
- Only work as instructed for your size. If the number for your size and gauge in the table is 0, omit those rows and/or stitches and move on to the next indicated stitch/row instructions.

PATTERN Cuff-Down Socks

CUFF

Cast on ___ sts:

Gauge	4" / 10cm	5¼" / 13.5cm	6¼" / 16cm	7¼" / 18.5cm	8" / 20.5cm	9" / 23cm
3	16	20	24	28	32	36
4	20	28	32	36	40	44
5	24	32	36	44	48	56
6	28	36	44	52	56	64
7	32	44	52	56	64	72
8	36	48	56	64	72	80

Rnd 1: *K3, p1; rep from * to end.
Rep Rnd 1 until cuff measures a finished length of 1½" / 4 cm.

LEG

Change to Fave patt and work even in pattern until sock measures a finished length of 7¾" / 19.5 cm or to desired length. Note the last round worked in Fave patt so that you can resume in the correct place after the heel flap.

HEEL

Heel Flap

Group the last ___ sts onto one needle to be worked for the heel flap:

Gauge	4" / 10cm	5¼" / 13.5cm	6¼" / 16cm	7¼" / 18.5cm	8" / 20.5cm	9" / 23cm
3	8	8	12	12	16	16
4	8	12	16	16	20	20
5	12	16	16	20	24	28
6	12	16	20	24	28	32
7	16	20	24	28	32	36
8	16	24	28	32	36	40

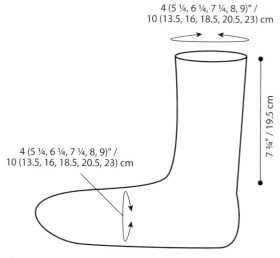

4 (5 ¼, 6 ¼, 7 ¼, 8, 9)" / 10 (13.5, 16, 18.5, 20.5, 23) cm

7 ¾" / 19.5 cm

4 (5 ¼, 6 ¼, 7 ¼, 8, 9)" / 10 (13.5, 16, 18.5, 20.5, 23) cm

*Measurements are an average of all the gauges listed.

Leave the remaining ___ sts on hold for the instep:

Gauge	4" / 10cm	5¼" / 13.5cm	6¼" / 16cm	7¼" / 18.5cm	8" / 20.5cm	9" / 23cm
3	8	12	12	16	16	20
4	12	16	16	20	20	24
5	12	16	20	24	24	28
6	16	20	24	28	28	32
7	16	24	28	28	32	36
8	20	24	28	32	36	40

With RS facing, work back and forth in rows on heel flap sts as follows:
Row 1 (RS): * Sl 1 wyib, k1; rep from * to end of heel flap.
Row 2 (WS): Sl 1 wyib, purl to last st of heel flap.
Rep Rows 1–2 ___ more times:

Gauge	4" / 10cm	5¼" / 13.5cm	6¼" / 16cm	7¼" / 18.5cm	8" / 20.5cm	9" / 23cm
3	3	4	5	6	7	8
4	4	6	7	8	9	10
5	5	7	8	10	11	13
6	6	8	10	12	13	15
7	7	10	12	13	15	17
8	8	11	13	15	17	19

Heel Turn

Row 1 (RS): Sl 1, k___, ssk, k1, turn:

Gauge	4" / 10cm	5¼" / 13.5cm	6¼" / 16cm	7¼" / 18.5cm	8" / 20.5cm	9" / 23cm
3	1	1	6	6	8	8
4	1	6	8	8	10	10
5	6	8	8	10	12	14
6	6	8	10	12	14	16
7	8	10	12	14	16	18
8	8	12	14	16	18	20

Row 2 (WS): Sl 1, p___, p2tog, p1, turn:

Gauge	4" / 10cm	5¼" / 13.5cm	6¼" / 16cm	7¼" / 18.5cm	8" / 20.5cm	9" / 23cm
3	1	1	3	3	3	3
4	1	3	3	3	3	3
5	3	3	3	3	3	3
6	3	3	3	3	3	3
7	3	3	3	3	3	3
8	3	3	3	3	3	3

There are ___ sts rem on either side of the turn gaps:

Gauge	4" / 10cm	5¼" / 13.5cm	6¼" / 16cm	7¼" / 18.5cm	8" / 20.5cm	9" / 23cm
3	1	1	2	2	4	4
4	1	2	4	4	6	6
5	2	4	4	6	8	10
6	2	4	6	8	10	12
7	4	6	8	10	12	14
8	4	8	10	12	14	16

Note: If there are only enough sts to work the decrease at the end of the following rows, just work the decrease and ignore the additional k1/p1 before the turn.
Row 3: Sl 1, knit to 1 st before the gap, ssk, k1, turn.
Row 4: Sl 1, purl to 1 st before the gap, p2tog, p1, turn.

Rep Rows 3–4 ___ more times:

Gauge	4" / 10cm	5¼" / 13.5cm	6¼" / 16cm	7¼" / 18.5cm	8" / 20.5cm	9" / 23cm
3	0	0	0	0	1	1
4	0	0	1	1	2	2
5	0	1	1	2	3	4
6	0	1	2	3	4	5
7	1	2	3	4	5	6
8	1	3	4	5	6	7

___ heel flap sts rem:

Gauge	4" / 10cm	5¼" / 13.5cm	6¼" / 16cm	7¼" / 18.5cm	8" / 20.5cm	9" / 23cm
3	4	4	8	8	10	10
4	4	8	10	10	12	12
5	8	10	10	12	14	16
6	8	10	12	14	16	18
7	10	12	14	16	18	20
8	10	14	16	18	20	22

Next Row (RS): Sl 1, knit to end of heel flap.

Gusset Decreases

Pick up and knit ___ sts along left edge of heel flap, pm:

Gauge	4" / 10cm	5¼" / 13.5cm	6¼" / 16cm	7¼" / 18.5cm	8" / 20.5cm	9" / 23cm
3	5	6	7	8	9	10
4	6	8	9	10	11	12
5	7	9	10	12	13	15
6	8	10	12	14	15	17
7	9	12	14	15	17	19
8	10	13	15	17	19	21

Work in est Fave patt across ___ sts of instep, pm:

Gauge	4" / 10cm	5¼" / 13.5cm	6¼" / 16cm	7¼" / 18.5cm	8" / 20.5cm	9" / 23cm
3	8	12	12	16	16	20
4	12	16	16	20	20	24
5	12	16	20	24	24	28
6	16	20	24	28	28	32
7	16	24	28	28	32	36
8	20	24	28	32	36	40

Pick up and knit ___ sts along right edge of heel flap:

Gauge	4" / 10cm	5¼" / 13.5cm	6¼" / 16cm	7¼" / 18.5cm	8" / 20.5cm	9" / 23cm
3	5	6	7	8	9	10
4	6	8	9	10	11	12
5	7	9	10	12	13	15
6	8	10	12	14	15	17
7	9	12	14	15	17	19
8	10	13	15	17	19	21

Then knit ___ sts across heel flap. Pm for new beg of rnd.

Gauge	4" / 10cm	5¼" / 13.5cm	6¼" / 16cm	7¼" / 18.5cm	8" / 20.5cm	9" / 23cm
3	2	2	4	4	5	5
4	2	4	5	5	6	6
5	4	5	5	6	7	8
6	4	5	6	7	8	9
7	5	6	7	8	9	10
8	5	7	8	9	10	11

___ total sts:

Gauge	4" / 10cm	5¼" / 13.5cm	6¼" / 16cm	7¼" / 18.5cm	8" / 20.5cm	9" / 23cm
3	22	28	34	40	44	50
4	28	40	44	50	54	60
5	34	44	50	60	64	74
6	40	50	60	70	74	84
7	44	60	70	74	84	94
8	50	64	74	84	94	104

Dec Rnd: Knit until 3 sts before 1st m, k2tog, k1, sm, work in est Fave patt to next m, sm, k1, ssk, knit to end of rnd. 2 sts dec'd; 1 st dec'd on each side of sole.

Rnd 2: Knit to m, sm, work in est Fave patt to next m, sm, knit to end of rnd.

Rep last 2 rnds ___ more times:

Gauge	4" / 10cm	5¼" / 13.5cm	6¼" / 16cm	7¼" / 18.5cm	8" / 20.5cm	9" / 23cm
3	2	3	4	5	5	6
4	3	5	5	6	6	7
5	4	5	6	7	7	8
6	5	6	7	8	8	9
7	5	7	8	8	9	10
8	6	7	8	9	10	11

___ sts rem:

Gauge	4" / 10cm	5¼" / 13.5cm	6¼" / 16cm	7¼" / 18.5cm	8" / 20.5cm	9" / 23cm
3	16	20	24	28	32	36
4	20	28	32	36	40	44
5	24	32	36	44	48	56
6	28	36	44	52	56	64
7	32	44	52	56	64	72
8	36	48	56	64	72	80

FOOT

Work even in patt as est (Fave patt between 1st and 2nd m, Stockinette st on sole) until foot meas ___" / ___ cm less than desired total foot length:

Gauge	4" / 10cm	5¼" / 13.5cm	6¼" / 16cm	7¼" / 18.5cm	8" / 20.5cm	9" / 23cm
3	1.25" / 3 cm	1.25" / 3 cm	1.75" / 4.5 cm	1.75" / 4.5 cm	2" / 5 cm	2.25" / 5.5 cm
4	1.25" / 3 cm	1.5" / 4 cm	1.75" / 4.5 cm	1.75" / 4.5 cm	2.25" / 5.5 cm	2.25" / 5.5 cm
5	1.25" / 3 cm	1.5" / 4 cm	1.75" / 4.5 cm	2" / 5 cm	2.25" / 5.5 cm	2.5" / 6.5 cm
6	1.25" / 3 cm	1.5" / 4 cm	1.75" / 4.5 cm	2" / 5 cm	2.25" / 5.5 cm	2.5" / 6.5 cm
7	1.25" / 3 cm	1.5" / 4 cm	1.75" / 4.5 cm	2" / 5 cm	2.25" / 5.5 cm	2.5" / 6.5 cm
8	1.25" / 3 cm	1.5" / 4 cm	1.75" / 4.5 cm	2" / 5 cm	2.25" / 5.5 cm	2.5" / 6.5 cm

TOE

Dec Rnd: [Knit until 3 sts before m, k2tog, k1, sm, k1, ssk] twice, knit to end of rnd. 4 sts dec'd.
Rnd 2: Knit.
Rep last 2 rnds ___ more times:

Gauge	4" / 10cm	5¼" / 13.5cm	6¼" / 16cm	7¼" / 18.5cm	8" / 20.5cm	9" / 23cm
3	1	1	3	3	3	3
4	1	3	3	3	5	5
5	3	3	3	5	5	7
6	3	3	5	5	7	7
7	3	5	5	7	7	9
8	3	5	7	7	9	9

___ sts rem:

Gauge	4" / 10cm	5¼" / 13.5cm	6¼" / 16cm	7¼" / 18.5cm	8" / 20.5cm	9" / 23cm
3	8	12	8	12	16	20
4	12	12	16	20	16	20
5	8	16	20	20	24	24
6	12	20	20	28	24	32
7	16	20	28	24	32	32
8	20	24	24	32	32	40

Rep Dec Rnd every rnd 4 times:

Gauge	4" / 10cm	5¼" / 13.5cm	6¼" / 16cm	7¼" / 18.5cm	8" / 20.5cm	9" / 23cm
3	1	2	0	1	2	3
4	2	1	2	3	1	2
5	0	2	3	2	3	2
6	1	3	2	4	2	4
7	2	2	4	2	4	3
8	3	3	2	4	3	5

___ sts rem:

Gauge	4" / 10cm	5¼" / 13.5cm	6¼" / 16cm	7¼" / 18.5cm	8" / 20.5cm	9" / 23cm
3	4	4	8	8	8	8
4	4	8	8	8	12	12
5	8	8	8	12	12	16
6	8	8	12	12	16	16
7	8	12	12	16	16	20
8	8	12	16	16	20	20

Knit to start of instep (first) m.
Close toe with Kitchener St (page 178).
Work Second Sock same as the first.

FINISHING
Block socks as desired. Weave in ends.

TWO-BUTTON CARDIGAN

Perfect for layering, this cardigan features a lush collar, an open front, and ample opportunity to play with a variety of stitches.

SKILL LEVEL
Intermediate

STITCH PATTERN
Choose one stitch pattern (the pattern recipe will refer to it as Fave patt) for the body and sleeves.
The sample shown uses Woven Herringbone (page 157).

FINISHED MEASUREMENTS
Bust Circumference (seamed and buttoned):

Gauge	34³/₄" / 88.5 cm	38³/₄" / 98.5 cm	42³/₄" / 108.5 cm	46³/₄" / 118.5cm	50³/₄" / 129cm	54³/₄" / 139cm	58³/₄" / 149cm
3	32.75" 83 cm	35.25" 89.5 cm	39.25" 99.5 cm	44.75" 113.5 cm	48.75" 124 cm	51.25" 130 cm	55.25" 140.5 cm
4	33.5" 85 cm	37.5" 95.5 cm	41.5" 105.5 cm	45.5" 115.5 cm	49.5" 125.5 cm	53.5" 136 cm	57.5" 146 cm
5	31.5" 80 cm	36.5" 92.5 cm	40.5" 103 cm	43.5" 110.5 cm	47.5" 120.5 cm	52.5" 133.5 cm	56.5" 143.5 cm
6	31.75" 80.5 cm	36.25" 92 cm	39.75" 101 cm	44.25" 112.5 cm	47.75" 121.5 cm	52.25" 132.5 cm	55.75" 141.5 cm
7	31.75" 80.5 cm	35.75" 91 cm	40.25" 102 cm	43.25" 110 cm	47.75" 121.5 cm	51.75" 131.5 cm	56.25" 143 cm
8	31.75" 80.5 cm	35.75" 91 cm	39.75" 101 cm	43.75" 111 cm	47.75" 121.5 cm	51.75" 131.5 cm	55.75" 141.5 cm

The pattern will reference the averaged bust circumference measurements throughout the pattern charts and lengths: 34¾ (38¾, 42¾, 46¾, 50¾, 54¾, 58¾)" / 88.5 (98.5, 108.5, 118.5, 129, 139, 149) cm.
Choose the size that is approx. 2–3" / 5–7.5 cm larger than your actual bust circumference.
Garment Length: 23¾ (24½, 25, 26¼, 26¾, 27½, 28¼)" / 60.5 (62, 63.5, 66.5, 68, 70, 72) cm
Sample size is 38¾" / 98.5 cm bust circumference.

YARN REQUIREMENTS

Gauge	34³/₄" / 88.5 cm	38³/₄" / 98.5 cm	42³/₄" / 108.5 cm	46³/₄" / 118.5cm	50³/₄" / 129cm	54³/₄" / 139cm	58³/₄" / 149cm
3	405 yds 370 m	465 yds 425 m	515 yds 471 m	580 yds 530 m	635 yds 581 m	685 yds 626 m	710 yds 649 m
4	580 yds 530 m	645 yds 590 m	720 yds 658 m	800 yds 732 m	860 yds 786 m	945 yds 864 m	1025 yds 937 m
5	1005 yds 919 m	1100 yds 1006 m	1215 yds 1111 m	1345 yds 1230 m	1485 yds 1358 m	1595 yds 1458 m	1760 yds 1609 m
6	1260 yds 1152 m	1420 yds 1298 m	1565 yds 1431 m	1755 yds 1605 m	1905 yds 1742 m	2070 yds 1893 m	2235 yds 2044 m
7	1400 yds 1280 m	1560 yds 1426 m	1740 yds 1591 m	1930 yds 1765 m	2115 yds 1934 m	2280 yds 2085 m	2485 yds 2272 m
8	1535 yds 1404 m	1725 yds 1577 m	1910 yds 1747 m	2140 yds 1957 m	2320 yds 2121 m	2525 yds 2309 m	2735 yds 2501 m

NEEDLES & NOTIONS

Choose a needle size that is slightly larger than recommended for your yarn so as to achieve a relaxed drape.

- Set of needles (for the body) in the size necessary to obtain the desired gauge
- Circular needles (for the collar), 24" / 60 cm in length, in the same size as the body set
- Yarn needle
- 2 stitch markers
- Two 1⅛" / 3 cm buttons

SAMPLE PROJECT

The sample cardigan shown is worked with 7 skeins Premier Everyday Soft Worsted in Chocolate #ED100-11 (203 yards / 186 m per 4 oz / 113 g skein; 100% anti-pilling acrylic) with a finished gauge of 6 sts and 10 rows = 1" / 2.5 cm.

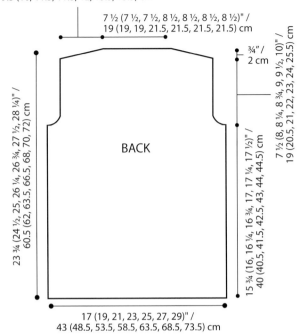

3 ¾ (4, 4 ½, 4 ½, 4 ¾, 5 ¼, 5 ¼)" /
9.5 (10, 11.5, 11.5, 12, 13.5, 13.5) cm

7 ½ (7 ½, 7 ½, 8 ½, 8 ½, 8 ½, 8 ½)" /
19 (19, 19, 21.5, 21.5, 21.5, 21.5) cm

¾" /
2 cm

BACK

7 ½ (8, 8 ¼, 8 ¾, 9, 9 ½, 10)" /
19 (20.5, 21, 22, 23, 24, 25.5) cm

23 ¾ (24 ½, 25, 26 ¼, 26 ¾, 27 ½, 28 ¼)" /
60.5 (62, 63.5, 66.5, 68, 70, 72) cm

15 ¾ (16, 16 ¼, 16 ¾, 17, 17 ¼, 17 ½)" /
40 (40.5, 41.5, 42.5, 43, 44, 44.5) cm

17 (19, 21, 23, 25, 27, 29)" /
43 (48.5, 53.5, 58.5, 63.5, 68.5, 73.5) cm

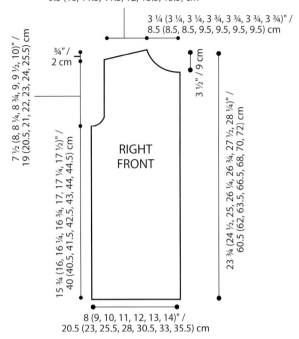

3 ¾ (4, 4 ½, 4 ½, 4 ¾, 5 ¼, 5 ¼)" /
9.5 (10, 11.5, 11.5, 12, 13.5, 13.5) cm

3 ¼ (3 ¼, 3 ¼, 3 ¾, 3 ¾, 3 ¾, 3 ¾)" /
8.5 (8.5, 8.5, 9.5, 9.5, 9.5, 9.5) cm

¾" /
2 cm

3 ½" / 9 cm

RIGHT
FRONT

7 ½ (8, 8 ¼, 8 ¾, 9, 9 ½, 10)" /
19 (20.5, 21, 22, 23, 24, 25.5) cm

23 ¾ (24 ½, 25, 26 ¼, 26 ¾, 27 ½, 28 ¼)" /
60.5 (62, 63.5, 66.5, 68, 70, 72) cm

15 ¾ (16, 16 ¼, 16 ¾, 17, 17 ¼, 17 ½)" /
40 (40.5, 41.5, 42.5, 43, 44, 44.5) cm

8 (9, 10, 11, 12, 13, 14)" /
20.5 (23, 25.5, 28, 30.5, 33, 35.5) cm

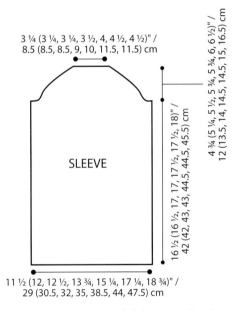

3 ¼ (3 ¼, 3 ¼, 3 ½, 4, 4 ½, 4 ½)" /
8.5 (8.5, 8.5, 9, 10, 11.5, 11.5) cm

4 ¾ (5 ¼, 5 ½, 5 ¾, 5 ¾, 6, 6 ½)" /
12 (13.5, 14, 14.5, 14.5, 15, 16.5) cm

SLEEVE

16 ½ (16 ½, 17, 17, 17 ¼, 17 ½, 18)" /
42 (42, 43, 43, 44.5, 44.5, 45.5) cm

11 ½ (12, 12 ½, 13 ¾, 15 ¼, 17 ¼, 18 ¾)" /
29 (30.5, 32, 35, 38.5, 44, 47.5) cm

*Measurements are an average of all the gauges listed.

PATTERN NOTES

- Cardigan is worked flat and then seamed together. Because of the seaming, 2 sts have been added to the instructions, 1 on either side of your desired stitch pattern, that you'll knit on every row.
- Only work as instructed for your size. If the number for your size and gauge in the table is 0, omit those rows and/or stitches and move on to the next indicated stitch/ row instructions.

PATTERN Two-Button Cardigan

BACK
Cast on ____ sts:

Gauge	34¾" / 88.5 cm	38¾" / 98.5 cm	42¾" / 108.5 cm	46¾" / 118.5cm	50¾" / 129cm	54¾" / 139cm	58¾" / 149cm
3	50	58	62	70	74	82	86
4	70	78	86	94	102	110	118
5	86	94	106	114	126	134	146
6	102	114	126	138	150	162	174
7	118	130	146	158	174	186	202
8	134	150	166	182	198	214	230

Rib Row: K1, *k2, p2; rep from * to last st, k1.
Rep Rib Row until hem measures a finished length of approx. 1½" / 4 cm from cast-on edge, ending with a WS row.

Body
Change to Fave patt for the body as follows:
Row 1 (RS): K1, work Fave patt RS row to last st, k1.
Row 2 (WS): K1, work Fave patt WS row to last st, k1.
Rep Rows 1–2 for every row, repeating rows of Fave patt as est, until back measures a finished length of 15¾ (16, 16¼, 16¾, 17, 17¼, 17½)" / 40 (40.5, 41.5, 42.5, 43, 44, 44.5) cm from cast-on edge, ending with a WS row.

Armhole
BO ____ sts at beg of next 2 rows:

Gauge	34¾" / 88.5 cm	38¾" / 98.5 cm	42¾" / 108.5 cm	46¾" / 118.5cm	50¾" / 129cm	54¾" / 139cm	58¾" / 149cm
3	1	3	3	4	5	6	7
4	3	4	5	6	7	9	11
5	3	4	6	7	9	10	13
6	4	5	7	8	11	13	16
7	4	6	8	9	12	14	18
8	4	7	9	11	14	17	21

____ sts rem:

Gauge	34¾" / 88.5 cm	38¾" / 98.5 cm	42¾" / 108.5 cm	46¾" / 118.5cm	50¾" / 129cm	54¾" / 139cm	58¾" / 149cm
3	48	52	56	62	64	70	72
4	64	70	76	82	88	92	96
5	80	86	94	100	108	114	120
6	94	104	112	122	128	136	142
7	110	118	130	140	150	158	166
8	126	136	148	160	170	180	188

Dec Row (RS): K1, ssk, maintain est Fave patt to last 3 sts, k2tog, k1. 2 sts dec'd at each armhole edge.
Rep Dec Row every RS row ____ more times:

Gauge	34¾" / 88.5 cm	38¾" / 98.5 cm	42¾" / 108.5 cm	46¾" / 118.5cm	50¾" / 129cm	54¾" / 139cm	58¾" / 149cm
3	0	2	2	3	4	5	6
4	2	3	4	5	6	8	10
5	2	3	5	6	8	9	12
6	3	4	6	7	10	12	15
7	3	5	7	8	11	13	17
8	3	6	8	10	13	16	20

___ sts rem:

Gauge	34¾" / 88.5 cm	38¾" / 98.5 cm	42¾" / 108.5 cm	46¾" / 118.5 cm	50¾" / 129 cm	54¾" / 139 cm	58¾" / 149 cm
3	46	46	50	54	54	58	58
4	58	62	66	70	74	74	74
5	74	78	82	86	90	94	94
6	86	94	98	106	106	110	110
7	102	106	114	122	126	130	130
8	118	122	130	138	142	146	146

Work even in est Fave patt, knitting the first and last st of every row, until armhole measures a finished length of 7½ (8, 8¼, 8¾, 9, 9½, 10)" / 19 (20.5, 21, 22, 23, 24, 25.5) cm from BO edge, ending with a WS row.

Shape Shoulders

Maintaining est Fave patt, BO ___ sts at beg of next 2 rows:

Gauge	34¾" / 88.5 cm	38¾" / 98.5 cm	42¾" / 108.5 cm	46¾" / 118.5 cm	50¾" / 129 cm	54¾" / 139 cm	58¾" / 149 cm
3	6	6	8	8	8	8	8
4	8	8	10	10	10	10	10
5	10	10	12	12	8	8	8
6	10	12	14	14	10	10	10
7	8	10	10	10	12	12	12
8	10	10	12	12	12	14	14

Maintaining est Fave patt, BO ___ more sts at beg of next 2 rows:

Gauge	34¾" / 88.5 cm	38¾" / 98.5 cm	42¾" / 108.5 cm	46¾" / 118.5 cm	50¾" / 129 cm	54¾" / 139 cm	58¾" / 149 cm
3	6	6	6	6	6	8	8
4	6	8	8	8	10	10	10
5	8	10	10	10	8	8	8
6	10	12	12	14	10	10	10
7	8	10	10	10	12	12	12
8	10	10	12	12	12	14	14

Maintaining est Fave patt, BO ___ more sts at beg of next 2 rows:

Gauge	34¾" / 88.5 cm	38¾" / 98.5 cm	42¾" / 108.5 cm	46¾" / 118.5 cm	50¾" / 129 cm	54¾" / 139 cm	58¾" / 149 cm
3	0	0	0	0	0	0	0
4	0	0	0	0	0	0	0
5	0	0	0	0	8	10	10
6	0	0	0	0	8	10	10
7	10	8	12	12	10	12	12
8	10	12	12	12	14	12	12

BO rem ___ sts on next RS row:

Gauge	34¾" / 88.5 cm	38¾" / 98.5 cm	42¾" / 108.5 cm	46¾" / 118.5 cm	50¾" / 129 cm	54¾" / 139 cm	58¾" / 149 cm
3	22	22	22	26	26	26	26
4	30	30	30	34	34	34	34
5	38	38	38	42	42	42	42
6	46	46	46	50	50	50	50
7	50	50	50	58	58	58	58
8	58	58	58	66	66	66	66

RIGHT FRONT

Cast on ____ sts:

Gauge	34¾" / 88.5 cm	38¾" / 98.5 cm	42¾" / 108.5 cm	46¾" / 118.5cm	50¾" / 129cm	54¾" / 139cm	58¾" / 149cm
3	26	26	30	34	38	38	42
4	34	38	42	46	50	54	58
5	38	46	50	54	58	66	70
6	46	54	58	66	70	78	82
7	54	62	70	74	82	90	98
8	62	70	78	86	94	102	110

Rib Row: K1, *k2, p2; rep from * to last st, k1.
Rep Rib Row until hem measures a finished length of approx. 1½" / 4 cm from cast-on edge, ending with a WS row.

Body

Change to Fave patt for the body as follows:
Row 1 (RS): K1, work Fave patt RS row to last st, k1.
Row 2 (WS): K1, work Fave patt WS row to last st, k1.
Rep Rows 1–2 for every row, repeating rows of Fave patt as est, until front measures a finished length of 15¾ (16, 16¼, 16¾, 17, 17¼, 17½)" / 40 (40.5, 41.5, 42.5, 43, 44, 44.5) cm from cast-on edge, ending with a RS row.

Armhole

BO ____ sts at beg of next WS row:

Gauge	34¾" / 88.5 cm	38¾" / 98.5 cm	42¾" / 108.5 cm	46¾" / 118.5cm	50¾" / 129cm	54¾" / 139cm	58¾" / 149cm
3	1	3	3	4	5	6	7
4	3	4	5	6	7	9	11
5	3	4	6	7	9	10	13
6	4	5	7	8	11	13	16
7	4	6	8	9	12	14	18
8	4	7	9	11	14	17	21

____ sts rem:

Gauge	34¾" / 88.5 cm	38¾" / 98.5 cm	42¾" / 108.5 cm	46¾" / 118.5cm	50¾" / 129cm	54¾" / 139cm	58¾" / 149cm
3	25	23	27	30	33	32	35
4	31	34	37	40	43	45	47
5	35	42	44	47	49	56	57
6	42	49	51	58	59	65	66
7	50	56	62	65	70	76	80
8	58	63	69	75	80	85	89

Dec Row (RS): K1, maintain est patt to last 3 sts, k2tog, k1. 1 st dec'd at armhole edge.
Rep Dec Row every RS row ____ more times:

Gauge	34¾" / 88.5 cm	38¾" / 98.5 cm	42¾" / 108.5 cm	46¾" / 118.5cm	50¾" / 129cm	54¾" / 139cm	58¾" / 149cm
3	0	2	2	3	4	5	6
4	2	3	4	5	6	8	10
5	2	3	5	6	8	9	12
6	3	4	6	7	10	12	15
7	3	5	7	8	11	13	17
8	3	6	8	10	13	16	20

___ sts rem:

Gauge	34¾" / 88.5 cm	38¾" / 98.5 cm	42¾" / 108.5 cm	46¾" / 118.5cm	50¾" /129cm	54¾" /139cm	58¾" /149cm
3	24	20	24	26	28	26	28
4	28	30	32	34	36	36	36
5	32	38	38	40	40	46	44
6	38	44	44	50	48	52	50
7	46	50	54	56	58	62	62
8	54	56	60	64	66	68	68

Work even in est Fave patt, knitting the first and last st of every row, until armhole measures a finished length of 4½ (5, 5¼, 5¾, 6, 6½, 7)" / 11.5 (12.5, 13.5, 14.5, 15, 16.5, 18) cm from BO edge, ending with a WS row.

Shape Front Neck

Cont in patt as est and BO ___ sts at beg of next RS row:

Gauge	34¾" / 88.5 cm	38¾" / 98.5 cm	42¾" / 108.5 cm	46¾" / 118.5cm	50¾" /129cm	54¾" /139cm	58¾" /149cm
3	9	6	8	9	11	8	9
4	11	11	11	11	11	11	11
5	10	13	11	13	11	14	13
6	13	13	13	15	16	15	13
7	13	15	15	15	15	17	17
8	15	15	15	18	18	18	18

Work 1 WS row in patt as est.
Neck Dec Row (RS): K1, ssk, work in est Fave patt to last st, k1. 1 st dec'd at neck edge.
Rep Neck Dec Row every RS row ___ more times:

Gauge	34¾" / 88.5 cm	38¾" / 98.5 cm	42¾" / 108.5 cm	46¾" / 118.5cm	50¾" /129cm	54¾" /139cm	58¾" /149cm
3	0	0	0	0	0	0	0
4	1	1	1	2	2	2	2
5	2	0	0	0	0	2	0
6	4	3	4	3	1	3	3
7	2	2	2	6	6	6	6
8	4	4	4	6	6	6	6

___ sts rem:

Gauge	34¾" / 88.5 cm	38¾" / 98.5 cm	42¾" / 108.5 cm	46¾" / 118.5cm	50¾" /129cm	54¾" /139cm	58¾" /149cm
3	14	13	15	16	16	17	18
4	15	17	19	20	22	22	22
5	19	24	26	26	28	29	30
6	20	27	26	31	30	33	33
7	30	32	36	34	36	38	38
8	34	36	40	39	41	43	43

Rep Neck Dec Row every OTHER RS row ___ times:

Gauge	34¾" / 88.5 cm	38¾" / 98.5 cm	42¾" / 108.5 cm	46¾" / 118.5cm	50¾" /129cm	54¾" /139cm	58¾" /149cm
3	2	1	1	2	2	1	2
4	1	1	1	2	2	2	2
5	1	4	4	4	4	3	4
6	0	3	0	3	2	3	3
7	4	4	4	2	2	2	2
8	4	4	4	3	3	3	3

Gauge	34³/₄" / 88.5 cm	38³/₄" / 98.5 cm	42³/₄" / 108.5 cm	46³/₄" / 118.5cm	50³/₄" / 129cm	54³/₄" / 139cm	58³/₄" / 149cm
3	12	12	14	14	14	16	16
4	14	16	18	18	20	20	20
5	18	20	22	22	24	26	26
6	20	24	26	28	28	30	30
7	26	28	32	32	34	36	36
8	30	32	36	36	38	40	40

Work even in est patt until armhole measures a finished length of 7½ (8, 8½, 9, 9, 9½, 10)" / 19 (20.5, 21.5, 23, 23, 24, 25.5) cm from BO edge, ending with a RS row.

Shape Shoulders

Maintaining est Fave patt, BO ___ sts at beg of next WS row:

Gauge	34³/₄" / 88.5 cm	38³/₄" / 98.5 cm	42³/₄" / 108.5 cm	46³/₄" / 118.5cm	50³/₄" / 129cm	54³/₄" / 139cm	58³/₄" / 149cm
3	6	6	8	8	8	8	8
4	8	8	10	10	10	10	10
5	10	10	12	12	8	8	8
6	10	12	14	14	10	10	10
7	8	10	10	10	12	12	12
8	10	10	12	12	12	14	14

Maintaining est Fave patt, BO ___ rem/more sts at beg of next WS row:

Gauge	34³/₄" / 88.5 cm	38³/₄" / 98.5 cm	42³/₄" / 108.5 cm	46³/₄" / 118.5cm	50³/₄" / 129cm	54³/₄" / 139cm	58³/₄" / 149cm
3	6	6	6	6	6	8	8
4	6	8	8	8	10	10	10
5	8	10	10	10	8	8	8
6	10	12	12	14	10	10	10
7	8	10	10	10	12	12	12
8	10	10	12	12	12	14	14

Maintaining est Fave patt, BO ___ rem sts at beg of next WS row:

Gauge	34³/₄" / 88.5 cm	38³/₄" / 98.5 cm	42³/₄" / 108.5 cm	46³/₄" / 118.5cm	50³/₄" / 129cm	54³/₄" / 139cm	58³/₄" / 149cm
3	0	0	0	0	0	0	0
4	0	0	0	0	0	0	0
5	0	0	0	0	8	10	10
6	0	0	0	0	8	10	10
7	10	8	12	12	10	12	12
8	10	12	12	12	14	12	12

LEFT FRONT

Cast on ___ sts:

Gauge	34³/₄" / 88.5 cm	38³/₄" / 98.5 cm	42³/₄" / 108.5 cm	46³/₄" / 118.5cm	50³/₄" / 129cm	54³/₄" / 139cm	58³/₄" / 149cm
3	26	26	30	34	38	38	42
4	34	38	42	46	50	54	58
5	38	46	50	54	58	66	70
6	46	54	58	66	70	78	82
7	54	62	70	74	82	90	98
8	62	70	78	86	94	102	110

Rib Row: K1, *k2, p2; rep from * to last st, k1.
Rep Rib Row until hem measures a finished length of approx. 1½" / 4 cm from cast-on edge, ending with a WS row.

Body

Change to Fave patt for the body as follows:
Row 1 (RS): K1, work Fave patt RS row to last st, k1.

Row 2 (WS): K1, work Fave patt WS row to last st, k1.
Rep Rows 1–2 for every row, repeating rows of Fave patt as est, until front measures a finished length of 15¾ (16, 16¼, 16¾, 17, 17¼, 17½)" / 40 (40.5, 41.5, 42.5, 43, 44, 44.5) cm from cast-on edge, ending with a WS row.

Armhole

BO ___ sts at beg of next RS row:

Gauge	34¾" / 88.5 cm	38¾" / 98.5 cm	42¾" / 108.5 cm	46¾" / 118.5cm	50¾" / 129cm	54¾" / 139cm	58¾" / 149cm
3	1	3	3	4	5	6	7
4	3	4	5	6	7	9	11
5	3	4	6	7	9	10	13
6	4	5	7	8	11	13	16
7	4	6	8	9	12	14	18
8	4	7	9	11	14	17	21

___ sts rem:

Gauge	34¾" / 88.5 cm	38¾" / 98.5 cm	42¾" / 108.5 cm	46¾" / 118.5cm	50¾" / 129cm	54¾" / 139cm	58¾" / 149cm
3	25	23	27	30	33	32	35
4	31	34	37	40	43	45	47
5	35	42	44	47	49	56	57
6	42	49	51	58	59	65	66
7	50	56	62	65	70	76	80
8	58	63	69	75	80	85	89

Dec Row (RS): K1, ssk, maintain est patt to last st, k1. 1 st dec'd at armhole edge.
Rep Dec Row every RS row ___ more times:

Gauge	34¾" / 88.5 cm	38¾" / 98.5 cm	42¾" / 108.5 cm	46¾" / 118.5cm	50¾" / 129cm	54¾" / 139cm	58¾" / 149cm
3	0	2	2	3	4	5	6
4	2	3	4	5	6	8	10
5	2	3	5	6	8	9	12
6	3	4	6	7	10	12	15
7	3	5	7	8	11	13	17
8	3	6	8	10	13	16	20

___ sts rem:

Gauge	34¾" / 88.5 cm	38¾" / 98.5 cm	42¾" / 108.5 cm	46¾" / 118.5cm	50¾" / 129cm	54¾" / 139cm	58¾" / 149cm
3	24	20	24	26	28	26	28
4	28	30	32	34	36	36	36
5	32	38	38	40	40	46	44
6	38	44	44	50	48	52	50
7	46	50	54	56	58	62	62
8	54	56	60	64	66	68	68

Work even in est Fave patt, knitting the first and last st of every row, until armhole measures a finished length of 4½ (5, 5¼, 5¾, 6, 6½, 7)" / 11.5 (12.5, 13.5, 14.5, 15, 16.5, 18) cm from BO edge, ending with a RS row.

Shape Front Neck

Cont in patt as est and BO ___ sts at beg of next WS row:

Gauge	34¾" / 88.5 cm	38¾" / 98.5 cm	42¾" / 108.5 cm	46¾" / 118.5cm	50¾" / 129cm	54¾" / 139cm	58¾" / 149cm
3	9	6	8	9	11	8	9
4	11	11	11	11	11	11	11
5	10	13	11	13	11	14	13
6	13	13	13	15	16	15	13
7	13	15	15	15	15	17	17
8	15	15	15	18	18	18	18

Neck Dec Row (RS): K1, work in est Fave patt to last 3 sts, k2tog, k1. 1 st dec'd at neck edge. Rep Neck Dec Row every RS row ___ more times:

Gauge	34¾" / 88.5 cm	38¾" / 98.5 cm	42¾" / 108.5 cm	46¾" / 118.5cm	50¾" / 129cm	54¾" / 139cm	58¾" / 149cm
3	0	0	0	0	0	0	0
4	1	1	1	2	2	2	2
5	2	0	0	0	0	2	0
6	4	3	4	3	1	3	3
7	2	2	2	6	6	6	6
8	4	4	4	6	6	6	6

___ sts rem:

Gauge	34¾" / 88.5 cm	38¾" / 98.5 cm	42¾" / 108.5 cm	46¾" / 118.5cm	50¾" / 129cm	54¾" / 139cm	58¾" / 149cm
3	14	13	15	16	16	17	18
4	15	17	19	20	22	22	22
5	19	24	26	26	28	29	30
6	20	27	26	31	30	33	33
7	30	32	36	34	36	38	38
8	34	36	40	39	41	43	43

Rep Neck Dec Row every OTHER RS row ___ times:

Gauge	34¾" / 88.5 cm	38¾" / 98.5 cm	42¾" / 108.5 cm	46¾" / 118.5cm	50¾" / 129cm	54¾" / 139cm	58¾" / 149cm
3	2	1	1	2	2	1	2
4	1	1	1	2	2	2	2
5	1	4	4	4	4	3	4
6	4	3	0	3	2	3	3
7	4	4	4	2	2	2	2
8	4	4	4	3	3	3	3

___ sts rem:

Gauge	34¾" / 88.5 cm	38¾" / 98.5 cm	42¾" / 108.5 cm	46¾" / 118.5cm	50¾" / 129cm	54¾" / 139cm	58¾" / 149cm
3	12	12	14	14	14	16	16
4	14	16	18	18	20	20	20
5	18	20	22	22	24	26	26
6	20	24	26	28	28	30	30
7	26	28	32	32	34	36	36
8	30	32	36	36	38	40	40

Work even in est patt until armhole measures a finished length of 7½ (8, 8½, 9, 9, 9½, 10)" / 19 (20.5, 21.5, 23, 23, 24, 25.5) cm from BO edge, ending with a WS row.

Shape Shoulders
Maintaining est Fave patt, BO ___ sts at beg of next RS row:

Gauge	34¾" / 88.5 cm	38¾" / 98.5 cm	42¾" / 108.5 cm	46¾" / 118.5cm	50¾" / 129cm	54¾" / 139cm	58¾" / 149cm
3	6	6	8	8	8	8	8
4	8	8	10	10	10	10	10
5	10	10	12	12	8	8	8
6	10	12	14	14	10	10	10
7	8	10	10	10	12	12	12
8	10	10	12	12	12	14	14

Maintaining est Fave patt, BO ___ rem/more sts at beg of next RS row:

Gauge	34¾" / 88.5 cm	38¾" / 98.5 cm	42¾" / 108.5 cm	46¾" / 118.5cm	50¾" / 129cm	54¾" / 139cm	58¾" / 149cm
3	6	6	6	6	6	8	8
4	6	8	8	8	10	10	10
5	8	10	10	10	8	8	8
6	10	12	12	14	10	10	10
7	8	10	10	10	12	12	12
8	10	10	12	12	12	14	14

Maintaining est Fave patt, BO ___ rem sts at beg of next RS row:

Gauge	34¾" / 88.5 cm	38¾" / 98.5 cm	42¾" / 108.5 cm	46¾" / 118.5 cm	50¾" / 129 cm	54¾" / 139 cm	58¾" / 149 cm
3	0	0	0	0	0	0	0
4	0	0	0	0	0	0	0
5	0	0	0	0	8	10	10
6	0	0	0	0	8	10	10
7	10	8	12	12	10	12	12
8	10	12	12	12	14	12	12

SLEEVES (MAKE 2)

Cuff

Cast on ___ sts:

Gauge	34¾" / 88.5 cm	38¾" / 98.5 cm	42¾" / 108.5 cm	46¾" / 118.5 cm	50¾" / 129 cm	54¾" / 139 cm	58¾" / 149 cm
3	34	38	38	42	46	54	58
4	46	50	50	54	62	70	74
5	58	58	62	70	74	86	94
6	70	70	74	82	90	102	110
7	78	82	86	94	106	118	130
8	90	94	102	110	122	138	150

Rib Row: K1, *k2, p2; rep from * to last st, k1.
Rep Rib Row until hem measures a finished length of approx 1½" / 4 cm from cast-on edge, ending with a WS row.

Body

Change to Fave patt for the body as follows:
Row 1 (RS): K1, work Fave patt RS row to last st, k1.
Row 2 (WS): K1, work Fave patt WS row to last st, k1.
Rep Rows 1–2 for every row, repeating rows of Fave patt as est, until sleeve measures a finished length of 16½ (16½, 17, 17, 17½, 17½, 18)" / 42 (42, 43, 43, 44.5, 44.5, 45.5) cm from cast-on edge, ending with a WS row.

Shape Sleeve Cap

BO ___ sts at beg of next 2 rows:

Gauge	34¾" / 88.5 cm	38¾" / 98.5 cm	42¾" / 108.5 cm	46¾" / 118.5 cm	50¾" / 129 cm	54¾" / 139 cm	58¾" / 149 cm
3	1	3	3	4	5	6	7
4	3	4	5	6	7	9	11
5	3	4	6	7	9	10	13
6	4	5	7	8	11	13	16
7	4	6	8	9	12	14	18
8	4	7	9	11	14	17	21

___ sts rem:

Gauge	34¾" / 88.5 cm	38¾" / 98.5 cm	42¾" / 108.5 cm	46¾" / 118.5 cm	50¾" / 129 cm	54¾" / 139 cm	58¾" / 149 cm
3	32	32	32	34	36	42	44
4	40	42	40	42	48	52	52
5	52	50	50	56	56	66	68
6	62	60	60	66	68	76	78
7	70	70	70	76	82	90	94
8	82	80	84	88	94	104	108

Dec Row (RS): K1, ssk, work in est Fave patt to last 3 sts, k2tog, k1. 2 sts dec'd.

Rep Dec Row every RS row ____ more times:

		34³/₄" / 88.5 cm	38³/₄" / 98.5 cm	42³/₄" / 108.5 cm	46³/₄" / 118.5 cm	50³/₄" / 129 cm	54³/₄" / 139 cm	58³/₄" / 149 cm
Gauge	3	6	5	5	6	4	8	9
	4	6	6	3	5	7	10	8
	5	11	8	7	8	8	13	13
	6	15	11	10	11	13	16	16
	7	17	14	13	18	20	23	25
	8	20	14	16	19	21	26	23

____ sts rem:

		34³/₄" / 88.5 cm	38³/₄" / 98.5 cm	42³/₄" / 108.5 cm	46³/₄" / 118.5 cm	50³/₄" / 129 cm	54³/₄" / 139 cm	58³/₄" / 149 cm
Gauge	3	18	20	20	20	26	24	24
	4	26	28	32	30	32	30	34
	5	28	32	34	38	38	38	40
	6	30	36	38	42	40	42	44
	7	34	40	42	38	40	42	42
	8	40	50	50	48	50	50	60

Rep Dec Row every OTHER RS row ____ times:

		34³/₄" / 88.5 cm	38³/₄" / 98.5 cm	42³/₄" / 108.5 cm	46³/₄" / 118.5 cm	50³/₄" / 129 cm	54³/₄" / 139 cm	58³/₄" / 149 cm
Gauge	3	0	1	1	1	2	0	0
	4	2	3	5	4	3	2	4
	5	1	3	4	4	4	2	3
	6	0	3	4	4	3	2	3
	7	0	3	4	2	1	0	0
	8	0	4	4	3	2	0	3

___ sts rem:

Gauge	34³/₄" / 88.5 cm	38³/₄" / 98.5 cm	42³/₄" / 108.5 cm	46³/₄" / 118.5cm	50³/₄" / 129cm	54³/₄" / 139cm	58³/₄" /149cm
3	18	18	18	18	22	24	24
4	22	22	22	22	26	26	26
5	26	26	26	30	30	34	34
6	30	30	30	34	34	38	38
7	34	34	34	34	38	42	42
8	40	42	42	42	46	50	54

BO ___ sts at beg of next 4 rows:

Gauge	34³/₄" / 88.5 cm	38³/₄" / 98.5 cm	42³/₄" / 108.5 cm	46³/₄" / 118.5cm	50³/₄" / 129cm	54³/₄" / 139cm	58³/₄" /149cm
3	2	2	2	2	2	2	2
4	2	2	2	2	2	2	2
5	3	3	3	3	3	3	3
6	3	3	3	3	3	3	3
7	3	3	3	3	3	3	3
8	4	4	4	4	4	4	4

BO rem ___ sts on next WS row:

Gauge	34³/₄" / 88.5 cm	38³/₄" / 98.5 cm	42³/₄" / 108.5 cm	46³/₄" / 118.5cm	50³/₄" / 129cm	54³/₄" / 139cm	58³/₄" /149cm
3	10	10	10	10	14	16	16
4	14	14	14	14	18	18	18
5	14	14	14	18	18	22	22
6	18	18	18	22	22	26	26
7	22	22	22	22	26	30	30
8	24	26	26	26	30	34	38

FINISHING

Block pieces to measurements. Sew shoulder seams. Sew sleeve caps into armholes. Sew side and sleeve seams.

Left Front Band

With RS facing and circular needle, beg at neck edge and pick up and knit ___ sts along left front edge, from neckline to hem:

Gauge	34³/₄" / 88.5 cm	38³/₄" / 98.5 cm	42³/₄" / 108.5 cm	46³/₄" / 118.5cm	50³/₄" / 129cm	54³/₄" / 139cm	58³/₄" /149cm
3	42	46	46	46	50	50	50
4	74	74	74	78	82	82	82
5	74	74	74	78	78	82	82
6	90	94	94	98	98	98	102
7	110	110	110	114	118	118	118
8	122	126	130	130	134	134	138

Row 1 (WS): Sl 1 wyif, *k2, p2; rep from * to last st, sl 1 wyif.
Row 2 (RS): K1, *k2, p2; rep from * to last st, k1.
Rep Rows 1–2 until Band measures 1½" / 3 cm from body.
BO in patt on next WS row.

Right Front Band

Mark position of 2 buttons on right front, the first 2" / 5 cm below the beg of neck shaping and the last 4" / 10 cm below the first.

With RS facing and circular needle, beg at hem edge and pick up and knit ___ sts left front edge, from hem to neckline.

Gauge	34¾" / 88.5 cm	38¾" / 98.5 cm	42¾" / 108.5 cm	46¾" / 118.5 cm	50¾" / 129cm	54¾" / 139cm	58¾" / 149cm
3	42	46	46	46	50	50	50
4	74	74	74	78	82	82	82
5	74	74	74	78	78	82	82
6	90	94	94	98	98	98	102
7	110	110	110	114	118	118	118
8	122	126	130	130	134	134	138

Row 1 (WS): Sl 1 wyif, *p2, k2; rep from * to last st, sl 1 wyif.
Row 2 (RS): K1, *p2, k2; rep from * to last st, k1.
Rep Rows 1–2 until Band measures just short of 1½" / 3 cm from body, approx. 2 rows less than worked for the Left Front Band.
Rep Row 1 once.
Buttonhole Row (RS): K1, [work in P2K2 to marker, CO 5 sts] twice, work in patt to last st, k1. ___ sts:

Gauge	34¾" / 88.5 cm	38¾" / 98.5 cm	42¾" / 108.5 cm	46¾" / 118.5 cm	50¾" / 129cm	54¾" / 139cm	58¾" / 149cm
3	52	56	56	56	60	60	60
4	84	84	84	88	92	92	92
5	84	84	84	88	88	92	92
6	100	104	104	108	108	108	112
7	120	120	120	124	128	128	128
8	132	136	140	140	144	144	148

BO knitwise on next WS row.

Collar

With WS facing and circular needle, beg at right front band and pick up and knit ___ sts evenly across band, right neck, back neck, left neck, to left band:

Gauge	34¾" / 88.5 cm	38¾" / 98.5 cm	42¾" / 108.5 cm	46¾" / 118.5 cm	50¾" / 129cm	54¾" / 139cm	58¾" / 149cm
3	60	60	64	68	72	64	68
4	88	88	88	92	92	92	92
5	96	104	100	108	108	112	112
6	116	116	116	124	128	128	124
7	128	132	132	140	140	144	144
8	148	148	148	164	164	164	164

Inc Row (RS): K___,

Gauge	34¾" / 88.5 cm	38¾" / 98.5 cm	42¾" / 108.5 cm	46¾" / 118.5 cm	50¾" / 129cm	54¾" / 139cm	58¾" / 149cm
3	8	8	4	4	6	10	4
4	4	4	6	8	8	8	8
5	8	6	4	8	8	10	10
6	4	4	4	8	10	10	8
7	10	4	4	8	8	8	10
8	4	4	4	4	4	4	4

*M1, k___; rep from *

Gauge	34¾" / 88.5 cm	38¾" / 98.5 cm	42¾" / 108.5 cm	46¾" / 118.5 cm	50¾" / 129cm	54¾" / 139cm	58¾" / 149cm
3	4	4	5	4	4	3	4
4	7	7	5	5	5	5	5
5	7	6	6	6	6	6	6
6	7	7	7	7	7	7	7
7	7	8	8	8	8	8	8
8	9	9	9	10	10	10	10

___ times:

Gauge	34³/₄" / 88.5 cm	38³/₄" / 98.5 cm	42³/₄" / 108.5 cm	46³/₄" / 118.5 cm	50³/₄" / 129 cm	54³/₄" / 139 cm	58³/₄" / 149 cm
3	12	12	12	16	16	16	16
4	12	12	16	16	16	16	16
5	12	16	16	16	16	16	16
6	16	16	16	16	16	16	16
7	16	16	16	16	16	16	16
8	16	16	16	16	16	16	16

K ___:

Gauge	34³/₄" / 88.5 cm	38³/₄" / 98.5 cm	42³/₄" / 108.5 cm	46³/₄" / 118.5 cm	50³/₄" / 129 cm	54³/₄" / 139 cm	58³/₄" / 149 cm
3	4	4	0	0	2	6	0
4	0	0	2	4	4	4	4
5	4	2	0	4	4	6	6
6	0	0	0	4	6	6	4
7	6	0	0	4	4	6	6
8	0	0	0	0	0	0	0

___ sts:

Gauge	34³/₄" / 88.5 cm	38³/₄" / 98.5 cm	42³/₄" / 108.5 cm	46³/₄" / 118.5 cm	50³/₄" / 129 cm	54³/₄" / 139 cm	58³/₄" / 149 cm
3	72	72	76	84	88	80	84
4	100	100	104	108	108	108	108
5	108	120	116	124	124	128	128
6	132	132	132	140	144	144	140
7	144	148	148	156	156	160	160
8	164	164	164	180	180	180	180

Row 1 (WS): Sl 1 wyif, *p2, k2; rep from * to last 3 sts, p2, sl 1 wyif.
Row 2 (RS): K3, *p2, k2; rep from * to last st, k1.
Rep Rows 1–2 until collar measures 1½" / 3 cm.
BO knitwise on next WS row.
Sew buttons to left front, approx. 2 sts to the right of the band, opposite button loops. Weave in all ends.

TWO-STITCH STOLE

This rectangular shawl features two stitch patterns, allowing you to mix and match to your heart's content. Whether knit in lace weight or soft worsted, with texture or with cables, the results are beautifully personal and exciting.

SKILL LEVEL
Intermediate

STITCH PATTERNS
Choose two stitch patterns (the pattern recipe will refer to them as Fave patt and Second patt). *The sample shown used Anchored Eyelets and Easy Zig-Zag Lace (page 124).*

FINISHED MEASUREMENTS
Width: 18 (20, 22, 24)" / 45.5 (51, 56, 61) cm
Length for all sizes: 54" / 137 cm
Sample size is 22" / 56 cm width.

YARN REQUIREMENTS

Gauge	18" / 45.5cm	20" / 51cm	22" / 56cm	24" / 61cm
3	485 yds / 443 m	540 yds / 494 m	595 yds / 544 m	650 yds / 594 m
4	780 yds / 713 m	865 yds / 791 m	950 yds / 869 m	1035 yds / 946 m
5	875 yds / 800 m	970 yds / 887 m	1070 yds / 978 m	1165 yds / 1065 m
6	970 yds / 887 m	1080 yds / 988 m	1190 yds / 1088 m	1295 yds / 1184 m
7	1070 yds / 978 m	1190 yds / 1088 m	1305 yds / 1193 m	1425 yds / 1303 m
8	1265 yds / 1157 m	1405 yds / 1285 m	1545 yds / 1413 m	1685 yds / 1541 m

NEEDLES & NOTIONS
A loose gauge will yield a lofty drape, so aim for the recommended needle size indicated for the yarn or one to two sizes larger.
- Set of circular needles, 32" / 80 cm in length, in the size necessary to obtain the desired gauge
- Yarn needle

SAMPLE PROJECT
The sample stole shown is worked with 4 skeins Patons Classic Wool Worsted in Jade Heather (210 yards / 192 m per 3.5 oz / 100 g skein; 100% wool) *with a finished gauge of* 4 sts and 6 rows = 1" / 2.5 cm.

PATTERN NOTES
- This rectangular stole is worked flat from side to side. Two stitch patterns are used.

PATTERN Two-Stitch Stole

BORDER

Cast on ____ sts:

	18" / 45.5cm	20" / 51cm	22" / 56cm	24" / 61cm
3	58	62	70	74
4	74	82	90	98
5	94	102	114	122
6	110	122	134	146
7	130	142	158	170
8	146	162	178	194

Row 1 (RS): K1, work Row 1 of Fave patt to last st, k1.
Row 2 (WS): Sl 1 wyif, work Row 2 of Fave patt to last st, sl 1 wyif.
Rep Rows 1–2, continuing through the remaining rows of Fave patt and then repeating them, until shawl measures 10" / 25.5 cm from cast-on.

BODY

Row 1 (RS): K1, work Row 1 of Second patt to last st, k1.
Row 2 (WS): Sl 1 wyif, work Row 2 of Second patt to last st, sl 1 wyif.
Rep Rows 1–2, continuing through the remaining rows of Second patt and then repeating them, until shawl measures 44" / 112 cm from cast-on.

BORDER

Row 1 (RS): K1, work Row 1 of Fave patt to last st, k1.
Row 2 (WS): Sl 1 wyif, work Row 2 of Fave patt to last st, sl 1 wyif.
Rep Rows 1–2, continuing through the remaining rows of Fave patt and then repeating them, until shawl measures 54" / 137 cm from cast-on.
Bind off loosely on next RS row.

FINISHING

Block as desired. Weave in ends.

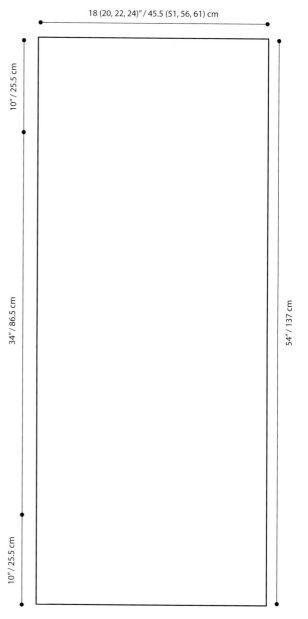

18 (20, 22, 24)" / 45.5 (51, 56, 61) cm

10" / 25.5 cm

34" / 86.5 cm

10" / 25.5 cm

54" / 137 cm

*Measurements are an average of all the gauges listed.

BASIC TOQUE

Comfy enough for year-round wear, this basic toque is just the ticket for every hat-loving knitter. Easy construction pairs perfectly with a variety of stitches, especially with the fun pom-pom topper.

SKILL LEVEL
Intermediate

STITCH PATTERN
Choose one stitch pattern (the pattern recipe will refer to it as Fave patt) for the hat body. *The sample shown uses High Lift (page 160).*

FINISHED MEASUREMENTS
Brim Circumference: approx. 14¾ (16, 17½, 19, 20½, 22¼)" / 37.5 (40.5, 44.5, 48.5, 52, 56.5) cm
Length: 6¾ (7, 7½, 8, 8¼, 8¾)" / 17 (18, 19, 20.5, 21, 22) cm
Sample size is 19" / 48.5 cm circumference.

YARN REQUIREMENTS

Gauge	14¾" / 37.5cm	16" / 40.5cm	17½" / 44.5cm	19" / 48.5cm	20½" / 52cm	22¼" / 56.5cm
3	60 yds / 55 m	65 yds / 59 m	80 yds / 73 m	90 yds / 82 m	100 yds / 91 m	120 yds / 110 m
4	100 yds / 91 m	110 yds / 101 m	135 yds / 123 m	150 yds / 137 m	175 yds / 160 m	195 yds / 178 m
5	110 yds / 101 m	125 yds / 114 m	145 yds / 133 m	170 yds / 155 m	190 yds / 174 m	215 yds / 197 m
6	130 yds / 119 m	145 yds / 133 m	170 yds / 155 m	200 yds / 183 m	225 yds / 206 m	250 yds / 229 m
7	135 yds / 123 m	155 yds / 142 m	185 yds / 169 m	210 yds / 192 m	235 yds / 215 m	275 yds / 251 m
8	155 yds / 142 m	180 yds / 165 m	210 yds / 192 m	245 yds / 224 m	270 yds / 247 m	310 yds / 283 m

NEEDLES & NOTIONS
Choose a needle size that is close to or slightly smaller than recommended for your yarn so as to achieve a long-wearing fabric.
- Circular needles, 16" / 40 cm in length, in the size necessary to obtain the desired gauge
- Set of double-pointed needles in the same size as circular needles
- Yarn needle

SAMPLE PROJECT
The sample hat shown is worked with 1 skein Red Heart Unforgettable in Meadow (270 yards / 247 m per 3.5 oz / 100 g skein; 100% acrylic) *with a finished gauge of 5 sts and 7 rnds = 1" / 2.5 cm.*

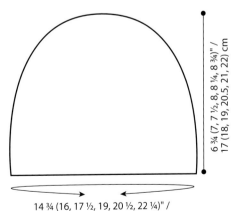

6¾ (7, 7½, 8, 8¼, 8¾)" / 17 (18, 19, 20.5, 21, 22) cm

14¾ (16, 17½, 19, 20½, 22¼)" / 37.5 (40.5, 44.5, 48.5, 52, 56.5) cm

Measurements are an average of all the gauges listed.

PATTERN NOTES

- This hat is worked in the round from the brim to the crown. After the crown shaping begins, change to double-pointed needles as needed to accommodate the decrease in stitches.
- Only work as instructed for your size. If the number for your size and gauge in the table is 0, omit those rows and/or stitches and move on to the next indicated stitch/ row instructions.

PATTERN Basic Toque

BRIM
Cast on _____ sts:

Gauge	14³/₄" / 37.5cm	16" / 40.5cm	17¹/₂" / 44.5cm	19" / 48.5cm	20¹/₂" / 52cm	22¹/₄" / 56.5cm
3	44	48	52	56	60	68
4	60	64	72	76	84	88
5	72	80	88	96	104	112
6	88	96	104	116	124	132
7	100	112	124	132	144	156
8	116	128	140	152	164	176

Rnd 1: *K2, p2; rep from * to end.
Rep Rnd 1 until Brim measures a finished length of 1" / 2.5 cm from cast-on edge.

BODY
Change to Fave patt and work even until hat measures a finished length of _____" / _____ cm:

Gauge	14³/₄" / 37.5cm	16" / 40.5cm	17¹/₂" / 44.5cm	19" / 48.5cm	20¹/₂" / 52cm	22¹/₄" / 56.5cm
3	5³/₄" 14.5 cm	6" 15 cm	6¹/₂" 16.5 cm	7" 18 cm	7¹/₄" 18.5 cm	7³/₄" 19.5 cm
4	6¹/₄" 16 cm	6¹/₂" 16.5 cm	7" 18 cm	7¹/₂" 19 cm	7³/₄" 19.5 cm	8¹/₄" 21 cm
5	6¹/₄" 16 cm	6¹/₂" 16.5 cm	7" 18 cm	7¹/₂" 19 cm	7³/₄" 19.5 cm	8¹/₄" 21 cm
6	6³/₄" 17 cm	7" 18 cm	7¹/₂" 19 cm	8" 20.5 cm	8¹/₄" 21 cm	8³/₄" 22 cm
7	6³/₄" 17 cm	7" 18 cm	7¹/₂" 19 cm	8" 20.5 cm	8¹/₄" 21 cm	8³/₄" 22 cm
8	6³/₄" 17 cm	7" 18 cm	7¹/₂" 19 cm	8" 20.5 cm	8¹/₄" 21 cm	8³/₄" 22 cm

CROWN
Rnd 1: *K2, k2tog; rep from * to end of rnd. _____ sts rem:

Gauge	14³/₄" / 37.5cm	16" / 40.5cm	17¹/₂" / 44.5cm	19" / 48.5cm	20¹/₂" / 52cm	22¹/₄" / 56.5cm
3	33	36	39	42	45	51
4	45	48	54	57	63	66
5	54	60	66	72	78	84
6	66	72	78	87	93	99
7	75	84	93	99	108	117
8	87	96	105	114	123	132

Rnd 2: *K1, k2tog; rep from * to end of rnd. _____ sts rem:

Gauge	14³/₄" / 37.5cm	16" / 40.5cm	17¹/₂" / 44.5cm	19" / 48.5cm	20¹/₂" / 52cm	22¹/₄" / 56.5cm
3	22	24	26	28	30	34
4	30	32	36	38	42	44
5	36	40	44	48	52	56
6	44	48	52	58	62	66
7	50	56	62	66	72	78
8	58	64	70	76	82	88

Rnd 3: *K2tog; rep from * to end of rnd. ___ sts rem:

Gauge	14³/₄" / 37.5cm	16" / 40.5cm	17¹/₂" / 44.5cm	19" / 48.5cm	20¹/₂" / 52cm	22¹/₄" / 56.5cm
3	11	12	13	14	15	17
4	15	16	18	19	21	22
5	18	20	22	24	26	28
6	22	24	26	29	31	33
7	25	28	31	33	36	39
8	29	32	35	38	41	44

Rnd 4: K___, *k2tog; rep from * to end of rnd:

Gauge	14³/₄" / 37.5cm	16" / 40.5cm	17¹/₂" / 44.5cm	19" / 48.5cm	20¹/₂" / 52cm	22¹/₄" / 56.5cm
3	1	0	1	0	1	1
4	1	0	0	1	1	0
5	0	0	0	0	0	0
6	0	0	0	1	1	1
7	1	0	1	1	0	1
8	1	0	1	0	1	0

___ sts rem:

Gauge	14³/₄" / 37.5cm	16" / 40.5cm	17¹/₂" / 44.5cm	19" / 48.5cm	20¹/₂" / 52cm	22¹/₄" / 56.5cm
3	6	6	7	7	8	9
4	8	8	9	10	11	11
5	9	10	11	12	13	14
6	11	12	13	15	16	17
7	13	14	16	17	18	20
8	15	16	18	19	21	22

If there are 10 sts or less rem after the last rnd, skip ahead to Finishing. If there are 11 and up sts rem after last rnd, then work Rnd 5 as follows:

Rnd 5: K___, *K2tog; rep from * to end of rnd:

Gauge	14³/₄" / 37.5cm	16" / 40.5cm	17¹/₂" / 44.5cm	19" / 48.5cm	20¹/₂" / 52cm	22¹/₄" / 56.5cm
3	N/A	N/A	N/A	N/A	N/A	N/A
4	N/A	N/A	N/A	N/A	1	1
5	N/A	N/A	1	0	1	0
6	1	0	1	1	0	1
7	1	0	0	1	0	0
8	1	0	0	1	1	0

___ sts rem:

Gauge	14³/₄" / 37.5cm	16" / 40.5cm	17¹/₂" / 44.5cm	19" / 48.5cm	20¹/₂" / 52cm	22¹/₄" / 56.5cm
3	N/A	N/A	N/A	N/A	N/A	N/A
4	N/A	N/A	N/A	N/A	6	6
5	N/A	N/A	6	6	7	7
6	6	6	7	8	8	9
7	7	7	8	9	9	10
8	8	8	9	10	11	11

FINISHING

Cut yarn, leaving a 6" / 15 cm tail, pull through remaining sts, and pull tight.
Block to measurements.
Make a pom-pom. Sew it to the top of the hat crown.
Weave in ends.

FINGERLESS MITTS

Whether it's the near-instant gratification or the cozy sensation on your hands, there's something wonderful about knitting a pair of fingerless mitts. This simple pattern is no exception, giving you plenty of ways to play with stitch patterning.

SKILL LEVEL
Advanced Beginner

STITCH PATTERN
Choose one stitch pattern (the pattern recipe will refer to it as Fave patt) for the body.
The sample shown uses Dot (page 106).

FINISHED MEASUREMENTS
Hand Circumference: 6 (6½, 7, 7½, 8, 8½, 9)" / 15 (16.5, 18, 19, 20.5, 21.5, 23) cm
Choose the size that is approx. 10% less than your actual hand circumference.
Length: 7¾ (8½, 9¼, 9½, 10¼, 11, 11½)" / 19.5 (21.5, 23.5, 24, 26, 28, 29) cm
Sample size is 6½" / 16.5 cm in circumference.

YARN REQUIREMENTS
Note: Yardage is calculated for a mitt length of approx. 8–11" / 20–28 cm in length. If you plan for longer mitts, adjust accordingly.

Gauge	6" / 15cm	6½" / 16.5cm	7" / 18cm	7½" / 19cm	8" / 20.5cm	8½" / 21.5cm	9" / 23cm
3	55 yds / 50 m	65 yds / 59 m	80 yds / 73 m	85 yds / 78 m	100 yds / 91 m	110 yds / 101 m	125 yds / 114 m
4	95 yds / 87 m	110 yds / 101 m	130 yds / 119 m	145 yds / 133 m	165 yds / 151 m	185 yds / 169 m	205 yds / 187 m
5	100 yds / 91 m	120 yds / 110 m	140 yds / 128 m	155 yds / 142 m	180 yds / 165 m	205 yds / 187 m	230 yds / 210 m
6	120 yds / 110 m	145 yds / 133 m	170 yds / 155 m	185 yds / 169 m	215 yds / 197 m	245 yds / 224 m	270 yds / 247 m
7	130 yds / 119 m	155 yds / 142 m	180 yds / 165 m	200 yds / 183 m	230 yds / 210 m	260 yds / 238 m	290 yds / 265 m
8	150 yds / 137 m	175 yds / 160 m	205 yds / 187 m	230 yds / 210 m	260 yds / 238 m	300 yds / 274 m	330 yds / 302 m

NEEDLES & NOTIONS
A firm gauge will yield a long-wearing fabric, so aim for the recommended needle size indicated for the yarn or one size smaller.
- Set of 4 double-pointed needles in the size necessary to obtain the desired gauge
- 2 stitch markers
- Yarn needle

SAMPLE PROJECT
The sample mitts shown are worked with 1 ball Lion Brand Collection Baby Alpaca in Fawn Heather #125 (146 yards / 133 m per 1.75 oz / 50 g skein; 100% baby alpaca) *with a finished gauge of 7 sts and 9 rnds = 1" / 2.5 cm.*

PATTERN NOTES
- These mitts are worked in the round from the cuff to the fingers. The thumb gusset stitches are placed on hold to finish after knitting the mitt.
- Only work as instructed for your size. If the number for your size and gauge in the table is 0, omit those rnds and/or stitches and move on to the next indicated stitch/rnd instructions.

PATTERN Fingerless Mitts

CUFF

CO ___ sts:

Gauge	6" / 15cm	6½" / 16.5cm	7" / 18cm	7½" / 19cm	8" / 20.5cm	8½" / 21.5cm	9" / 23cm
3	20	20	20	24	24	24	28
4	24	28	28	32	32	36	36
5	32	32	36	36	40	44	44
6	36	40	44	44	48	52	56
7	44	44	48	52	56	60	64
8	48	52	56	60	64	68	72

Arrange stitches evenly on 3 dpns. PM and join to work in the rnd, being careful not to twist the stitches.

Cuff Rnd: *K2, p2; rep from * to end of rnd.

Rep Cuff Rnd until cuff measures approx. ½" / 3.5 cm from CO edge.

SLEEVE

Change to Fave patt, repeating the indicated rows until the mitt measures a finished length of 3 (3½, 4, 4, 4½, 4½, 5)" / 7.5 (9, 10, 10, 11.5, 11.5, 12.5) cm or to desired arm length to thumb.

HAND

Work in patt across ___ sts, pm, M1L, pm, work in patt to end. 1 st inc'd between gusset markers:

Gauge	6" / 15cm	6½" / 16.5cm	7" / 18cm	7½" / 19cm	8" / 20.5cm	8½" / 21.5cm	9" / 23cm
3	10	10	10	12	12	12	14
4	12	14	14	16	16	18	18
5	16	16	18	18	20	22	22
6	18	20	22	22	24	26	28
7	22	22	24	26	28	30	32
8	24	26	28	30	32	34	36

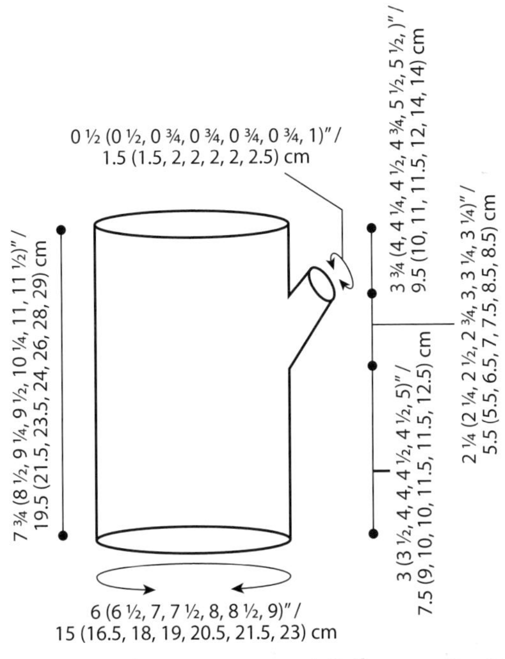
0 ½ (0 ½, 0 ¾, 0 ¾, 0 ¾, 0 ¾, 1)"/
1.5 (1.5, 2, 2, 2, 2, 2.5) cm
3 ¾ (4, 4 ¼, 4 ½, 4 ¾, 5 ½, 5 ½,)"/
9.5 (10, 11, 11.5, 12, 14, 14) cm
7 ¾ (8 ½, 9 ¼, 9 ½, 10 ¼, 11, 11 ½)"/
19.5 (21.5, 23.5, 24, 26, 28, 29) cm
2 ¼ (2 ¼, 2 ½, 2 ¾, 3, 3 ¼, 3 ¼)"/
5.5 (5.5, 6.5, 7, 7.5, 8.5, 8.5) cm
3 (3 ½, 4, 4, 4 ½, 4 ½, 5)"/
7.5 (9, 10, 10, 11.5, 11.5, 12.5) cm
6 (6 ½, 7, 7 ½, 8, 8 ½, 9)"/
15 (16.5, 18, 19, 20.5, 21.5, 23) cm

*Measurements are an average of all the gauges listed.

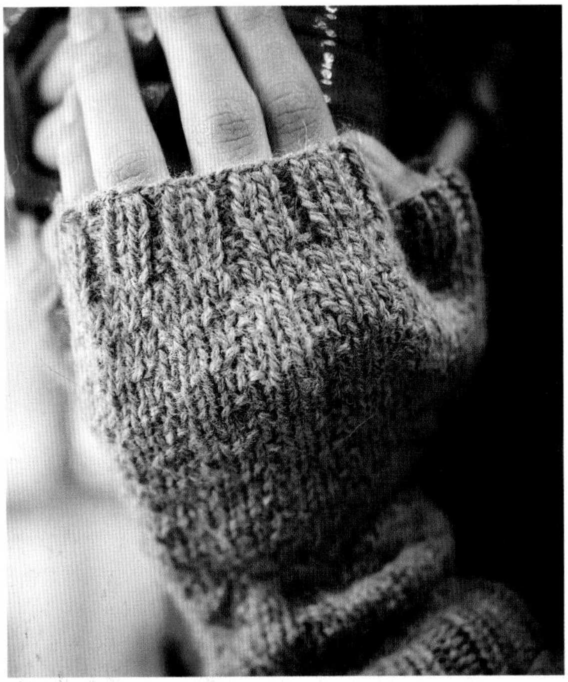

Next Rnd: Work in patt to first m, sm, knit to second m, sm, work in patt to end of rnd.

Thumb Gusset

Inc Rnd: Work in patt to first m, sm, M1L, knit to second m, M1R, sm, work in patt to end of rnd. 2 sts inc'd between gusset markers.

Rep Inc Rnd every ___ rnds:

Gauge	6" / 15cm	6½" / 16.5cm	7" / 18cm	7½" / 19cm	8" / 20.5cm	8½" / 21.5cm	9" / 23cm
3	0	0	2	2	2	2	2
4	4	0	2	2	2	2	2
5	2	2	2	2	2	2	2
6	2	2	2	2	2	2	2
7	0	2	2	2	2	2	2
8	2	2	2	2	2	2	2

___ more times:

Gauge	6" / 15cm	6½" / 16.5cm	7" / 18cm	7½" / 19cm	8" / 20.5cm	8½" / 21.5cm	9" / 23cm
3	0	0	2	1	1	2	2
4	1	0	1	1	2	1	3
5	1	1	2	3	2	4	4
6	2	2	3	4	5	4	6
7	0	2	2	3	4	5	7
8	1	3	3	4	4	5	7

Then rep Inc Rnd every ___ rnds:

Gauge	6" / 15cm	6½" / 16.5cm	7" / 18cm	7½" / 19cm	8" / 20.5cm	8½" / 21.5cm	9" / 23cm
3	4	4	4	4	4	4	4
4	6	4	4	4	4	4	4
5	4	4	4	4	4	4	4
6	4	4	4	4	4	4	4
7	4	4	4	4	4	4	4
8	4	4	4	4	4	4	4

___ times:

Gauge	6" / 15cm	6½" / 16.5cm	7" / 18cm	7½" / 19cm	8" / 20.5cm	8½" / 21.5cm	9" / 23cm
3	2	2	1	2	2	2	2
4	1	3	3	3	3	4	3
5	3	3	3	3	4	3	3
6	3	3	3	3	3	4	3
7	5	4	5	5	5	5	4
8	5	4	5	5	6	6	5

There are ___ sts between the two gusset markers:

Gauge	6" / 15cm	6½" / 16.5cm	7" / 18cm	7½" / 19cm	8" / 20.5cm	8½" / 21.5cm	9" / 23cm
3	7	7	9	9	9	11	11
4	7	9	11	11	13	13	15
5	11	11	13	15	15	17	17
6	13	13	15	17	19	19	21
7	13	15	17	19	21	23	25
8	15	17	19	21	23	25	27

Next Rnd: Work in patt to first m, remove m, place gusset sts on scrap yarn, remove second m, rejoin and continue working patt to end of rnd.

___ sts rem for the hand:

Gauge	6" / 15cm	6½" / 16.5cm	7" / 18cm	7½" / 19cm	8" / 20.5cm	8½" / 21.5cm	9" / 23cm
3	20	20	20	24	24	24	28
4	24	28	28	32	32	36	36
5	32	32	36	36	40	44	44
6	36	40	44	44	48	52	56
7	44	44	48	52	56	60	64
8	48	52	56	60	64	68	72

Work even in patt as est until hand measures approx. 1½" / 3.5 cm from rejoin location or as desired.

Cuff Rnd: *K2, p2; rep from * to end of rnd.

Rep Cuff Rnd until the border measures a finished length of 1½" / 3.5 cm.

Bind off loosely in pattern.

THUMB

Place gusset stitches onto a dpn. Pick up and knit ___ st(s) from between the thumb and the hand:

Gauge	6" / 15cm	6½" / 16.5cm	7" / 18cm	7½" / 19cm	8" / 20.5cm	8½" / 21.5cm	9" / 23cm
3	1	1	3	3	3	1	1
4	1	3	1	1	3	3	1
5	1	1	3	1	1	3	3
6	3	3	1	3	1	1	3
7	3	1	3	1	3	1	3
8	1	3	1	3	1	3	1

___ sts:

Gauge	6" / 15cm	6½" / 16.5cm	7" / 18cm	7½" / 19cm	8" / 20.5cm	8½" / 21.5cm	9" / 23cm
3	8	8	12	12	12	12	12
4	8	12	12	12	16	16	16
5	12	12	16	16	16	20	20
6	16	16	16	20	20	20	24
7	16	16	20	20	24	24	28
8	16	20	20	24	24	28	28

Arrange sts evenly on 3 dpns, place m, and join for working in the rnd.

Knit 2 rnds.

Cuff Rnd: *K2, p2; rep from * to end of rnd.

Rep Cuff Rnd until desired thumb length.

Bind off loosely in patt.

FINISHING

Block as desired. Weave in ends, closing gaps at base of the thumb as necessary.

TOE-UP SOCKS

Branch out in your sock-making skills with toe-up socks. Featuring a short-row heel and wedge toe, they are the perfect palette to try out a variety of stitches. In other words, cozy foot comfort just got a little more fun!

SKILL LEVEL
Intermediate

STITCH PATTERN
Choose one stitch pattern (the pattern recipe will refer to it as Fave patt).
The sample shown uses Split Rib (page 148).

FINISHED MEASUREMENTS
Foot Circumference: approx. 4 (5¼, 6¼, 7¼, 8, 9)" / 10 (13.5, 16, 18.5, 20.5, 23) cm
Choose the size that is approx. 10% smaller than your actual foot circumference.
Foot Length is adjustable.
Sample size is 8" / 20.5 cm foot circumference.

YARN REQUIREMENTS

Gauge	4" / 10cm	5¼" / 13.5cm	6¼" / 16cm	7¼" / 18.5cm	8" / 20.5cm	9" / 23cm
3	45 yds / 41 m	90 yds / 82 m	140 yds / 128 m	170 yds / 155 m	205 yds / 187 m	275 yds / 251 m
4	50 yds / 46 m	115 yds / 105 m	175 yds / 160 m	205 yds / 187 m	235 yds / 215 m	310 yds / 283 m
5	60 yds / 55 m	125 yds / 114 m	185 yds / 169 m	230 yds / 210 m	265 yds / 242 m	370 yds / 338 m
6	75 yds / 69 m	150 yds / 137 m	235 yds / 215 m	295 yds / 270 m	325 yds / 297 m	455 yds / 416 m
7	80 yds / 73 m	175 yds / 160 m	265 yds / 242 m	300 yds / 274 m	355 yds / 325 m	485 yds / 443 m
8	85 yds / 78 m	180 yds / 165 m	280 yds / 256 m	325 yds / 297 m	385 yds / 352 m	525 yds / 480 m

NEEDLES & NOTIONS
A smaller gauge will provide good stability, so choose a needle size that is the same or slightly smaller than recommended for your yarn.

- Set of needles in the size necessary to obtain the desired gauge: set of 4 dpns; 32" / 80 cm circular for magic loop; or two 24" / 60 cm circulars for two-needle method
- 4 stitch markers (1 distinct for BOR)
- Yarn needle
- Cable needle (optional)

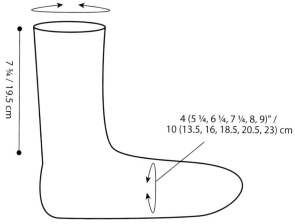

4 (5 ¼, 6 ¼, 7 ¼, 8, 9)" / 10 (13.5, 16, 18.5, 20.5, 23) cm

7 ¾ / 19.5 cm

4 (5 ¼, 6 ¼, 7 ¼, 8, 9)" / 10 (13.5, 16, 18.5, 20.5, 23) cm

Measurements are an average of all the gauges listed.

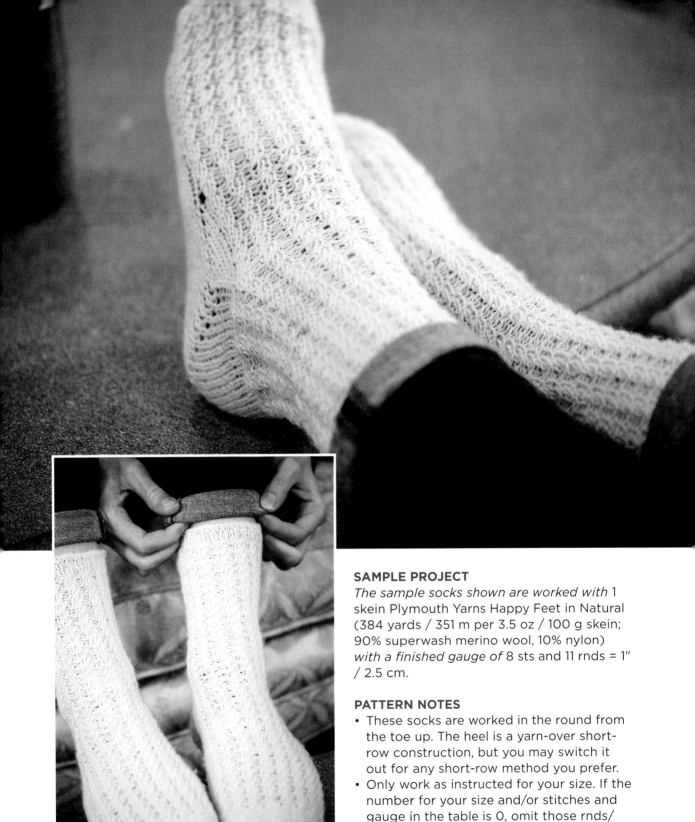

SAMPLE PROJECT
The sample socks shown are worked with 1 skein Plymouth Yarns Happy Feet in Natural (384 yards / 351 m per 3.5 oz / 100 g skein; 90% superwash merino wool, 10% nylon) *with a finished gauge of* 8 sts and 11 rnds = 1″ / 2.5 cm.

PATTERN NOTES
- These socks are worked in the round from the toe up. The heel is a yarn-over short-row construction, but you may switch it out for any short-row method you prefer.
- Only work as instructed for your size. If the number for your size and/or stitches and gauge in the table is 0, omit those rnds/rows and move on to the next indicated stitch/row instructions.

PATTERN Toe-Up Socks

TOE

With favorite toe-up cast-on technique, such as Judy's Magic Cast-On, CO ____ sts:

Gauge	4" / 10cm	5¼" / 13.5cm	6¼" / 16cm	7¼" / 18.5cm	8" / 20.5cm	9" / 23cm
3	4	4	8	8	8	8
4	4	8	8	8	12	12
5	8	8	8	12	12	16
6	8	8	12	12	16	16
7	8	12	12	16	16	20
8	8	12	16	16	20	20

There are ____ sts divided between two needles. Pm to mark beg of rnd:

Gauge	4" / 10cm	5¼" / 13.5cm	6¼" / 16cm	7¼" / 18.5cm	8" / 20.5cm	9" / 23cm
3	2	2	4	4	4	4
4	2	4	4	4	6	6
5	4	4	4	6	6	8
6	4	4	6	6	8	8
7	4	6	6	8	8	10
8	4	6	8	8	10	10

Rnd 1: K ____, pm (Instep m), knit to end of rnd:

Gauge	4" / 10cm	5¼" / 13.5cm	6¼" / 16cm	7¼" / 18.5cm	8" / 20.5cm	9" / 23cm
3	2	2	4	4	4	4
4	2	4	4	4	6	6
5	4	4	4	6	6	8
6	4	4	6	6	8	8
7	4	6	6	8	8	10
8	4	6	8	8	10	10

Inc Rnd: K1, M1L, knit until 1 st before Instep m, M1R, k1, sm, k1, M1L, knit until 1 st before end of rnd, M1R, k1. 4 sts inc'd.
Rep Inc Rnd ____ more times:

Gauge	4" / 10cm	5¼" / 13.5cm	6¼" / 16cm	7¼" / 18.5cm	8" / 20.5cm	9" / 23cm
3	0	1	1	0	1	2
4	1	0	1	2	0	1
5	1	1	2	1	2	1
6	0	2	1	3	1	3
7	1	1	3	1	3	2
8	2	2	1	3	2	4

____ sts:

Gauge	4" / 10cm	5¼" / 13.5cm	6¼" / 16cm	7¼" / 18.5cm	8" / 20.5cm	9" / 23cm
3	8	12	16	12	16	20
4	12	12	16	20	16	20
5	16	16	20	20	24	24
6	12	20	20	28	24	32
7	16	20	28	24	32	32
8	20	24	24	32	32	40

Rnd 3: Knit.
Rnd 4: K1, M1L, knit until 1 st before Instep m, M1R, k1, sm, k1, M1L, knit until 1 st before end of rnd, M1R, k1. 4 sts inc'd.
Rep Rnds 3-4 ____ more times:

Gauge	4" / 10cm	5¼" / 13.5cm	6¼" / 16cm	7¼" / 18.5cm	8" / 20.5cm	9" / 23cm
3	1	1	1	3	3	3
4	1	3	3	3	5	5
5	1	3	3	5	5	7
6	3	3	5	5	7	7
7	3	5	5	7	7	9
8	3	5	7	7	9	9

____ sts:

Gauge	4" / 10cm	5¼" / 13.5cm	6¼" / 16cm	7¼" / 18.5cm	8" / 20.5cm	9" / 23cm
3	16	20	24	28	32	36
4	20	28	32	36	40	44
5	24	32	36	44	48	56
6	28	36	44	52	56	64
7	32	44	52	56	64	72
8	36	48	56	64	72	80

FOOT

The first ____ sts before the Instep m are the heel sts:

Gauge	4" / 10cm	5¼" / 13.5cm	6¼" / 16cm	7¼" / 18.5cm	8" / 20.5cm	9" / 23cm
3	8	8	12	12	16	16
4	8	12	16	16	20	20
5	12	16	16	20	24	28
6	12	16	20	24	28	32
7	16	20	24	28	32	36
8	16	24	28	32	36	40

and the next ____ sts are the instep sts:

Gauge	4" / 10cm	5¼" / 13.5cm	6¼" / 16cm	7¼" / 18.5cm	8" / 20.5cm	9" / 23cm
3	8	12	12	16	16	20
4	12	16	16	20	20	24
5	12	16	20	24	24	28
6	16	20	24	28	28	32
7	16	24	28	28	32	36
8	20	24	28	32	36	40

Every Rnd: Knit to Instep m, sm, work Fave patt to end.

Work even in patt as est until foot meas approx. ____" / ____ cm less than desired total foot length:

Gauge	4" / 10cm	5¹/₄" / 13.5cm	6¹/₄" / 16cm	7¹/₄" / 18.5cm	8" / 20.5cm	9" / 23cm
3	1.75" 4.5 cm	1.75" 4.5 cm	2" 5 cm	2.75" 7 cm	2.75" 7 cm	3.25" 8.5 cm
4	1.25" 3 cm	2.25" 5.5 cm	2.25" 5.5 cm	3" 7.5 cm	3.25" 8.5 cm	3.25" 8.5 cm
5	1.5" 4 cm	2" 5 cm	2.5" 6.5 cm	2.75" 7 cm	3.25" 8.5 cm	3.75" 9.5 cm
6	1.75" 4.5 cm	2.25" 5.5 cm	2.5" 6.5 cm	3" 7.5 cm	3.25" 8.5 cm	3.75" 9.5 cm
7	1.5" 4 cm	2.25" 5.5 cm	2.75" 7 cm	3" 7.5 cm	3.5" 9 cm	4" 10 cm
8	1.75" 4.5 cm	2.5" 6.5 cm	2.75" 7 cm	3" 7.5 cm	3.5" 9 cm	3.75" 9.5 cm

HEEL

Gusset Increases

Rnd 1: Knit to Instep m, sm, M1L, pm (G1), work in Fave patt to end of rnd, pm (G2), M1R. 2 sts inc'd.

Rnd 2: Knit to G1 m, sm, work in Fave patt to G2 m, sm, knit to end.

Rnd 3: Knit to Instep (first) m, sm, M1L, knit to G1 m, sm, work in Fave patt to G2 m, sm, knit to end, M1R. 2 sts inc'd.

Rep Rnds 2–3 ____ more times:

Gauge	4" / 10cm	5¹/₄" / 13.5cm	6¹/₄" / 16cm	7¹/₄" / 18.5cm	8" / 20.5cm	9" / 23cm
3	0	0	0	1	1	2
4	0	1	1	2	2	2
5	0	1	2	2	3	4
6	1	2	2	3	4	4
7	1	2	3	4	4	5
8	2	3	4	4	5	6

____ sts total:

Gauge	4" / 10cm	5¹/₄" / 13.5cm	6¹/₄" / 16cm	7¹/₄" / 18.5cm	8" / 20.5cm	9" / 23cm
3	20	24	28	34	38	44
4	24	34	38	44	48	52
5	28	38	44	52	58	68
6	34	44	52	62	68	76
7	38	52	62	68	76	86
8	44	58	68	76	86	96

____ sts on instep:

Gauge	4" / 10cm	5¹/₄" / 13.5cm	6¹/₄" / 16cm	7¹/₄" / 18.5cm	8" / 20.5cm	9" / 23cm
3	12	16	16	22	22	28
4	16	22	22	28	28	32
5	16	22	28	32	34	40
6	22	28	32	38	40	44
7	22	32	38	40	44	50
8	28	34	40	44	50	56

Rep Rnd 2 once.

Short Row Heel

Make a note of last rnd worked on Fave patt to resume after the heel is completed. The instep sts will be left unworked while working short rows over the first heel sts.

Short Row 1 (RS): Knit until 1 st before Instep m, turn.
Short Row 2 (WS): Yo, purl until 1 st before BOR m, turn.
Short Row 3: Yo, knit until 1 st before yo, turn.
Short Row 4: Yo, purl until 1 st before yo, turn.
Rep last 2 rows ___ more times:

Gauge	4" / 10cm	5¼" / 13.5cm	6¼" / 16cm	7¼" / 18.5cm	8" / 20.5cm	9" / 23cm
3	1	1	2	3	3	4
4	1	3	3	4	5	5
5	2	3	4	5	6	7
6	3	4	5	7	7	9
7	3	5	7	7	9	10
8	4	6	7	9	10	11

___ sts rem unworked in the center between the last 2 turns:

Gauge	4" / 10cm	5¼" / 13.5cm	6¼" / 16cm	7¼" / 18.5cm	8" / 20.5cm	9" / 23cm
3	2	4	4	4	6	6
4	4	4	6	6	6	8
5	4	6	6	8	8	10
6	4	6	8	8	10	10
7	6	8	8	10	10	12
8	6	8	10	10	12	14

Short Row 5: Yo, knit to yo, k2tog (yarn over and next st), turn.
Short Row 6: Yo (this results in two yarn overs in a row), purl to yo, ssp (yarn over and next st), turn.
The last row worked has set up "double" yarn overs that we will close moving forward.
Short Row 7: Yo, knit to first yo, k3tog (both yarn overs and next st), turn.
Short Row 8: Yo, purl to first yo, sssp (both yarn overs and next st), turn.
Rep last 2 rows ___ more times:

Gauge	4" / 10cm	5¼" / 13.5cm	6¼" / 16cm	7¼" / 18.5cm	8" / 20.5cm	9" / 23cm
3	0	0	1	2	2	3
4	0	2	2	3	4	4
5	1	2	3	4	5	6
6	2	3	4	6	6	8
7	2	4	6	6	8	9
8	3	5	6	8	9	10

Next Rnd: Yo, knit to first yo, k3tog (both yarn overs and next st), sm (Instep), knit to G1 m, sm, work in Fave patt to G2 m, sm, knit to end of rnd m, remove m, sssk (st from the start of rnd and 2 yarn overs), pm for new start of rnd.
Move Instep m 1 st to the right so that there are ___ heel sts before Instep m:

Gauge	4" / 10cm	5¼" / 13.5cm	6¼" / 16cm	7¼" / 18.5cm	8" / 20.5cm	9" / 23cm
3	6	6	10	10	14	14
4	6	10	14	14	18	18
5	10	14	14	18	22	26
6	10	14	18	22	26	30
7	14	18	22	26	30	34
8	14	22	26	30	34	38

and ___ instep sts:

Gauge	4" / 10cm	5¼" / 13.5cm	6¼" / 16cm	7¼" / 18.5cm	8" / 20.5cm	9" / 23cm
3	14	18	18	24	24	30
4	18	24	24	30	30	34
5	18	24	30	34	36	42
6	24	30	34	40	42	46
7	24	34	40	42	46	52
8	30	36	42	46	52	58

Gusset Decreases

Dec Rnd: Knit to Instep m, sm, ssk, knit to G1 m, work in Fave patt as est to G2 m, sm, knit to last 2 sts, k2tog. 2 sts dec'd on instep.

Rep Dec Rnd ___ more times:

Gauge	4" / 10cm	5¼" / 13.5cm	6¼" / 16cm	7¼" / 18.5cm	8" / 20.5cm	9" / 23cm
3	1	1	1	2	2	3
4	1	2	2	3	3	3
5	1	2	3	3	4	5
6	2	3	3	4	5	5
7	2	3	4	5	5	6
8	3	4	5	5	6	7

___ sts rem:

Gauge	4" / 10cm	5¼" / 13.5cm	6¼" / 16cm	7¼" / 18.5cm	8" / 20.5cm	9" / 23cm
3	16	20	24	28	32	36
4	20	28	32	36	40	44
5	24	32	36	44	48	56
6	28	36	44	52	56	64
7	32	44	52	56	64	72
8	36	48	56	64	72	80

Remove gusset and instep stitch markers.

LEG

Even Rnd: Cont in Fave patt as est until leg meas 1" / 2.5 cm less than desired leg length from top of heel.

Cuff

Every Rnd: *K1, p1; rep from * to end of rnd. Rep Every Rnd until cuff meas approx. 1" / 2.5 cm in length. BO loosely in favorite stretchy bind-off.

Repeat instructions for second sock.

FINISHING

Block socks as desired. Weave in ends.

EASY TEE

An easy tee makes for a wardrobe staple! This simple one boasts a flattering v-neck and simple shaping. Pair it with your favorite stitch pattern for a top that is beautiful dressed up or down.

SKILL LEVEL
Intermediate

STITCH PATTERN
Choose one stitch pattern (the pattern recipe will refer to it as Fave patt) for the body and sleeves.
The sample shown uses Scattered Lace (page 131).

FINISHED MEASUREMENTS
Bust Circumference:

Gauge	33½" / 85 cm	37½" / 95.5 cm	41½" / 105.5 cm	45½" / 115.5 cm	49½" / 125.5 cm	53½" / 136 cm	57½" / 146 cm
3	32" 81.5 cm	37.25" 94.5 cm	40" 101.5 cm	45.25" 115 cm	48" 122 cm	53.25" 135.5 cm	56" 142 cm
4	34" 86.5 cm	38" 96.5 cm	42" 106.5 cm	46" 117 cm	50" 127 cm	54" 137 cm	58" 147.5 cm
5	33.5" 85 cm	36.75" 93.5 cm	41.5" 105.5 cm	44.75" 113.5 cm	49.5" 125.5 cm	52.75" 134 cm	57.5" 146 cm
6	33.25" 84.5 cm	37.25" 94.5 cm	41.25" 105 cm	45.25" 115 cm	49.25" 125 cm	53.25" 135.5 cm	57.25" 145.5 cm
7	33.25" 84.5 cm	36.5" 92.5 cm	41.25" 105 cm	44.5" 113 cm	49.25" 125 cm	52.5" 133.5 cm	57.25" 145.5 cm
8	33" 84 cm	37" 94 cm	41" 104 cm	45" 114.5 cm	49" 124.5 cm	53" 134.5 cm	57" 145 cm

The pattern will reference the averaged bust circumference measurements throughout the pattern charts and lengths: 33½ (37½, 41½, 45½, 49½, 53½, 57½)" / 85 (95.5, 105.5, 115.5, 125.5, 136, 146) cm.
Choose the size that is approx. 2-3" / 5-7.5 cm larger than your actual bust circumference.
Garment Length: 23¾ (24¼, 24¾, 25¾, 26½, 27¼, 28)" / 60.5 (61.5, 63, 65.5, 67.5, 69, 71) cm
Sample size is 37½" / 95.5 cm bust circumference.

YARN REQUIREMENTS

Gauge	33½" / 85 cm	37½" / 95.5 cm	41½" / 105.5 cm	45½" / 115.5 cm	49½" / 125.5 cm	53½" / 136 cm	57½" / 146 cm
3	410 yds 375 m	450 yds 411 m	510 yds 466 m	580 yds 530 m	645 yds 590 m	715 yds 654 m	785 yds 718 m
4	575 yds 526 m	635 yds 581 m	725 yds 663 m	815 yds 745 m	905 yds 828 m	995 yds 910 m	1100 yds 1006 m
5	750 yds 686 m	816 yds 746 m	935 yds 855 m	1055 yds 965 m	1185 yds 1084 m	1295 yds 1184 m	1435 yds 1312 m
6	1175 yds 1074 m	1320 yds 1207 m	1490 yds 1362 m	1690 yds 1545 m	1875 yds 1715 m	2075 yds 1897 m	2285 yds 2089 m
7	1355 yds 1239 m	1480 yds 1353 m	1695 yds 1550 m	1915 yds 1751 m	2145 yds 1961 m	2355 yds 2153 m	2620 yds 2396 m
8	1695 yds 1550 m	1875 yds 1715 m	2135 yds 1952 m	2425 yds 2217 m	2695 yds 2464 m	2990 yds 2734 m	3290 yds 3008 m

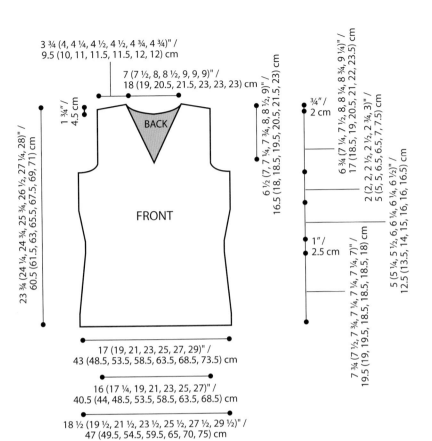

3 ¾ (4, 4 ¼, 4 ½, 4 ½, 4 ¾, 4 ¾)" /
9.5 (10, 11, 11.5, 11.5, 12, 12) cm

1 ¾" /
4.5 cm

7 (7 ½, 8, 8 ½, 9, 9, 9)" /
18 (19, 20.5, 21.5, 23, 23, 23) cm

BACK

FRONT

23 ¾ (24 ¼, 24 ¾, 25 ¾, 26 ½, 27 ¼, 28)" /
60.5 (61.5, 63, 65.5, 67.5, 69, 71) cm

6 ½ (7, 7 ¼, 7 ¾, 8, 8 ½, 9)" /
16.5 (18, 18.5, 19.5, 20.5, 21.5, 23) cm

¾" /
2 cm

6 ¾ (7 ¼, 7 ½, 8, 8 ¼, 8 ¾, 9 ¼)" /
17 (18.5, 19, 20.5, 21, 22, 23.5) cm

2 (2, 2, 2 ½, 2 ¾, 3)" /
5 (5, 5, 6.5, 6.5, 7, 7.5) cm

1" /
2.5 cm

7 ¾ (7 ½, 7 ¾, 7 ¼, 7 ¼, 7 ¼, 7)" /
19.5 (19, 19.5, 18.5, 18.5, 18.5, 18) cm

5 (5 ¼, 5 ½, 6, 6 ¼, 6 ¼, 6 ½)" /
12.5 (13.5, 14, 15, 16, 16, 16.5) cm

17 (19, 21, 23, 25, 27, 29)" /
43 (48.5, 53.5, 58.5, 63.5, 68.5, 73.5) cm

16 (17 ¼, 19, 21, 23, 25, 27)" /
40.5 (44, 48.5, 53.5, 58.5, 63.5, 68.5) cm

18 ½ (19 ½, 21 ½, 23 ½, 25 ½, 27 ½, 29 ½)" /
47 (49.5, 54.5, 59.5, 65, 70, 75) cm

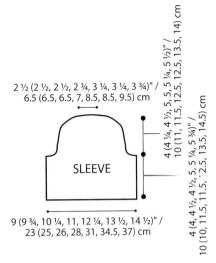

2 ½ (2 ½, 2 ½, 2 ¾, 3 ¼, 3 ¼, 3 ¾)" /
6.5 (6.5, 6.5, 7, 8.5, 8.5, 9.5) cm

SLEEVE

4 (4 ¼, 4 ½, 4 ½, 5, 5 ¼, 5 ½)" /
10 (11, 11.5, 11.5, 12.5, 13.5, 14) cm

9 (9 ¾, 10 ¼, 11, 12 ¼, 13 ½, 14 ½)" /
23 (25, 26, 28, 31, 34.5, 37) cm

4 (4, 4 ½, 4 ½, 5, 5 ¼, 5 ¾)" /
10 (10, 11.5, 11.5, 12.5, 13.5, 14.5) cm

NEEDLES & NOTIONS

Choose a needle size that is the same or slightly smaller than recommended for your yarn so as to achieve nice stitch definition.

- Set of needles (for the body) in the size necessary to obtain the desired gauge
- Circular needles (for the collar), 24" / 60 cm in length, in the same size as the body set
- Yarn needle

SAMPLE PROJECT

The sample tee shown is worked with 3 skeins Knit One Crochet Too Daisy in Salmon #209 (272 yards / 248 m per 3.5 oz / 100 g skein; 38% linen, 32% silk, 30% hemp) *with a finished gauge of* 5 sts and 7 rows = 1" / 2.5 cm.

PATTERN NOTES

- The tee is worked flat in pieces and then seamed. Because of the seaming, 2 sts have been added to the instructions, 1 on either side of your desired stitch pattern, that you'll knit on every row.
- Only work as instructed for your size. If the number for your size and gauge in the table is 0, omit those rows and/or stitches and move on to the next indicated stitch/ row instructions.

PATTERN Easy Tee

Hem

Cast on ____ sts:

Gauge	33½" / 85 cm	37½" / 95.5 cm	41½" / 105.5 cm	45½" / 115.5 cm	49½" / 125.5 cm	53½" / 136 cm	57½" / 146 cm
3	58	58	66	70	78	82	90
4	74	78	86	94	102	110	118
5	94	98	106	118	126	138	146
6	110	118	130	142	154	166	178
7	130	134	150	162	178	190	206
8	146	154	170	186	202	218	234

Rib Row (RS): K1, *k1, p1; rep from * to last st, k1.
Rep Rib Row until back measures a finished length of approx. 1″ / 2.5 cm from cast-on edge, ending with a WS row.

Body

Change to Fave patt for the body as follows:
Row 1 (RS): K1, work RS row of Fave patt to last st, k1.
Row 2 (WS): K1, work WS row of Fave patt to last st, k1.
Rep Rows 1–2, continuing the rows of Fave patt to the end and then repeating, until back measures a finished length of 1″ / 2.5 cm from cast-on edge, ending with a WS row.

Shape Waist

Dec Row (RS): K1, ssk, maintain est Fave patt to last 3 sts, k2tog, k1. 2 sts dec'd.
Rep Dec Row every ____ rows:

Gauge	33½" / 85 cm	37½" / 95.5 cm	41½" / 105.5 cm	45½" / 115.5 cm	49½" / 125.5 cm	53½" / 136 cm	57½" / 146 cm
3	6	0	6	0	0	0	4
4	0	0	8	8	8	8	0
5	4	6	6	6	6	6	6
6	6	6	6	4	4	4	4
7	0	6	4	6	4	6	4
8	6	0	6	4	4	4	4

____ more time(s):

Gauge	33½" / 85 cm	37½" / 95.5 cm	41½" / 105.5 cm	45½" / 115.5 cm	49½" / 125.5 cm	53½" / 136 cm	57½" / 146 cm
3	2	0	3	0	0	0	1
4	0	0	1	2	2	3	0
5	1	1	1	3	3	4	5
6	6	6	7	1	1	2	3
7	0	2	1	6	4	7	6
8	8	0	9	1	1	3	4

Then rep Dec Row every ____ rows:

Gauge	33½" / 85 cm	37½" / 95.5 cm	41½" / 105.5 cm	45½" / 115.5 cm	49½" / 125.5 cm	53½" / 136 cm	57½" / 146 cm
3	8	14	0	6	6	6	6
4	10	10	10	10	10	0	8
5	6	8	8	8	8	8	0
6	8	8	0	6	6	6	6
7	6	8	6	8	6	0	6
8	8	8	0	6	6	6	6

___ more times:

Gauge	33½" / 85 cm	37½" / 95.5 cm	41½" / 105.5 cm	45½" / 115.5 cm	49½" / 125.5 cm	53½" / 136 cm	57½" / 146 cm
3	1	1	0	3	3	3	2
4	3	3	2	1	1	0	3
5	6	4	4	2	2	1	0
6	1	1	0	6	6	5	4
7	9	5	8	1	5	0	3
8	1	7	0	8	8	6	5

___ sts rem:

Gauge	33½" / 85 cm	37½" / 95.5 cm	41½" / 105.5 cm	45½" / 115.5 cm	49½" / 125.5 cm	53½" / 136 cm	57½" / 146 cm
3	50	54	58	62	70	74	82
4	66	70	78	86	94	102	110
5	78	86	94	106	114	126	134
6	94	102	114	126	138	150	162
7	110	118	130	146	158	174	186
8	126	138	150	166	182	198	214

Work even in est pattern until back measures a finished length of 8¾ (8½, 8¾, 8¼, 8¼, 8¼, 8)" / 22 (21.5, 22, 21, 21, 21, 20.5) cm from cast-on edge, ending with a WS row.

Inc Row (RS): K1, M1, maintain est Fave patt to last st, M1, k1. 2 sts inc'd.

Rep Inc Row every ___ rows:

Gauge	33½" / 85 cm	37½" / 95.5 cm	41½" / 105.5 cm	45½" / 115.5 cm	49½" / 125.5 cm	53½" / 136 cm	57½" / 146 cm
3	0	0	0	6	0	6	0
4	0	8	8	8	0	0	10
5	8	8	6	10	6	10	0
6	10	6	6	8	8	8	8
7	0	8	6	8	6	8	6
8	12	8	6	6	0	0	8

___ more time(s):

Gauge	33½" / 85 cm	37½" / 95.5 cm	41½" / 105.5 cm	45½" / 115.5 cm	49½" / 125.5 cm	53½" / 136 cm	57½" / 146 cm
3	0	0	0	3	0	2	0
4	0	3	2	1	0	0	3
5	1	1	4	2	1	1	0
6	3	2	1	5	4	4	3
7	0	5	6	2	3	1	2
8	2	3	3	1	0	0	6

Then rep Inc Row every ___ rows:

Gauge	33½" / 85 cm	37½" / 95.5 cm	41½" / 105.5 cm	45½" / 115.5 cm	49½" / 125.5 cm	53½" / 136 cm	57½" / 146 cm
3	0	12	12	0	14	8	14
4	16	0	10	10	10	10	0
5	10	10	8	12	8	12	8
6	0	8	8	0	10	10	10
7	12	0	8	10	8	10	8
8	14	10	8	8	8	8	10

___ more times:

Gauge	33½" / 85 cm	37½" / 95.5 cm	41½" / 105.5 cm	45½" / 115.5 cm	49½" / 125.5 cm	53½" / 136 cm	57½" / 146 cm
3	0	1	1	0	1	1	1
4	1	0	1	2	3	3	0
5	2	2	1	1	4	2	5
6	0	3	4	0	1	1	2
7	3	0	1	3	4	4	5
8	1	2	4	6	7	7	1

___ sts rem:

Gauge	33½" / 85 cm	37½" / 95.5 cm	41½" / 105.5 cm	45½" / 115.5 cm	49½" / 125.5 cm	53½" / 136 cm	57½" / 146 cm
3	50	58	62	70	74	82	86
4	70	78	86	94	102	110	118
5	86	94	106	114	126	134	146
6	102	114	126	138	150	162	174
7	118	130	146	158	174	186	202
8	134	150	166	182	198	214	230

Work even in est pattern until back measures a finished length of 16 (16, 16½, 17, 17¼, 17½, 17¾)" / 40.5 (40.5, 42, 43, 44, 44.5, 45) cm from cast-on edge, ending with a WS row.

Armhole

BO ___ sts at beg of next 2 rows:

Gauge	33½" / 85 cm	37½" / 95.5 cm	41½" / 105.5 cm	45½" / 115.5 cm	49½" / 125.5 cm	53½" / 136 cm	57½" / 146 cm
3	1	3	3	4	5	6	7
4	3	4	5	6	7	9	11
5	3	4	6	7	9	10	13
6	4	5	7	8	11	13	16
7	4	6	8	9	12	14	18
8	5	7	9	11	14	17	21

___ sts rem:

Gauge	33½" / 85 cm	37½" / 95.5 cm	41½" / 105.5 cm	45½" / 115.5 cm	49½" / 125.5 cm	53½" / 136 cm	57½" / 146 cm
3	48	52	56	62	64	70	72
4	64	70	76	82	88	92	96
5	80	86	94	100	108	114	120
6	94	104	112	122	128	136	142
7	110	118	130	140	150	158	166
8	124	136	148	160	170	180	188

Dec Row (RS): K1, ssk, maintain est Fave patt to last 3 sts, k2tog, k1. 2 sts dec'd.
Rep Dec Row every RS row ___ more times:

Gauge	33½" / 85 cm	37½" / 95.5 cm	41½" / 105.5 cm	45½" / 115.5 cm	49½" / 125.5 cm	53½" / 136 cm	57½" / 146 cm
3	0	2	2	3	4	5	6
4	2	3	4	5	6	8	10
5	2	3	5	6	8	9	12
6	3	4	6	7	10	12	15
7	3	5	7	8	11	13	17
8	4	6	8	10	13	16	20

___ sts rem:

Gauge	33½" / 85 cm	37½" / 95.5 cm	41½" / 105.5 cm	45½" / 115.5 cm	49½" / 125.5 cm	53½" / 136 cm	57½" / 146 cm
3	46	46	50	54	54	58	58
4	58	62	66	70	74	74	74
5	74	78	82	86	90	94	94
6	86	94	98	106	106	110	110
7	102	106	114	122	126	130	130
8	114	122	130	138	142	146	146

Work even in est Fave patt, knitting the first and last st of every row, until armhole measures a finished 6 (6½, 6½, 7, 7½, 8, 8½)" / 15 (16.5, 16.5, 18, 19, 20.5, 21.5) cm from bind-off edge, ending with a WS row.

Shape Back Neck

Maintaining est patt, work ___ sts:

Gauge	33½" / 85 cm	37½" / 95.5 cm	41½" / 105.5 cm	45½" / 115.5 cm	49½" / 125.5 cm	53½" / 136 cm	57½" / 146 cm
3	18	17	19	21	20	22	22
4	22	23	25	26	28	28	28
5	28	30	31	32	34	36	36
6	32	36	37	40	40	41	41
7	39	40	43	46	48	49	49
8	43	46	49	52	53	55	55

BO center ___ sts:

Gauge	33½" / 85 cm	37½" / 95.5 cm	41½" / 105.5 cm	45½" / 115.5 cm	49½" / 125.5 cm	53½" / 136 cm	57½" / 146 cm
3	10	12	12	12	14	14	14
4	14	16	16	18	18	18	18
5	18	18	20	22	22	22	22
6	22	22	24	26	26	28	28
7	24	26	28	30	30	32	32
8	28	30	32	34	36	36	36

Continue in patt to end of row.

Row 2 (WS): Work in patt across right shoulder to neck edge, join new ball of yarn on the other side of the neck (left shoulder).

Working both sides of the neck AT THE SAME TIME, BO ___ sts at EACH neck edge once:

Gauge	33½" / 85 cm	37½" / 95.5 cm	41½" / 105.5 cm	45½" / 115.5 cm	49½" / 125.5 cm	53½" / 136 cm	57½" / 146 cm
3	5	6	6	6	7	7	7
4	7	8	8	9	9	9	9
5	9	9	5	6	6	6	6
6	6	6	6	7	7	7	7
7	6	7	7	8	8	8	8
8	7	8	8	9	9	9	9

BO ___ sts at EACH neck edge once:

Gauge	33½" / 85 cm	37½" / 95.5 cm	41½" / 105.5 cm	45½" / 115.5 cm	49½" / 125.5 cm	53½" / 136 cm	57½" / 146 cm
3	0	0	0	0	0	0	0
4	0	0	0	0	0	0	0
5	0	0	5	5	5	5	5
6	5	5	6	6	6	7	7
7	6	6	7	7	7	8	8
8	7	7	8	8	9	9	9

___ sts rem on each shoulder / side of neck:

Gauge	33½" / 85 cm	37½" / 95.5 cm	41½" / 105.5 cm	45½" / 115.5 cm	49½" / 125.5 cm	53½" / 136 cm	57½" / 146 cm
3	13	11	13	15	13	15	15
4	15	15	17	17	19	19	19
5	19	21	21	21	23	25	25
6	21	25	25	27	27	27	27
7	27	27	29	31	33	33	33
8	29	31	33	35	35	37	37

Shape Shoulders

Maintaining est Fave patt, BO ___ sts at beg of next 2 rows:

Gauge	33½" / 85 cm	37½" / 95.5 cm	41½" / 105.5 cm	45½" / 115.5 cm	49½" / 125.5 cm	53½" / 136 cm	57½" / 146 cm
3	6	6	6	8	6	8	8
4	8	8	8	8	10	10	10
5	10	10	8	8	8	8	8
6	8	8	8	10	10	10	10
7	10	10	10	10	12	12	12
8	10	10	12	12	12	12	12

Then BO ___ sts at beg of next 2 rows:

Gauge	33½" / 85 cm	37½" / 95.5 cm	41½" / 105.5 cm	45½" / 115.5 cm	49½" / 125.5 cm	53½" / 136 cm	57½" / 146 cm
3	7	5	7	7	7	7	7
4	7	7	9	9	9	9	9
5	9	11	8	8	8	8	8
6	8	8	8	10	10	10	10
7	10	10	10	10	12	12	12
8	10	10	12	12	12	12	12

BO ___ more sts at beg of next 2 rows:

Gauge	33½" / 85 cm	37½" / 95.5 cm	41½" / 105.5 cm	45½" / 115.5 cm	49½" / 125.5 cm	53½" / 136 cm	57½" / 146 cm
3	0	0	0	0	0	0	0
4	0	0	0	0	0	0	0
5	0	0	5	5	7	9	9
6	5	9	9	7	7	7	7
7	7	7	9	11	9	9	9
8	9	11	9	11	11	13	13

FRONT

Work as for Back to Armhole.

Armhole

BO ___ sts at beg of next 2 rows:

Gauge	33½" / 85 cm	37½" / 95.5 cm	41½" / 105.5 cm	45½" / 115.5 cm	49½" / 125.5 cm	53½" / 136 cm	57½" / 146 cm
3	1	3	3	4	5	6	7
4	3	4	5	6	7	9	11
5	3	4	6	7	9	10	13
6	4	5	7	8	11	13	16
7	4	6	8	9	12	14	18
8	5	7	9	11	14	17	21

___ sts rem:

Gauge	33½" / 85 cm	37½" / 95.5 cm	41½" / 105.5 cm	45½" / 115.5 cm	49½" / 125.5 cm	53½" / 136 cm	57½" / 146 cm
3	48	52	56	62	64	70	72
4	64	70	76	82	88	92	96
5	80	86	94	100	108	114	120
6	94	104	112	122	128	136	142
7	110	118	130	140	150	158	166
8	124	136	148	160	170	180	188

Dec Row (RS): K1, ssk, maintain est Fave patt to last 3 sts, k2tog, k1. 2 sts dec'd.

Rep Dec Row every RS row ___ more times:

Gauge	33½" / 85 cm	37½" / 95.5 cm	41½" / 105.5 cm	45½" / 115.5 cm	49½" / 125.5 cm	53½" / 136 cm	57½" / 146 cm
3	0	2	2	3	4	5	6
4	2	3	4	5	6	8	10
5	2	3	5	6	8	9	12
6	3	4	6	7	10	12	15
7	3	5	7	8	11	13	17
8	4	6	8	10	13	16	20

___ sts rem:

Gauge	33½" / 85 cm	37½" / 95.5 cm	41½" / 105.5 cm	45½" / 115.5 cm	49½" / 125.5 cm	53½" / 136 cm	57½" / 146 cm
3	46	46	50	54	54	58	58
4	58	62	66	70	74	74	74
5	74	78	82	86	90	94	94
6	86	94	98	106	106	110	110
7	102	106	114	122	126	130	130
8	114	122	130	138	142	146	146

Work even in est Fave patt, knitting the first and last st of every row, until armhole measures a finished 1″ / 2.5 cm from bind-off edge, ending with a WS row.

Shape Front Neck

Row 1 (RS): Maintaining est patt, work ___ sts, BO center 2 sts, cont in patt to end of row:

Gauge	33½" / 85 cm	37½" / 95.5 cm	41½" / 105.5 cm	45½" / 115.5 cm	49½" / 125.5 cm	53½" / 136 cm	57½" / 146 cm
3	22	22	24	26	26	28	28
4	28	30	32	34	36	36	36
5	36	38	40	42	44	46	46
6	42	46	48	52	52	54	54
7	50	52	56	60	62	64	64
8	56	60	64	68	70	72	72

Row 2 (WS): Work in patt across right shoulder to neck edge, join new ball of yarn on the other side of the neck (left shoulder), work in patt to end.
Both sides of the neck will be worked AT THE SAME TIME as follows:
Neck Dec Row (RS): Work in patt until 3 sts before neck edge, k2tog, k1, change yarns to work right shoulder, k1, ssk, work in patt to end.
Rep Neck Dec Row every RS row:

Gauge	33½" / 85 cm	37½" / 95.5 cm	41½" / 105.5 cm	45½" / 115.5 cm	49½" / 125.5 cm	53½" / 136 cm	57½" / 146 cm
3	6	9	9	8	11	10	9
4	9	11	10	13	12	11	9
5	14	12	15	17	17	15	13
6	19	17	20	22	21	23	21
7	20	22	25	26	25	27	25
8	25	27	29	31	34	31	29

Rep Neck Dec Row every OTHER RS row ___ times:

Gauge	33½" / 85 cm	37½" / 95.5 cm	41½" / 105.5 cm	45½" / 115.5 cm	49½" / 125.5 cm	53½" / 136 cm	57½" / 146 cm
3	2	1	1	2	1	2	3
4	3	3	4	3	4	5	7
5	2	4	3	3	3	5	7
6	1	3	2	2	3	3	5
7	2	2	1	2	3	3	5
8	1	1	1	1	0	3	5

_____ sts rem on each shoulder / side of neck:

Gauge	33¹/₂" / 85 cm	37¹/₂" / 95.5 cm	41¹/₂" / 105.5 cm	45¹/₂" / 115.5 cm	49¹/₂" / 125.5 cm	53¹/₂" / 136 cm	57¹/₂" / 146 cm
3	13	11	13	15	13	15	15
4	15	15	17	17	19	19	19
5	19	21	21	21	23	25	25
6	21	25	25	27	27	27	27
7	27	27	29	31	33	33	33
8	29	31	33	35	35	37	37

Shape Shoulders

Maintaining est Fave patt, BO _____ sts at beg of next 2 rows:

Gauge	33¹/₂" / 85 cm	37¹/₂" / 95.5 cm	41¹/₂" / 105.5 cm	45¹/₂" / 115.5 cm	49¹/₂" / 125.5 cm	53¹/₂" / 136 cm	57¹/₂" / 146 cm
3	6	6	6	8	6	8	8
4	8	8	8	8	10	10	10
5	10	10	8	8	8	8	8
6	8	8	8	10	10	10	10
7	10	10	10	10	12	12	12
8	10	10	12	12	12	12	12

Then BO _____ sts at beg of next 2 rows:

Gauge	33¹/₂" / 85 cm	37¹/₂" / 95.5 cm	41¹/₂" / 105.5 cm	45¹/₂" / 115.5 cm	49¹/₂" / 125.5 cm	53¹/₂" / 136 cm	57¹/₂" / 146 cm
3	7	5	7	7	7	7	7
4	7	7	9	9	9	9	9
5	9	11	8	8	8	8	8
6	8	8	8	10	10	10	10
7	10	10	10	10	12	12	12
8	10	10	12	12	12	12	12

BO ____ more sts at beg of next 2 rows:

Gauge	33½" / 85 cm	37½" / 95.5 cm	41½" / 105.5 cm	45½" / 115.5 cm	49½" / 125.5 cm	53½" / 136 cm	57½" / 146 cm
3	0	0	0	0	0	0	0
4	0	0	0	0	0	0	0
5	0	0	5	5	7	9	9
6	5	9	9	7	7	7	7
7	7	7	9	11	9	9	9
8	9	11	9	11	11	13	13

SLEEVES (MAKE 2)

Cuff
Cast on ____ sts:

Gauge	33½" / 85 cm	37½" / 95.5 cm	41½" / 105.5 cm	45½" / 115.5 cm	49½" / 125.5 cm	53½" / 136 cm	57½" / 146 cm
3	34	38	42	46	50	54	58
4	50	54	54	58	66	74	78
5	62	66	70	74	82	90	98
6	74	78	82	86	98	110	118
7	86	90	94	102	114	126	138
8	98	102	110	118	130	146	158

Rib Row (RS): K1, *k1, p1; rep from * to last st, k1.
Rep Rib Row until back measures a finished length of approx. 1" / 2.5 cm from cast-on edge, ending with a WS row.

Sleeve
Change to Fave patt for the sleeve as follows:
Row 1 (RS): K1, work RS row of Fave patt to last st, k1.
Row 2 (WS): K1, work WS row of Fave patt to last st, k1.
Rep Rows 1–2, continuing the rows of Fave patt to the end and then repeating, until sleeve measures a finished length of 4 (4, 4½, 4½, 5, 5¼, 5¾)" / 10 (10, 11.5, 11.5, 12.5, 13.5, 14.5) cm from cast-on edge, ending with a WS row.

Cap
BO ____ sts at beg of next 2 rows:

Gauge	33½" / 85 cm	37½" / 95.5 cm	41½" / 105.5 cm	45½" / 115.5 cm	49½" / 125.5 cm	53½" / 136 cm	57½" / 146 cm
3	1	3	3	4	5	6	7
4	3	4	5	6	7	9	11
5	3	4	6	7	9	10	13
6	4	5	7	8	11	13	16
7	4	6	8	9	12	14	18
8	5	7	9	11	14	17	21

____ sts rem:

Gauge	33½" / 85 cm	37½" / 95.5 cm	41½" / 105.5 cm	45½" / 115.5 cm	49½" / 125.5 cm	53½" / 136 cm	57½" / 146 cm
3	32	32	36	38	40	42	44
4	44	46	44	46	52	56	56
5	56	58	58	60	64	70	72
6	66	68	68	70	76	84	86
7	78	78	78	84	90	98	102
8	88	88	92	96	102	112	116

Dec Row 1 (RS): K1, sssk, work in est patt to last 4 sts, k3tog, k1. 4 sts dec'd.
Rep Dec Row 1 every RS row ____ more times:

Gauge	33½" / 85 cm	37½" / 95.5 cm	41½" / 105.5 cm	45½" / 115.5 cm	49½" / 125.5 cm	53½" / 136 cm	57½" / 146 cm
3	2	1	3	3	3	3	4
4	3	3	1	1	2	3	0
5	6	4	3	2	2	5	3
6	7	5	4	3	4	7	5
7	9	8	7	5	6	9	8
8	9	8	8	6	7	9	9

____ sts rem:

Gauge	33½" / 85 cm	37½" / 95.5 cm	41½" / 105.5 cm	45½" / 115.5 cm	49½" / 125.5 cm	53½" / 136 cm	57½" / 146 cm
3	20	24	20	22	24	26	24
4	28	30	36	38	40	40	52
5	28	38	42	48	52	46	56
6	34	44	48	54	56	52	62
7	38	42	46	60	62	58	66
8	48	52	56	68	70	72	76

Dec Row 2 (RS): K1, ssk, work in est patt to last 3 sts, k2tog, k1. 2 sts dec'd.
Rep Dec Row 2 every RS row ____ more times:

Gauge	33½" / 85 cm	37½" / 95.5 cm	41½" / 105.5 cm	45½" / 115.5 cm	49½" / 125.5 cm	53½" / 136 cm	57½" / 146 cm
3	1	3	1	2	2	3	2
4	4	5	8	9	8	8	12
5	3	6	8	11	11	8	11
6	4	7	9	12	11	9	12
7	4	6	8	13	12	10	12
8	6	8	10	14	13	12	14

____ sts:

Gauge	33½" / 85 cm	37½" / 95.5 cm	41½" / 105.5 cm	45½" / 115.5 cm	49½" / 125.5 cm	53½" / 136 cm	57½" / 146 cm
3	16	16	16	16	18	18	18
4	18	18	18	18	22	22	26
5	20	24	24	24	28	28	32
6	24	28	28	28	32	32	36
7	28	28	28	32	36	36	40
8	34	34	34	38	42	46	46

BO ____ sts at the beg of the next 4 rows:

Gauge	33½" / 85 cm	37½" / 95.5 cm	41½" / 105.5 cm	45½" / 115.5 cm	49½" / 125.5 cm	53½" / 136 cm	57½" / 146 cm
3	2	1	2	2	2	2	2
4	2	2	1	1	2	2	1
5	3	3	3	2	2	3	3
6	3	3	3	3	3	3	3
7	3	3	3	3	3	3	3
8	4	4	4	4	4	4	4

BO the remaining ____ sts on the next RS row:

Gauge	33½" / 85 cm	37½" / 95.5 cm	41½" / 105.5 cm	45½" / 115.5 cm	49½" / 125.5 cm	53½" / 136 cm	57½" / 146 cm
3	12	12	12	12	14	14	14
4	14	14	14	14	18	18	22
5	14	18	18	18	22	22	26
6	18	22	22	22	26	26	30
7	22	22	22	26	30	30	34
8	26	26	26	30	34	38	38

FINISHING

Block pieces to measurements. Sew shoulder seams. Sew sleeve caps into armholes. Sew side and sleeve seams.

Trim Neckline

Note: When working around, insert needle into 3 sts per 4 rows or into every BO stitch.
With circular needle and RS facing, beg at right shoulder and pick up and knit ____ sts along back neck:

Gauge	33½" / 85 cm	37½" / 95.5 cm	41½" / 105.5 cm	45½" / 115.5 cm	49½" / 125.5 cm	53½" / 136 cm	57½" / 146 cm
3	20	24	24	24	28	28	28
4	28	32	32	36	36	36	36
5	36	36	40	44	44	44	44
6	44	44	48	52	52	56	56
7	48	52	56	60	60	64	64
8	56	60	64	68	72	72	72

____ along each side of front neck:

Gauge	33½" / 85 cm	37½" / 95.5 cm	41½" / 105.5 cm	45½" / 115.5 cm	49½" / 125.5 cm	53½" / 136 cm	57½" / 146 cm
3	18	20	20	22	22	24	26
4	26	28	30	30	32	34	36
5	34	36	40	42	42	46	48
6	40	42	44	46	48	52	54
7	44	46	48	52	54	58	60
8	48	52	54	58	58	64	66

____ total sts picked up:

Gauge	33½" / 85 cm	37½" / 95.5 cm	41½" / 105.5 cm	45½" / 115.5 cm	49½" / 125.5 cm	53½" / 136 cm	57½" / 146 cm
3	56	64	64	68	72	76	80
4	80	88	92	96	100	104	108
5	104	108	120	128	128	136	140
6	124	128	136	144	148	160	164
7	136	144	152	164	168	180	184
8	152	164	172	184	188	200	204

Do not join in the rnd. The Neckline is worked flat in rows.
Rib Row (WS): *K1, p1; rep from * to end.
Rep Rib Row every row until collar measures 1" / 2.5 cm in length from neck edge.
BO loosely in pattern.
Overlap the ends at the front of the "V," aligning the edge of the collar to the edge of the decreases along the neckline and sew to secure.
Weave in ends.

DRAPEY COWL

Long and decadent, this squishy infinity scarf wraps around the neck for the ultimate comfort year-round. Play it up with cables or texture, or opt for a more warm-weather-suited accessory by using a lighter yarn and lace. Either way, this cowl will be your new go-to project.

SKILL LEVEL
Advanced Beginner

STITCH PATTERN
Choose one stitch pattern (the pattern recipe will refer to it as Fave patt) for the body. *The sample shown uses Tiny Twist Rib (page 138).*

FINISHED MEASUREMENTS
Circumference: 26 (30, 48, 52)" / 66 (76, 122, 132) cm
Height: 10 (15)" / 25.5 (38) cm
Sample size is 48" / 122 cm by 10" / 25.5 cm.

YARN REQUIREMENTS
Yardage amounts vary with the smaller yardage requirements indicated for the 10" / 25.5 cm height and the larger yardage requirements indicated for the 15" / 38 cm height.

Gauge	26" / 66 cm	30" / 76 cm	48" / 122 cm	52" / 132 cm
3	155 - 235 yds *142 - 215 m*	180 - 270 yds *165 - 247 m*	290 - 430 yds *265 - 393 m*	310 - 470 yds *283 - 430 m*
4	260 - 390 yds *238 - 357 m*	300 - 450 yds *274 - 411 m*	480 - 720 yds *439 - 658 m*	520 - 780 yds *475 - 713 m*
5	285 - 430 yds *261 - 393 m*	330 - 495 yds *302 - 453 m*	530 - 790 yds *485 - 722 m*	570 - 860 yds *521 - 786 m*
6	340 - 505 yds *311 - 462 m*	390 - 585 yds *357 - 535 m*	625 - 935 yds *572 - 855 m*	675 - 1015 yds *617 - 928 m*
7	365 - 545 yds *334 - 498 m*	420 - 630 yds *384 - 576 m*	670 - 1010 yds *613 - 924 m*	730 - 1090 yds *668 - 997 m*
8	415 - 625 yds *379 - 572 m*	480 - 720 yds *439 - 658 m*	770 - 1150 yds *704 - 1052 m*	830 - 1250 yds *759 - 1143 m*

NEEDLES & NOTIONS
For a lovely drape, choose a needle size that is 1–2 sizes larger than recommended for the yarn weight.
- Circular needles, 32" / 80 cm long, in the size necessary to obtain the desired gauge
- Stitch marker
- Yarn needle

SAMPLE PROJECT
The sample scarf shown is worked with 2 skeins Lion Brand Wool-Ease Chunky in Eggplant #144 (153 yards / 140 m per 5 oz / 140 g skein; 80% acrylic, 20% wool) with a finished gauge of 3 sts and 4 rows = 1" / 2.5 cm.

PATTERN NOTES
- This cowl is worked in the round from the bottom up. A simple border of Garter stitch surrounds your Fave patt.
- Only work as instructed for your size. If the number for your size and gauge in the table is 0, omit those rows and/or stitches and move on to the next indicated stitch/row instructions.

PATTERN Drapey Cowl

BORDER

Cast on ___ sts:

	26" / 66 cm	30" / 76 cm	48" / 122 cm	52" 132 cm
3	80	92	144	156
4	104	120	192	208
5	132	152	240	260
6	156	180	288	312
7	184	212	336	364
8	208	240	384	416

Place marker and join for working in the rnd.
Rnd 1: Purl.
Rnd 2: Knit.
Rep Rnds 1–2 twice more.

BODY

Change to Fave patt, repeating the indicated rows until the cowl measures a finished length of 9½ (14½)" / 24 (37) cm or until ½" / 2 cm less than desired length.

BORDER

Rep Border Rnds 1–2 three times.
BO loosely.

FINISHING

Block as desired. Weave in ends.

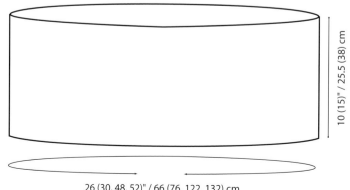

26 (30, 48, 52)" / 66 (76, 122, 132) cm

10 (15)" / 25.5 (38) cm

CRESCENT SHAWLETTE

This cozy shawlette offers up a lovely palette to explore lace or textured stitch patterns, all with only one or two skeins of yarn. It has the most wrappable shape for the neck, while the construction promises ease for every level of knitter.

SKILL LEVEL
Intermediate

STITCH PATTERN
Choose one stitch pattern (the pattern recipe will refer to it as Fave patt).
The sample shown uses Wedge Lace (page 126).

FINISHED MEASUREMENTS
Top Wingspan: approx. 43¼ (50¼, 60¼)" / 110 (127.5, 153) cm
Border Edge Length: approx. 56¾ (66½, 79¾)" / 144 (169, 202.5) cm
Width at Deepest Point: approx. 13½ (16¼, 19½)" / 34.5 (41.5, 49.5) cm
Sample size is 43½" / 110 cm wingspan.

YARN REQUIREMENTS

Gauge	43¼" / 110 cm	50¼" / 127.5 cm	60¼" / 153 cm
3	360 yds / *329 m*	475 yds / *434 m*	645 yds / *590 m*
4	420 yds / *384 m*	565 yds / *517 m*	755 yds / *690 m*
5	480 yds / *439 m*	630 yds / *576 m*	865 yds / *791 m*
6	610 yds / *558 m*	785 yds / *718 m*	1090 yds / *997 m*
7	665 yds / *608 m*	870 yds / *796 m*	1190 yds / *1088 m*
8	725 yds / *663 m*	945 yds / *864 m*	1300 yds / *1189 m*

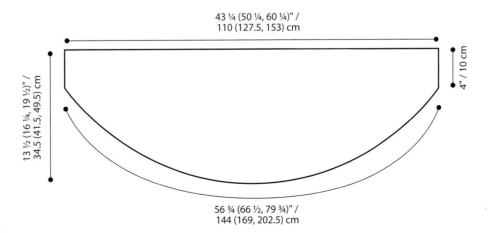

43 ¼ (50 ¼, 60 ¼)" / 110 (127.5, 153) cm

4" / 10 cm

13 ½ (16 ¼, 19 ½)" / 34.5 (41.5, 49.5) cm

56 ¾ (66 ½, 79 ¾)" / 144 (169, 202.5) cm

*Measurements are an average of all the gauges listed.

NEEDLES & NOTIONS

Choose a needle size that is larger than recommended for your yarn so as to achieve a moderate drape.

- Circular needles, 24" / 60 cm in length, in the size necessary to obtain the desired gauge
- Yarn needle

SAMPLE PROJECT

The sample shawl shown is worked with 1 skein SweetGeorgia Yarns Bulletproof Sock in Jasmine (437 yards / 400 m per 3.5 oz / 100 g skein; 50% superwash merino wool, 15% silk, 15% mohair, 20% nylon) *with a finished gauge of* 4 sts and 6 rows = 1" / 2.5 cm.

PATTERN NOTES

- This crescent-shaped shawl is worked from the bottom up, beginning with the border pattern and then utilizing short rows to shape the body.
- Only work as instructed for your size. If the number for your size and gauge in the table is 0, omit those rows and/or stitches and move on to the next indicated stitch/ row instructions.

PATTERN Crescent Shawlette

BORDER
Cast on ____ sts:

Gauge	43¹⁄₄" / 110 cm	50¹⁄₄" / 127.5 cm	60¹⁄₄" / 153 cm
3	172	200	240
4	228	268	320
5	284	332	400
6	340	396	480
7	396	464	556
8	452	528	636

Note: The pattern below indicates an additional two stitches worked in your chosen Fave patt so as to center the design on the border. When working those additional two stitches, work them in pattern except when you cannot match a decrease with an increase (such as having a k2tog without a paired yo). When that is the case, simply work those 2 stitches in Stockinette stitch).

Row 1 (RS): K1, work Fave patt to last 3 sts, work first 2 sts of Fave patt, k1.

Row 2 (WS): Sl 1 wyif, work last 2 sts of Fave patt, work Fave patt to last st, sl 1 wyif.

Rep Rows 1–2, continuing the Fave patt as established through the remaining pattern rows, until border measures 4" / 10 cm from cast-on edge, ending with a WS row.

BODY
Row 1 (RS): K____, turn:

Gauge	43¹⁄₄" / 110 cm	50¹⁄₄" / 127.5 cm	60¹⁄₄" / 153 cm
3	92	104	124
4	120	136	164
5	148	172	204
6	176	200	244
7	204	236	280
8	232	268	320

Row 2 (WS): K____, turn:

Gauge	43¹⁄₄" / 110 cm	50¹⁄₄" / 127.5 cm	60¹⁄₄" / 153 cm
3	12	8	8
4	12	4	8
5	12	12	8
6	12	4	8
7	12	8	4
8	12	8	4

Row 3: Knit until 1 st before gap (made at the turn point), ssk, k3, turn.

Row 4: Purl until 1 st before gap (made at the turn point), p2tog, p3, turn.

Rep Rows 3–4 ____ more times:

Gauge	43¹/₄" / 110 cm	50¹/₄" / 127.5 cm	60¹/₄" / 153 cm
3	19	23	28
4	26	32	38
5	33	39	48
6	40	48	58
7	47	56	68
8	54	64	78

____ sts rem:

Gauge	43¹/₄" / 110 cm	50¹/₄" / 127.5 cm	60¹/₄" / 153 cm
3	132	152	182
4	174	202	242
5	216	252	302
6	258	298	362
7	300	350	418
8	342	398	478

Knit 4 rows.
BO knitwise in patt.

FINISHING
Block to measurements. Weave in ends.

CHAPTER 3

KNITS AND PURLS

The foundation stitches of any pattern come down to simple knits and purls. Simple, yes, but these two stitches offer ample opportunity for texture, variation, and delight. The 2- and 4-stitch-multiple patterns you'll find in this chapter offer a wealth of exploration, such as ribbing, diagonals, triangles, columns and rows, and subtle transitions. The best part is that *almost* all of these are reversible.

There are two super basic stitch patterns you'll see references to in some of the pattern recipes earlier in the book: Stockinette Stitch and Garter Stitch.

Stockinette Stitch

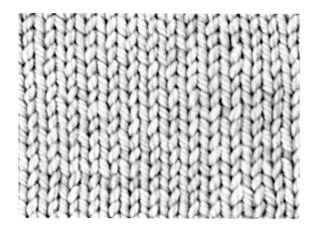

Flat
Row 1 (RS): Knit.
Row 2 (WS): Purl.

Round
Knit every rnd.

Garter Stitch

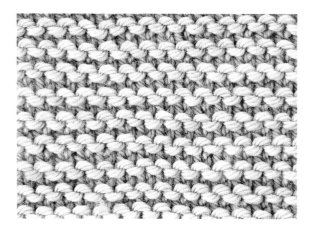

Flat
Knit every row.

Round
Rnd 1: Knit.
Rnd 2: Purl.

K2P2 Rib

Flat
Every Row: *K2, p2; rep from * to end.
Repeat Every Row for pattern.

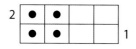

Stitches

	k on the RS; p on the WS
●	p on the RS; k on the WS

Round
Every Rnd: *K2, p2; rep from * to end.
Repeat Every Rnd for pattern.

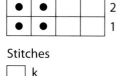

Stitches

	k
●	p

*Another simple rib stitch is the K1p1 Rib, which is worked every row/rnd as: *K1, p1; rep from * to end.

Diagonal Dots

Flat

Row 1 (RS): *P1, k3; rep from * to end.
Row 2 (WS): *P2, k1, p1; rep from * to end.
Row 3: *K2, p1, k1; rep from * to end.
Row 4: *K1, p3; rep from * to end.
Repeat Rows 1–4 for pattern.

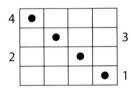

Stitches

	k on the RS; p on the WS
●	p on the RS; k on the WS

Round

Rnd 1: *P1, k3; rep from * to end.
Rnd 2: *K1, p1, k2; rep from * to end.
Rnd 3: *K2, p1, k1; rep from * to end.
Rnd 4: *K3, p1; rep from * to end.
Repeat Rnds 1–4 for pattern.

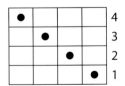

Stitches

	k
●	p

Double Seed

Flat

Rows 1–2: *P2, k2; rep from * to end.
Rows 3–4: *K2, p2; rep from * to end.
Repeat Rows 1–4 for pattern.

Stitches

	k on the RS; p on the WS
●	p on the RS; k on the WS

Round

Rnds 1–2: *P2, k2; rep from * to end.
Rnds 3–4: *K2, p2; rep from * to end.
Repeat Rnds 1–4 for pattern.

Stitches

	k
●	p

Garter Rib

Flat

Row 1 (RS): *K2, p2; rep from * to end.
Row 2 (WS): Purl.
Repeat Rows 1–2 for pattern.

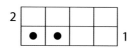

Stitches

☐ k on the RS; p on the WS
⊡ p on the RS; k on the WS

Round

Rnd 1: *K2, p2; rep from * to end.
Rnd 2: Knit.
Repeat Rnds 1–2 for pattern.

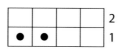

Stitches

☐ k
⊡ p

Waffle Rib

Flat

Rows 1–3: *K2, p2; rep from * to end.
Row 4: Knit.
Repeat Rows 1–4 for pattern.

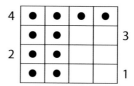

Stitches

☐ k on the RS; p on the WS
⊡ p on the RS; k on the WS

Round

Rnds 1–3: *K2, p2; rep from * to end.
Rnd 4: Purl.
Repeat Rnds 1–4 for pattern.

Stitches

☐ k
⊡ p

Garter Ladder

Flat
Row 1 (RS): *K1, p2, k1; rep from * to end.
Row 2 (WS): Knit.
Row 3: Rep Row 1.
Row 4: *P1, k2, p1; rep from * to end.
Repeat Rows 1–4 for pattern.

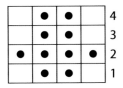

Stitches

| | k on the RS; p on the WS |
| | p on the RS; k on the WS |

Round
Rnd 1: *K1, p2, k1; rep from * to end.
Rnd 2: Purl.
Rnds 3–4: *K1, p2, k1; rep from * to end.
Repeat Rnds 1–4 for pattern.

Stitches

| | k |
| | p |

Single Point Chevron

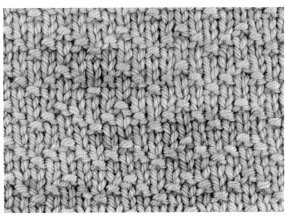

Flat
Row 1 (RS): *K3, p1; rep from * to end.
Row 2 (WS): *P1, k1; rep from * to end.
Row 3: *K1, p1, k2; rep from * to end.
Row 4: Purl.
Repeat Rows 1–4 for pattern.

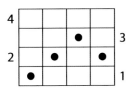

Stitches

| | k on the RS; p on the WS |
| | p on the RS; k on the WS |

Round
Rnd 1: *K3, p1; rep from * to end.
Rnd 2: *P1, k1; rep from * to end.
Rnd 3: *K1, p1, k2; rep from * to end.
Rnd 4: Knit.
Repeat Rnds 1–4 for pattern.

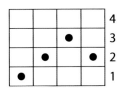

Stitches

| | k |
| | p |

Dot

Flat
Row 1 (RS): *P1, k3; rep from * to end.
Row 2 (WS): Purl.
Row 3: *K3, p1; rep from * to end.
Row 4: Purl.
Repeat Rows 1–4 for pattern.

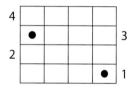

Stitches
☐ k on the RS; p on the WS
▣ p on the RS; k on the WS

Round
Rnd 1: *P1, k3; rep from * to end.
Rnd 2: Knit.
Rnd 3: *K3, p1; rep from * to end.
Rnd 4: Knit.
Repeat Rnds 1–4 for pattern.

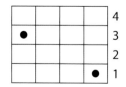

Stitches
☐ k
▣ p

Hint

Flat
Row 1 (RS): *P2, k2; rep from * to end.
Row 2 (WS): Purl.
Row 3: *K2, p2; rep from * to end.
Row 4: Purl.
Repeat Rows 1–4 for pattern.

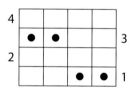

Stitches
☐ k on the RS; p on the WS
▣ p on the RS; k on the WS

Round
Rnd 1: *P2, k2; rep from * to end.
Rnd 2: Knit.
Rnd 3: *K2, p2; rep from * to end.
Rnd 4: Knit.
Repeat Rnds 1–4 for pattern.

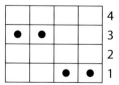

Stitches
☐ k
▣ p

Oblique Rib

Flat

Row 1 (RS): *K2, p2; rep from * to end.
Row 2 (WS): *K1, p2, k1; rep from * to end.
Row 3: *P2, k2; rep from * to end.
Row 4: *P1, k2, p1; rep from * to end.
Repeat Rows 1–4 for pattern.

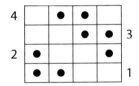

Stitches

☐ k on the RS; p on the WS
◉ p on the RS; k on the WS

Round

Rnd 1: *K2, p2; rep from * to end.
Rnd 2: *P1, k2, p1; rep from * to end.
Rnd 3: *P2, k2; rep from * to end.
Rnd 4: *K1, p2, k1; rep from * to end.
Repeat Rnds 1–4 for pattern.

Stitches

☐ k
◉ p

Right-Pointing Triangles

Flat

Row 1 (RS): *K3, p1; rep from * to end.
Row 2 (WS): *K2, p2; rep from * to end.
Row 3: *K1, p3; rep from * to end.
Row 4: *K2, p2; rep from * to end.
Repeat Rows 1–4 for pattern.

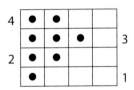

Stitches

☐ k on the RS; p on the WS
◉ p on the RS; k on the WS

Round

Rnd 1: *K3, p1; rep from * to end.
Rnd 2: *K2, p2; rep from * to end.
Rnd 3: *K1, p3; rep from * to end.
Rnd 4: *K2, p2; rep from * to end.
Repeat Rnds 1–4 for pattern.

Stitches

☐ k
◉ p

Left-Pointing Triangles

Flat

Row 1 (RS): *P1, k3; rep from * to end.
Row 2 (WS): *P2, k2; rep from * to end.
Row 3: *P3, k1; rep from * to end.
Row 4: *P2, k2; rep from * to end.
Repeat Rows 1–4 for pattern.

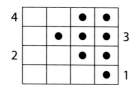

Stitches

☐ k on the RS; p on the WS
☒ p on the RS; k on the WS

Round

Rnd 1: *P1, k3; rep from * to end.
Rnd 2: *P2, k2; rep from * to end.
Rnd 3: *P3, k1; rep from * to end.
Rnd 4: *P2, k2; rep from * to end.
Repeat Rnds 1–4 for pattern.

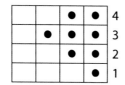

Stitches

☐ k
☒ p

K1P3 Rib

Flat

Row 1 (RS): *K1, p3; rep from * to end.
Row 2 (WS): *K3, p1; rep from * to end.
Repeat Rows 1–2 for pattern.

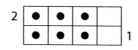

Stitches

☐ k on the RS; p on the WS
☒ p on the RS; k on the WS

Round

Every Rnd: *K1, p3; rep from * to end.
Repeat Every Rnd for pattern.

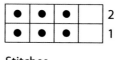

Stitches

☐ k
☒ p

Staggered Singles

Round

Rnds 1–4: *K1, p3; rep from * to end.
Rnds 5–8: *P1, k1, p2; rep from * to end.
Rnds 9–12: *P2, k1, p1; rep from * to end.
Rnds 13–16: *P3, k1; rep from * to end.
Repeat Rnds 1–16 for pattern.

	●	●	●	16
	●	●	●	15
	●	●	●	14
	●	●	●	13
●		●	●	12
●		●	●	11
●		●	●	10
●		●	●	9
●	●		●	8
●	●		●	7
●	●		●	6
●	●		●	5
●	●	●		4
●	●	●		3
●	●	●		2
●	●	●		1

Stitches

☐	k
●	p

Flat

Row 1 (RS): *K1, p3; rep from * to end.
Row 2 (WS): *K3, p1; rep from * to end.
Rows 3–4: Repeat Rows 1–2.
Row 5: *P1, k1, p2; rep from * to end.
Row 6: *K2, p1, k1; rep from * to end.
Rows 7–8: Repeat Rows 5–6.
Row 9: *P2, k1, p1; rep from * to end.
Row 10: *K1, p1, k2; rep from * to end.
Rows 11–12: Repeat Rows 9–10.
Row 13: *P3, k1; rep from * to end.
Row 14: *P1, k3; rep from * to end.
Rows 15–16: Repeat Rows 13–14.
Repeat Rows 1–16 for pattern.

16		●	●	●	
		●	●	●	15
14		●	●	●	
		●	●	●	13
12	●		●	●	
	●		●	●	11
10	●		●	●	
	●		●	●	9
8	●	●		●	
	●	●		●	7
6	●	●		●	
	●	●		●	5
4	●	●	●		
	●	●	●		3
2	●	●	●		
	●	●	●		1

Stitches

☐	k on the RS; p on the WS
●	p on the RS; k on the WS

Moss Rib

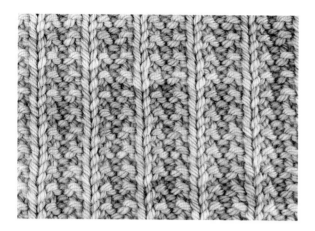

Flat

Row 1 (RS): *K1, p1; rep from * to end.
Row 2 (WS): *P1, k1, p2; rep from * to end.
Repeat Rows 1–2 for pattern.

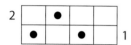

Stitches

☐ k on the RS; p on the WS
⬛ p on the RS; k on the WS

Round

Rnd 1: *K1, p1; rep from * to end.
Rnd 2: *K2, p1, k1; rep from * to end.
Repeat Rnds 1–2 for pattern.

Stitches

☐ k
⬛ p

Zig-Zag Purls

Flat

Row 1 (RS): *K2, p2; rep from * to end.
Row 2 (WS): *P1, k2, p1; rep from * to end.
Row 3: *P2, k2; rep from * to end.
Row 4: *K1, p2, k1; rep from * to end.
Row 5: *P2, k2; rep from * to end.
Row 6: *P1, k2, p1; rep from * to end.
Repeat Rows 1–6 for pattern.

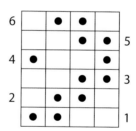

Stitches

☐ k on the RS; p on the WS
⬛ p on the RS; k on the WS

Rnd 1: *K2, p2; rep from * to end.
Rnd 2: *K1, p2, k1; rep from * to end.
Rnd 3: *P2, k2; rep from * to end.
Rnd 4: *P1, k2, p1; rep from * to end.
Rnd 5: *P2, k2; rep from * to end.
Rnd 6: *K1, p2, k1; rep from * to end.
Repeat Rnds 1–6 for pattern.

Stitches

☐ k

⊡ p

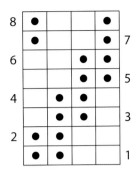

Stitches

☐ k on the RS; p on the WS

⊡ p on the RS; k on the WS

Round

Rnds 1–2: *K2, p2; rep from * to end.
Rnds 3–4: *K1, p2, k1; rep from * to end.
Rnds 5–6: *P2, k2; rep from * to end.
Rnds 7–8: *P1, k2, p1; rep from * to end.
Repeat Rnds 1–8 for pattern.

Stitches

☐ k

⊡ p

Diagonal Rib

Flat

Rows 1–2: *K2, p2; rep from * to end.
Row 3: *K1, p2, k1; rep from * to end.
Row 4: *P1, k2, p1; rep from * to end.
Rows 5–6: *P2, k2; rep from * to end.
Row 7: *P1, k2, p1; rep from * to end.
Row 8: *K1, p2, k1; rep from * to end.
Repeat Rows 1–8 for pattern.

Ladder

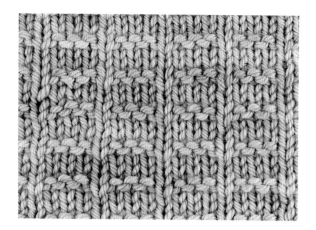

Flat
Row 1 (RS): Knit.
Row 2 (WS): Purl.
Row 3: *K1, p3; rep from * to end.
Row 4: Purl.
Repeat Rows 1–4 for pattern.

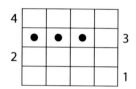

Stitches

☐ k on the RS; p on the WS
▢• p on the RS; k on the WS

Round
Rnds 1–2: Knit.
Rnd 3: *K1, p3; rep from * to end.
Rnd 4: Knit.
Repeat Rnds 1–4 for pattern.

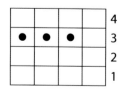

Stitches

☐ k
▢• p

Double Step

Flat
Row 1 (RS): *K1, p3; rep from * to end.
Row 2 (WS): *K3, p1; rep from * to end.
Row 3: Knit.
Row 4: Purl.
Repeat Rows 1–4 for pattern.

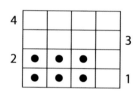

Stitches

☐ k on the RS; p on the WS
▢• p on the RS; k on the WS

Round
Rnds 1–2: *K1, p3; rep from * to end.
Rnds 3–4: Knit.
Repeat Rnds 1–4 for pattern.

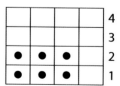

Stitches

☐ k
▢• p

Basketweave

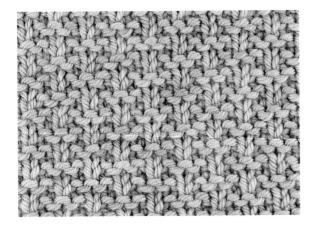

Flat

Row 1 (RS): *K1, p3; rep from * to end.
Row 2 (WS): Purl.
Row 3: *P2, k1, p1; rep from * to end.
Row 4: Purl.
Repeat Rows 1–4 for pattern.

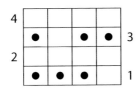

Stitches

☐ k on the RS; p on the WS
▣ p on the RS; k on the WS

Round

Rnd 1: *K1, p3; rep from * to end.
Rnd 2: Knit.
Rnd 3: *P2, k1, p1; rep from * to end.
Rnd 4: Knit.
Repeat Rnds 1–4 for pattern.

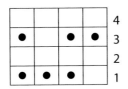

Stitches

☐ k
▣ p

Step Stool

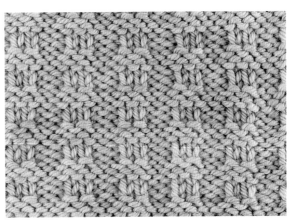

Flat

Row 1 (RS): Purl.
Row 2 (WS): Knit.
Rows 3–4: *K2, p2; rep from * to end.
Repeat Rows 1–4 for pattern.

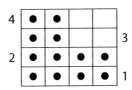

Stitches

☐ k on the RS; p on the WS
▣ p on the RS; k on the WS

Round

Rnds 1–2: Purl.
Rnds 3–4: *K2, p2; rep from * to end.
Repeat Rnds 1–4 for pattern.

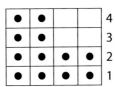

Stitches

☐ k
▣ p

Pillars

Round

Rnds 1–2: *P1, k1, p2; rep from * to end.
Rnds 3–4: *P1, k1; rep from * to end.
Rnds 5–6: *P3, k1; rep from * to end.
Rnds 7–8: *P1, k1; rep from * to end.
Repeat Rnds 1–8 for pattern.

Stitches

	k
●	p

Flat

Row 1 (RS): *P1, k1, p2; rep from * to end.
Row 2 (WS): *K2, p1, k1; rep from * to end.
Rows 3–4: *P1, k1; rep from * to end.
Row 5: *P3, k1; rep from * to end.
Row 6: *P1, k3; rep from * to end.
Rows 7–8: *P1, k1; rep from * to end.
Repeat Rows 1–8 for pattern.

Stitches

	k on the RS; p on the WS
●	p on the RS; k on the WS

Ripple Rib

Flat

Rows 1–2: *P2, k2; rep from * to end.
Row 3: *P1, k2, p1; rep from * to end.
Row 4: *K1, p2, k1; rep from * to end.
Rows 5–6: *K2, p2; rep from * to end.
Row 7: *K1, p2, k1; rep from * to end.
Row 8: *P1, k2, p1; rep from * to end.
Rows 9–10: *P2, k2; rep from * to end.
Row 11: *K1, p2, k1; rep from * to end.
Row 12: *P1, k2, p1; rep from * to end.
Rows 13–14: *K2, p2; rep from * to end.
Row 15: *P1, k2, p1; rep from * to end.
Row 16: *K1, p2, k1; rep from * to end.
Repeat Rows 1–16 for pattern.

Round

Rnds 1–2: *P2, k2; rep from * to end.
Rnds 3–4: *P1, k2, p1; rep from * to end.
Rnds 5–6: *K2, p2; rep from * to end.
Rnds 7–8: *K1, p2, k1; rep from * to end.
Rnds 9–10: Rep Rnds 1–2.
Rnds 11–12: Rep Rnds 7–8.
Rnds 13–14: Rep Rnds 5–6.
Rnds 15–16: Rep Rnds 3–4.
Repeat Rnds 1–16 for pattern.

Stitches

☐ k

⊡ p

Stitches

☐ k on the RS; p on the WS

⊡ p on the RS; k on the WS

Seeded Rib

Rnd 1: *K3, p1; rep from * to end.
Rnd 2: *P1, k1, p2; rep from * to end.
Repeat Rnds 1–2 for pattern.

•	•		•	2
•				1

Stitches

	k
•	p

Flat

Row 1 (RS): *K3, p1; rep from * to end.
Row 2 (WS): *K2, p1, k1; rep from * to end.
Repeat Rows 1–2 for pattern.

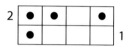

Stitches

	k on the RS; p on the WS
•	p on the RS; k on the WS

CHAPTER 4

LACE

Oh, how lace can take over the show. With its airy eyelets and soft appeal, lace is the grace of knitting. When worked in a small stitch multiple, as presented here, knitters will find a wealth of delicate, easy-to-memorize patterns to suit projects and fabrics of every kind. Zig-zags, columns, rows, or tiny eyelets offer ample opportunity to explore the richness of lace and openwork.

Ridged Eyelets

Round

Rnd 1: Knit.
Rnd 2: Purl.
Rnd 3: Knit.
Rnd 4: *K2tog, yo; rep from * to end.
Rnds 5–6: Repeat Rnds 1–2.
Rnd 7: Knit.
Rnd 8: *Yo, k2tog; rep from * to end.
Repeat Rnds 1–8 for pattern.

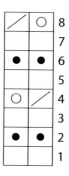

Stitches

☐ k
⬛ p
◯ yo
⟋ k2tog

Flat

Rows 1–3: Knit.
Row 4: *Yo, p2tog; rep from * to end.
Rows 5–7: Knit.
Row 8: *P2tog, yo; rep from * to end.
Repeat Rows 1–8 for pattern.

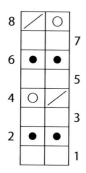

Stitches

☐ k on the RS; p on the WS
⬛ p on the RS; k on the WS
◯ yo
⟋ p2tog on the WS

Wide Open

Flat

Row 1 (RS): *Ssk, yo twice, k2tog; rep from *
to end.
Row 2 (WS): *P2, k1, p1; rep from * to end.
Repeat Rows 1–2 for pattern.

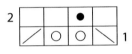

Stitches

☐	k on the RS; p on the WS
☐•	p on the RS; k on the WS
○	yo
╱	k2tog
╲	ssk

Round

Rnd 1: *Ssk, yo twice, k2tog; rep from *
to end.
Rnd 2: *K1, p1, k2; rep from * to end.
Repeat Rnds 1–2 for pattern.

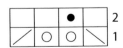

Stitches

☐	k
☐•	p
○	yo
╱	k2tog
╲	ssk

Light Eyelet Rows

Flat

Row 1 (RS): Knit.
Row 2 (WS): Purl.
Row 3: *Yo, ssk; rep from * to end.
Row 4: Purl.
Row 5: Knit.
Rows 6–7: Repeat Rows 4–5.
Row 8: Purl.
Row 9: *K1, yo, ssk, k1; rep from * to end.
Row 10: Purl.
Row 11: Knit.
Row 12: Purl.
Repeat Rows 1–8 for pattern.

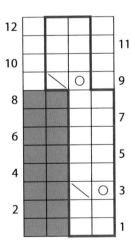

Stitches

▩	No stitch
☐	k on the RS; p on the WS
○	yo
╲	ssk

Borders

— rep

Round

Rnds 1–2: Knit.
Rnd 3: *Yo, ssk; rep from * to end.
Rnds 4–8: Knit.
Rnd 9: *K1, yo, ssk, k1; rep from * to end.
Rnds 10–12: Knit.
Repeat Rnds 1–8 for pattern.

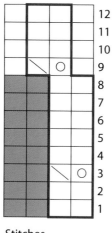

Stitches

▨	No stitch
☐	k
○	yo
◹	ssk

Borders
— rep

Grand Lace

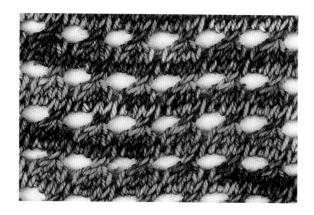

Flat

Row 1 (RS): Knit.
Row 2 (WS): *P4tog, yo; rep from * to end.
Row 3: *K1, (k1, p1, k1) in 1; rep from * to end.
Row 4: Purl.
Repeat Rows 1–4 for pattern.

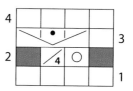

Stitches

▨	WS: No stitch
☐	k on the RS; p on the WS
○	yo
⟍•⟋	(k1, p1, k1) in 1
◢4	p4tog on the WS

Round

Rnd 1: Knit.
Rnd 2: *Yo, k4tog; rep from * to end.
Rnd 3: *K1, (k1, p1, k1) in 1; rep from * to end.
Rnd 4: Knit.
Repeat Rnds 1–4 for pattern.

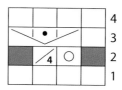

Stitches

▨	No stitch
☐	k
○	yo
⟍•⟋	(k1, p1, k1) in 1
◢4	k4tog

Special Stitches:

(K1, p1, k1) in 1 Knit, leaving the stitch on the needle, then purl, and then knit into the same stitch.
K4tog Knit 4 stitches together.
P4tog Purl 4 stitches together.

Twisty Ridges

Flat

Rows 1–4: Purl.
Row 5: *Yo, k2tog; rep from * to end.
Row 6: Purl.
Row 7: *K2tog, yo; rep from * to end.
Row 8: Purl.
Row 9: *Yo, k2tog; rep from * to end.
Row 10: Purl.
Repeat Rows 1–10 for pattern.

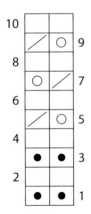

Stitches

☐ k on the RS; p on the WS
⊡ p on the RS; k on the WS
⊙ yo
⟋ k2tog

Round

Rnd 1: Purl.
Rnd 2: Knit.
Rnds 3–4: Repeat Rnds 1–2.
Rnd 5: *Yo, k2tog; rep from * to end.
Rnd 6: Knit.
Rnd 7: *K2tog, yo; rep from * to end.
Rnd 8: Knit.
Rnd 9: *Yo, k2tog; rep from * to end.
Rnd 10: Knit.
Repeat Rnds 1–10 for pattern.

Stitches

☐ k
⊡ p
⊙ yo
⟋ k2tog

Little Fountain

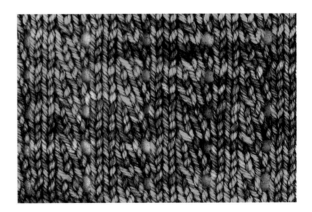

Flat

Row 1 (RS): Knit.
Row 2 (WS): *P3, yo, p1; rep from * to end.
Row 3: *K5; rep from * to end.
Row 4: *P1, sssp, p2; rep from * to end.
Row 5: Knit.

Repeat Rows 2–5 for pattern.

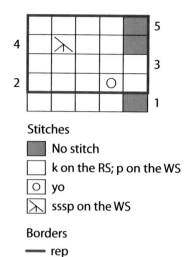

Stitches

▨ No stitch

☐ k on the RS; p on the WS

☐O yo

⧄ sssp on the WS

Borders

— rep

Round

Rnd 1: Knit.
Rnd 2: *K1, yo, k3; rep from * to end.
Rnd 3: Knit.
Rnd 4: *K2, sk2p, k1; rep from * to end.
Rnd 5: Knit.
Repeat Rnds 2–5 for pattern.

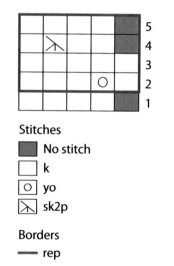

Stitches

▨ No stitch

☐ k

☐O yo

⧄ sk2p

Borders

— rep

Special Stitches:

Sk2p Slip one stitch knitwise, then knit 2 stitches together and pass the slipped stitch over.

Sssp Slip 3 stitches knitwise, then return slipped stitches to left needle and purl 3 together through back loop.

Twisted Lace

Flat

Row 1 (RS): *Yo, k2tog-tbl; rep from * to end.
Row 2 (WS): *Yo, p2tog; rep from * to end.
Repeat Rows 1–2 for pattern.

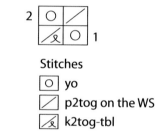

Stitches

☐O yo

⧄ p2tog on the WS

⧄ k2tog-tbl

Round

Rnd 1: *Yo, k2tog-tbl; rep from * to end.
Rnd 2: *K2tog, yo; rep from * to end.
Repeat Rnds 1–2 for pattern.

Stitches

☐O yo

⧄ k2tog

⧄ k2tog-tbl

Special Stitch:

K2tog-tbl Knit two stitches together through the back loop.

Wavy Column

Flat

Row 1 (RS): *K2, yo, ssk; rep from * to end.
Row 2 (WS): Purl.
Row 3: *K2, yo, k2tog; rep from * to end.
Row 4: Purl.
Repeat Rows 1–4 for pattern.

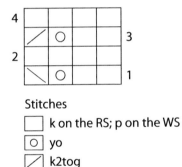

Stitches

	k on the RS; p on the WS
O	yo
/	k2tog
\	ssk

Round

Rnd 1: *K2, yo, ssk; rep from * to end.
Rnd 2: Knit.
Rnd 3: *K2, yo, k2tog; rep from * to end.
Rnd 4: Knit.
Repeat Rnds 1–4 for pattern.

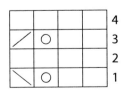

Stitches

	k
O	yo
/	k2tog
\	ssk

Eyelet Column

Flat

Row 1 (RS): *P1, yo, ssk, p1; rep from * to end.
Row 2 (WS): *K1, p2, k1; rep from * to end.
Row 3: *P1, k2tog, yo, p1; rep from * to end.
Row 4: *K1, p2, k1; rep from * to end.
Repeat Rows 1–4 for pattern.

Stitches

	k on the RS; p on the WS
●	p on the RS; k on the WS
O	yo
/	k2tog
\	ssk

Rnd 1: *P1, yo, ssk, p1; rep from * to end.
Rnd 2: *P1, k2, p1; rep from * to end.
Rnd 3: *P1, k2tog, yo, p1; rep from * to end.
Rnd 4: Rep Rnd 2.
Repeat Rnds 1–4 for pattern.

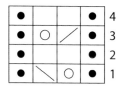

Stitches

☐	k
●	p
○	yo
╱	k2tog
╲	ssk

Easy Zig-Zag Lace

Row 1 (RS): *K2, k2tog, yo; rep from * to end.
Row 2 (WS): Purl.
Rows 3–8: Repeat Rows 1–2.
Row 9: *Yo, ssk, k2; rep from * to end.
Row 10: Purl.
Rows 11–16: Repeat Rows 9–10.
Repeat Rows 1–16 for pattern.

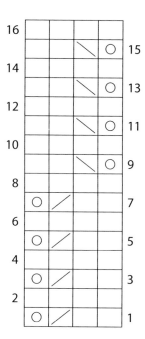

Stitches

☐	k on the RS; p on the WS
○	yo
╱	k2tog
╲	ssk

Rnd 1: *K2, k2tog, yo; rep from * to end.
Rnd 2: Knit.
Rnds 3–8: Repeat Rnds 1–2.
Rnd 9: *Yo, ssk, k2; rep from * to end.
Rnd 10: Knit.
Rnds 11–16: Repeat Rnds 9–10.
Repeat Rnds 1–16 for pattern.

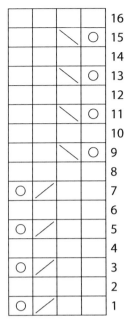

Stitches

- ☐ k
- ⊙ yo
- ◹ k2tog
- ◺ ssk

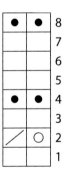

Stitches

- ☐ k on the RS; p on the WS
- ● p on the RS; k on the WS
- ⊙ yo
- ◹ p2tog on the WS

Round

Rnd 1: Knit.
Rnd 2: *Yo, k2tog; rep from * to end.
Rnd 3: Knit.
Rnd 4: Purl.
Rnds 5–7: Knit.
Rnd 8: Purl.
Repeat Rnds 1–8 for pattern.

Double Ridge Lace

Stitches

- ☐ k
- ● p
- ⊙ yo
- ◹ k2tog

Flat

Row 1 (RS): Knit.
Row 2 (WS): *P2tog, yo; rep from * to end.
Rows 3–5: Knit.
Row 6: Purl.
Rows 7–8: Knit.
Repeat Rows 1–8 for pattern.

Wedge Lace

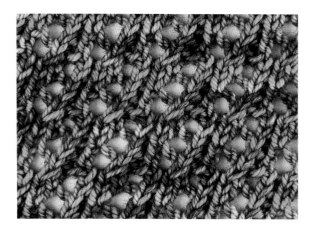

Flat

Row 1 (RS): *P2, k2tog, yo; rep from * to end.
Row 2 (WS): *P2, k2; rep from * to end.
Row 3: *P1, k2tog, yo, k1; rep from * to end.
Row 4: *P3, k1; rep from * to end.
Row 5: *K2tog, yo, k2; rep from * to end.
Row 6: Purl.
Repeat Rows 1–6 for pattern.

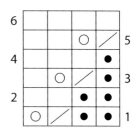

Stitches

☐	k on the RS; p on the WS
⦿	p on the RS; k on the WS
⊙	yo
⟋	k2tog

Round

Rnd 1: *P2, k2tog, yo; rep from * to end.
Rnd 2: *P2, k2; rep from * to end.
Rnd 3: *P1, k2tog, yo, k1; rep from * to end.
Rnd 4: *P1, k3; rep from * to end.
Rnd 5: *K2tog, yo, k2; rep from * to end.
Rnd 6: Knit.
Repeat Rnds 1–6 for pattern.

Stitches

☐	k
⦿	p
⊙	yo
⟋	k2tog

Starred Columns

Flat

Row 1 (RS): *P1, yo, sk2p, yo; rep from * to end.
Row 2 (WS): *P3, k1; rep from * to end.
Row 3: *P1, k3; rep from * to end.
Row 4: *P3, k1; rep from * to end.
Repeat Rows 1–4 for pattern.

Stitches

☐	k on the RS; p on the WS
⦿	p on the RS; k on the WS
⊙	yo
⋊	sk2p

Round

Rnd 1: *P1, yo, sk2p, yo; rep from * to end.
Rnds 2–4: *P1, k3; rep from * to end.
Repeat Rnds 1–4 for pattern.

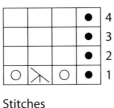

Stitches

- ☐ k
- ⊡ p
- ⊙ yo
- ⊠ sk2p

Special Stitch:

Sk2p Slip one stitch knitwise, then knit 2 stitches together and pass the slipped stitch over.

Bold Yarn Over

Flat

Row 1 (RS): Knit.
Row 2 (WS): Purl.
Rows 3–4: Knit.
Row 5: *P2, k2tog, yo; rep from * to end.
Row 6: Purl.
Row 7: Knit.
Row 8: Purl.
Repeat Rows 1–8 for pattern.

Stitches

- ☐ k on the RS; p on the WS
- ⊡ p on the RS; k on the WS
- ⊙ yo
- ⊘ k2tog

Round

Rnds 1–3: Knit.
Rnd 4: Purl.
Rnd 5: *P2, k2tog, yo; rep from * to end.
Rnds 6–8: Knit.
Repeat Rnds 1–8 for pattern.

Stitches

- ☐ k
- ⊡ p
- ⊙ yo
- ⊘ k2tog

Bamboo Eyelets

Flat

Row 1 (RS): *K2, k2tog, yo; rep from * to end.
Rows 2–4: Purl.
Repeat Rows 1–4 for pattern.

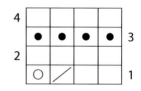

Stitches

☐	k on the RS; p on the WS
●	p on the RS; k on the WS
○	yo
╱	k2tog

Round

Rnd 1: *K2, k2tog, yo; rep from * to end.
Rnd 2: Knit.
Rnd 3: Purl.
Rnd 4: Knit.
Repeat Rnds 1–4 for pattern.

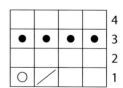

Stitches

☐	k
●	p
○	yo
╱	k2tog

More Eyelet Ridges

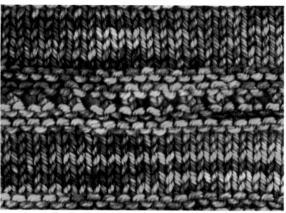

Flat

Rows 1–4: Knit.
Row 5: *K2tog, yo; rep from * to end.
Rows 6–9: Knit.
Row 10: Purl.
Row 11: Knit.
Rows 12–13: Repeat Rows 10–11.
Row 14: Purl.
Repeat Rows 1–14 for pattern.

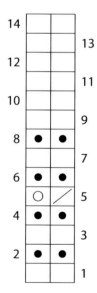

Stitches

☐	k on the RS; p on the WS
●	p on the RS; k on the WS
○	yo
╱	k2tog

Round

Rnd 1: Knit.
Rnd 2: Purl.
Rnds 3–4: Repeat Rnds 1–2.
Rnd 5: *K2tog, yo; rep from * to end.
Rnd 6: Purl.
Rnd 7: Knit.
Rnd 8: Purl.
Rnds 9–14: Knit.
Repeat Rnds 1–14 for pattern.

Stitches

☐ k
[•] p
[O] yo
[╱] k2tog

Faux Cable Lace

Flat

Row 1 (RS): *P1, k3; rep from * to end.
Row 2 (WS): *P3, k1; rep from * to end.
Row 3: *P1, Wrap KYOK; rep from * to end.
Row 4: *P3, k1; rep from * to end.
Repeat Rows 1–4 for pattern.

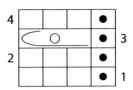

Stitches

☐ k on the RS; p on the WS
[•] p on the RS; k on the WS
[⊂ O] Wrap KYOK

Round

Rnds 1–2: *P1, k3; rep from * to end.
Rnd 3: *P1, Wrap KYOK; rep from * to end.
Rnd 4: *P1, k3; rep from * to end.
Repeat Rnds 1–4 for pattern.

Stitches

☐ k
[•] p
[⊂ O] Wrap KYOK

Special Stitch:

Wrap KYOK Slip the next 3 sts, as if to purl, to the right-hand needle. Lift the 1st slipped st up and over the last 2 sts, off the needle. Slide the 2 wrapped sts back to the left-hand needle; k1, yo, k1.

Tiny Eyelets

Flat

Row 1 (RS): *K2, k2tog, yo; rep from * to end.
Row 2 (WS): Purl.
Row 3: Knit.
Row 4: *P2, yo, p2tog; rep from * to end.
Row 5: Knit.
Row 6: Purl.
Repeat Rows 1–6 for pattern.

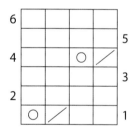

Stitches

☐ k on the RS; p on the WS
⊙ yo
⧄ k2tog on the RS; p2tog on the WS

Round

Rnd 1: *K2, k2tog, yo; rep from * to end.
Rnds 2–3: Knit.
Rnd 4: *K2tog, yo, k2; rep from * to end.
Rnds 5–6: Knit.
Repeat Rnds 1–6 for pattern.

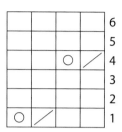

Stitches

☐ k
⊙ yo
⧄ k2tog

Simple Mesh

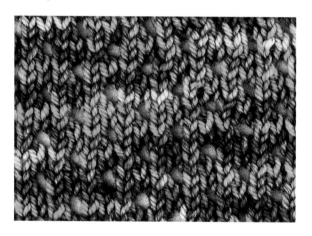

Flat

Row 1 (RS): *Yo, k2tog, k2; rep from * to end.
Row 2 (WS): Purl.
Row 3: *K2, yo, k2tog; rep from * to end.
Row 4: Purl.
Repeat Rows 1–4 for pattern.

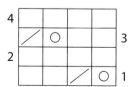

Stitches

☐ k on the RS; p on the WS
⊙ yo
⧄ k2tog

Round

Rnd 1: *Yo, k2tog, k2; rep from * to end.
Rnd 2: Knit.
Rnd 3: *K2, yo, k2tog; rep from * to end.
Rnd 4: Knit.
Repeat Rnds 1–4 for pattern.

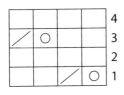

Stitches

☐ k
◯ yo
◺ k2tog

Scattered Lace

Stitches

☐ k on the RS; p on the WS
◯ yo
◺ k2tog
◻ ssk

Flat

Row 1 (RS): Knit.
Row 2 (WS): Purl.
Rows 3–4: Repeat Rows 1–2.
Row 5: *K2, k2tog, yo; rep from * to end.
Row 6: Purl.
Row 7: *K1, k2tog, yo, k1; rep from * to end.
Row 8: Purl.
Row 9: Knit.
Rows 10–13: Repeat Rows 8–9.
Row 14: Purl.
Row 15: *Yo, ssk, k2; rep from * to end.
Row 16: Purl.
Row 17: *K1, yo, ssk, k1; rep from * to end.
Row 18: Purl.
Row 19: Knit.
Row 20: Purl.
Repeat Rows 1–20 for pattern.

Round

Rnds 1–4: Knit.
Rnd 5: *K2, k2tog, yo; rep from * to end.
Rnd 6: Knit.
Rnd 7: *K1, k2tog, yo, k1; rep from * to end.
Rnds 8–14: Knit.
Rnd 15: *Yo, ssk, k2; rep from * to end.
Rnd 16: Knit.
Rnd 17: *K1, yo, ssk, k1; rep from * to end.
Rnds 18–20: Knit.
Repeat Rnds 1–20 for pattern.

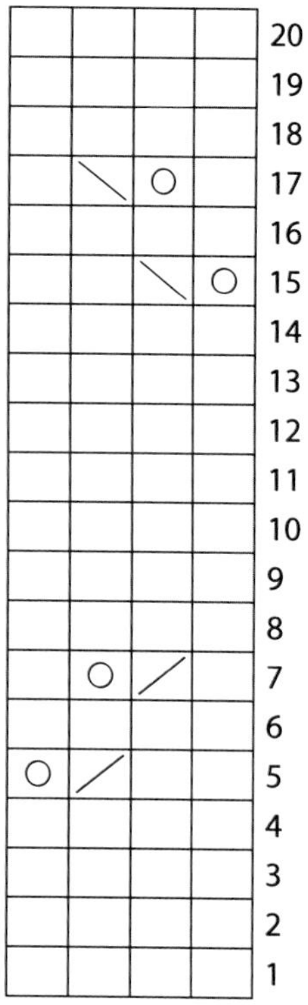

Stitches

k

yo

k2tog

ssk

Anchored Eyelets

Flat

Row 1 (RS): *K3, p1; rep from * to end.
Row 2 (WS): *K1, p3; rep from * to end.
Rows 3–4: Repeat Rows 1–2.
Row 5: *Yo, s2k1p, yo, p1; rep from * to end.
Row 6: Knit.
Repeat Rows 1–6 for pattern.

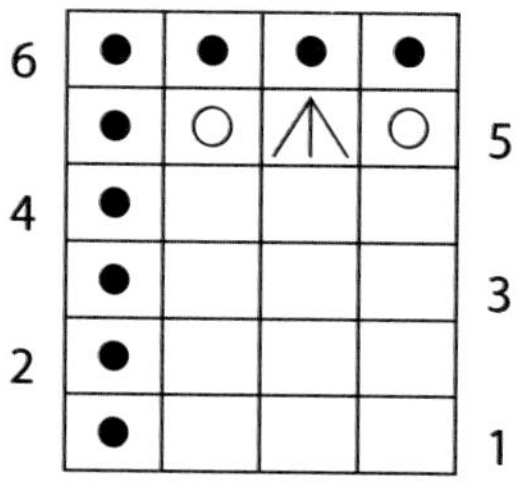

Stitches

k on the RS; p on the WS

p on the RS; k on the WS

yo

s2k1p

Round

Rnds 1–4: *K3, p1; rep from * to end.
Rnd 5: *Yo, s2k1p, yo, p1; rep from * to end.
Rnd 6: Purl.
Repeat Rnds 1–6 for pattern.

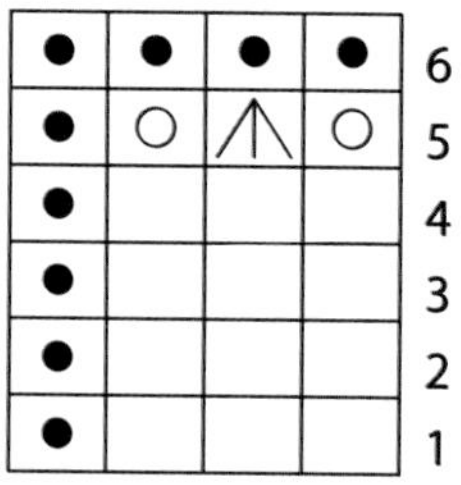

Stitches

k

p

yo

s2k1p

Special Stitch:

S2k1p Slip 2 stitches together knitwise, knit 1, then pass slipped stitches over.

Step Up Lace

Flat

Row 1 (RS): *K3, p1; rep from * to end.
Row 2 (WS): *K1, p3; rep from * to end.
Row 3: *Yo, s2k1p, yo, p1; rep from * to end.
Row 4: *P3, k1; rep from * to end.
Row 5: *P1, k3; rep from * to end.
Row 6: *P3, k1; rep from * to end.
Row 7: *P1, yo, s2k1p, yo; rep from * to end.
Row 8: *K1, p3; rep from * to end.
Repeat Rows 1–8 for pattern.

Stitches

	k on the RS; p on the WS
•	p on the RS; k on the WS
○	yo
⋀	s2k1p

Round

Rnds 1–2: *K3, p1; rep from * to end.
Rnd 3: *Yo, s2k1p, yo, p1; rep from * to end.
Rnds 4–6: *P1, k3; rep from * to end.
Rnd 7: *P1, yo, s2k1p, yo; rep from * to end.
Rnd 8: *K3, p1; rep from * to end.
Repeat Rnds 1–8 for pattern.

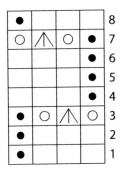

Stitches

	k
•	p
○	yo
⋀	s2k1p

Special Stitch:
S2k1p Slip 2 stitches together knitwise, knit 1, then pass slipped stitches over.

Sharp Turns

Flat

Row 1 (RS): *K1, k2tog, yo, p1; rep from * to end.
Row 2 (WS): *K1, yo, p1, p2tog; rep from * to end.
Row 3: *Yo, ssk, k1, p1; rep from * to end.
Row 4: *K1, ssp, p1, yo; rep from * to end.
Repeat Rows 1–4 for pattern.

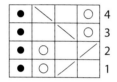

Stitches

- ☐ k on the RS; p on the WS
- ● p on the RS; k on the WS
- ○ yo
- ╱ k2tog on the RS; p2tog on the WS
- ╲ ssk on the RS; ssp on the WS

Round

Rnd 1: *K1, k2tog, yo, p1; rep from * to end.
Rnd 2: *K2tog, k1, yo, p1; rep from * to end.
Rnd 3: *Yo, ssk, k1, p1; rep from * to end.
Rnd 4: *Yo, k1, ssk, p1; rep from * to end.
Repeat Rnds 1–4 for pattern.

Stitches

- ☐ k
- ● p
- ○ yo
- ╱ k2tog
- ╲ ssk

Special Stitch:

Ssp Slip 2 stitches knitwise, then return slipped stitches to left needle and purl 2 together through back loop.

Lace Rib

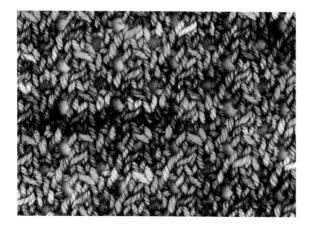

Flat

Row 1 (RS): *K1, k2tog, yo, p1; rep from * to end.
Row 2 (WS): *K1, p3; rep from * to end.
Row 3: *Yo, ssk, k1, p1; rep from * to end.
Row 4: *K1, p3; rep from * to end.
Repeat Rows 1–4 for pattern.

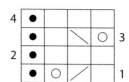

Stitches

- ☐ k on the RS; p on the WS
- ● p on the RS; k on the WS
- ○ yo
- ╱ k2tog
- ╲ ssk

Round

Rnd 1: *K1, k2tog, yo, p1; rep from * to end.
Rnd 2: *K3, p1; rep from * to end.
Rnd 3: *Yo, ssk, k1, p1; rep from * to end.
Rnd 4: *K3, p1; rep from * to end.
Repeat Rnds 1–4 for pattern.

Stitches

- ☐ k
- ● p
- ○ yo
- ╱ k2tog
- ╲ ssk

CHAPTER 5

CABLES

Dreamy, luscious cables are often viewed as the "pinnacle skill" in knitting—the technique that seems to showcase all our knitter-ly prowess. And indeed, with a vibrant texture that pops off the fabric, it is easy to see why cables maintain such a reputation. With only a multiple of four stitches to worry about, the cable patterns found in this chapter are beautifully accessible for every level of knitter.

The joy of cables comes from their versatility, and, even with a small stitch multiple, there is a lovely range of types to explore, from 1-stitch on up to 3-stitch cables. Whether worked all over a sweater or just plugged into a column, the results are always classic, textural, and wholly addictive.

Tiny Cable Rib

Round

Rnds 1–2: *K2, p2; rep from * to end.
Rnd 3: *1/1 RC, p2; rep from * to end.
Rnd 4: *K2, p2; rep from * to end.
Repeat Rnds 1–4 for pattern.

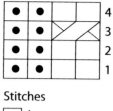

Stitches

☐ k

[•] p

▱ 1/1 RC

*Note: You may optionally change the right-crossing cable to a left-crossing one by changing 1/1 RC to 1/1 LC.

Special Stitches:

1/1 RC Slip 1 stitch to cable needle and hold in back; k1, k1 from cable needle.
1/1 LC Slip 1 stitch to cable needle and hold to front; k1, k1 from cable needle.

Flat

Rows 1–2: *K2, p2; rep from * to end.
Row 3: *1/1 RC, p2; rep from * to end.
Row 4: *K2, p2; rep from * to end.
Repeat Rows 1–4 for pattern.

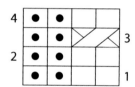

Stitches

☐ k on the RS; p on the WS

[•] p on the RS; k on the WS

 1/1 RC

Shifting Rib

Round

Rnds 1–4: *K2, p2; rep from * to end.
Rnd 5: *1/1 RC, p2; rep from * to end.
Rnds 6–10: *P2, k2; rep from * to end.
Rnd 11: *P2, 1/1 RC; rep from * to end.
Rnd 12: Rep Rnd 1.
Repeat Rnds 1–12 for pattern.

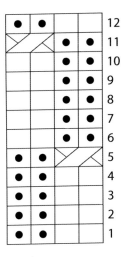

Stitches

☐ k

⊡ p

▷◁ 1/1 RC

*Note: You may optionally change the right-crossing cable to a left-crossing one by changing 1/1 RC to 1/1 LC.

Special Stitches:

1/1 RC Slip 1 stitch to cable needle and hold in back; k1, k1 from cable needle.
1/1 LC Slip 1 stitch to cable needle and hold to front; k1, k1 from cable needle.

Flat

Rows 1–4: *K2, p2; rep from * to end.
Row 5: *1/1 RC, p2; rep from * to end.
Rows 6–10: *P2, k2; rep from * to end.
Row 11: *P2, 1/1 RC; rep from * to end.
Row 12: Rep Row 1.
Repeat Rows 1–12 for pattern.

Stitches

☐ k on the RS; p on the WS

⊡ p on the RS; k on the WS

▷◁ 1/1 RC

Larger Cable Rib

Flat

Row 1 (RS): *K3, p1; rep from * to end.
Row 2 (WS): *K1, p3; rep from * to end.
Row 3: *2/1 RC, p1; rep from * to end.
Row 4: *K1, p3; rep from * to end.
Repeat Rows 1–4 for pattern.

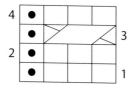

Stitches

☐ k on the RS; p on the WS

● p on the RS; k on the WS

⟋⟍ 2/1 RC

Round

Rnds 1–2: *K3, p1; rep from * to end.
Rnd 3: *2/1 RC, p1; rep from * to end.
Rnd 4: *K3, p1; rep from * to end.
Repeat Rnds 1–4 for pattern.

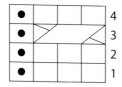

Stitches

☐ k

● p

⟋⟍ 2/1 RC

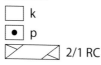

*Note: You may optionally change the right-crossing cable to a left-crossing one by changing 2/1 RC to 2/1 LC.

Special Stitches:

2/1 RC Slip 1 stitch to cable needle and hold in back; k2, k1 from cable needle.
2/1 LC Slip 2 stitches to cable needle and hold in front; k1, k2 from cable needle.

Tiny Twist Rib

Flat

Row 1 (RS): *P1, k3; rep from * to end.
Row 2 (WS): *P3, k1; rep from * to end.
Row 3: *P1, k1, 1/1 RC; rep from * to end.
Row 4: Rep Row 2.
Row 5: *P1, 1/2 RC; rep from * to end.
Row 6: Rep Row 2.
Row 7: *P1, 1/1 RC, k1; rep from * to end.
Row 8: Rep Row 2.
Row 9: Rep Row 1.
Rows 10–11: Repeat Rows 8–9.
Row 12: Rep Row 2.
Repeat Rows 1–12 for pattern.

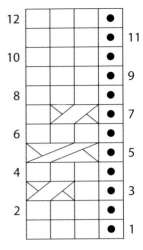

Stitches

☐ k on the RS; p on the WS

● p on the RS; k on the WS

◧ 1/1 RC

◨ 1/2 RC

Round

Rnds 1–2: *P1, k3; rep from * to end.
Rnd 3: *P1, k1, 1/1 RC; rep from * to end.
Rnd 4: Rep Row 1.
Rnd 5: *P1, 1/2 RC; rep from * to end.
Rnd 6: Rep Row 1.
Row 7: *P1, 1/1 RC, k1; rep from * to end.
Rnds 8–12: Rep Row 1.
Repeat Rnds 1–12 for pattern.

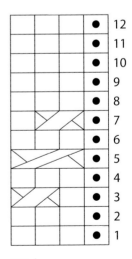

Stitches

☐ k

● p

◧ 1/1 RC

◨ 1/2 RC

Special Stitches:

1/1 RC Slip 1 stitch to cable needle and hold in back; k1, k1 from cable needle.
1/2 RC Slip 2 stitches to cable needle and hold in back; k1, k2, from cable needle.

Crossing Over

Flat

Row 1 (RS): *P2, 1/1 RC; rep from * to end.
Row 2 (WS): *P2, k2; rep from * to end.
Row 3: *P1, 1/1 RC, p1; rep from * to end.
Row 4: *K1, p2, k1; rep from * to end.
Row 5: *1/1 RC, p2; rep from * to end.
Row 6: *K2, p2; rep from * to end.
Repeat Rows 1–6 for pattern.

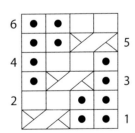

Stitches

☐ k on the RS; p on the WS

● p on the RS; k on the WS

◧ 1/1 RC

Round

Rnd 1: *P2, 1/1 RC; rep from * to end.
Rnd 2: *P2, k2; rep from * to end.
Rnd 3: *P1, 1/1 RC, p1; rep from * to end.
Rnd 4: *K1, p2, k1; rep from * to end.
Rnd 5: *1/1 RC, p2; rep from * to end.
Rnd 6: *K2, p2; rep from * to end.
Repeat Rnds 1–6 for pattern.

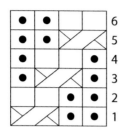

Stitches

☐ k
☑ p
◪ 1/1 RC

*Note: You may optionally change the right-crossing cable to a left-crossing one by changing 1/1 RC to 1/1 LC.

Special Stitches:

1/1 RC Slip 1 stitch to cable needle and hold in back; k1, k1 from cable needle.
1/1 LC Slip 1 stitch to cable needle and hold to front; k1, k1 from cable needle.

Formal Diagonal

Flat

Row 1 (RS): *1/1 LPC, p2; rep from * to end.
Row 2 (WS): *K2, p1, k1; rep from * to end.
Row 3: *P1, 1/1 LPC, p1; rep from * to end.
Row 4: *K1, p1, k2.
Row 5: *P2, 1/1 LPC; rep from * to end.
Row 6: *P1, k3; rep from * to end.
Repeat Rows 1–6 for pattern.

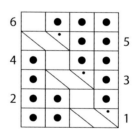

Stitches

☐ k on the RS; p on the WS
☑ p on the RS; k on the WS
◪ 1/1 LPC

Round

Rnd 1: *1/1 LPC, p2; rep from * to end.
Rnd 2: *P1, k1, p2; rep from * to end.
Rnd 3: *P1, 1/1 LPC, p1; rep from * to end.
Rnd 4: *P2, k1, p1; rep from * to end.
Rnd 5: *P2, 1/1 LPC; rep from * to end.
Rnd 6: *P3, k1; rep from * to end.
Repeat Rnds 1–6 for pattern.

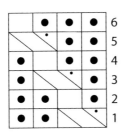

Stitches

	k
•	p
⟋	1/1 LPC

Special Stitch:

1/1 LPC Slip 1 stitch to cable needle and hold in front; p1, k1 from cable needle.

Tight Twist

Flat

Row 1 (RS): *P1, 2/1 RC; rep from * to end.
Row 2 (WS): *P3, k1; rep from * to end.
Rows 3–6: Repeat Rows 1–2.
Row 7: *P1, k3; rep from * to end.
Row 8: *P3, k1; rep from * to end.
Repeat Rows 1–8 for pattern.

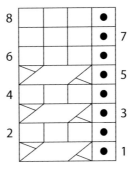

Stitches

	k on the RS; p on the WS
•	p on the RS; k on the WS
⟋⟍	2/1 RC

Round

Rnd 1: *P1, 2/1 RC; rep from * to end.
Rnd 2: *P1, k3; rep from * to end.
Rnds 3–4: Repeat Rnds 1–2.
Rnd 5: *P1, 2/1 RC; rep from * to end.
Rnds 6–8: *P1, k3; rep from * to end.
Repeat Rnds 1–8 for pattern.

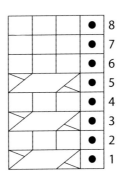

Stitches

	k
•	p
⟋⟍	2/1 RC

*Note: You may optionally change the right-crossing cable to a left-crossing one by changing 2/1 RC to 2/1 LC.

Special Stitches:

2/1 RC Slip 1 stitch to cable needle and hold in back; k2, k1 from cable needle.
2/1 LC Slip 2 stitches to cable needle and hold in front; k1, k2 from cable needle.

Laddered Cable

Flat

Row 1 (RS): *1/1 LC, k1, p1; rep from * to end.
Row 2 (WS): *K1, p3; rep from * to end.
Row 3: *K1, 1/1 LC, p1; rep from * to end.
Row 4: Rep Row 2.
Rows 5–8: Repeat Rows 1–4.
Row 9: *K1, 1/1 RC, p1; rep from * to end.
Row 10: Rep Row 2.
Row 11: *1/1 RC, k1, p1; rep from * to end.
Row 12: Rep Row 2.
Rows 13–16: Repeat Rows 9–12.
Repeat Rows 1–16 for pattern.

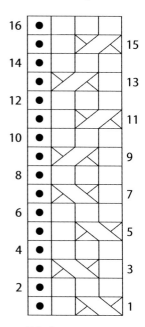

Stitches

- ☐ k on the RS; p on the WS
- ☐• p on the RS; k on the WS
- ⧄ 1/1 RC
- ⧅ 1/1 LC

Round

Rnd 1: *1/1 LC, k1, p1; rep from * to end.
Rnd 2: *K3, p1; rep from * to end.
Rnd 3: *K1, 1/1 LC, p1; rep from * to end.
Rnd 4: Rep Rnd 2.
Rnd 5–8: Repeat Rnds 1–4.
Rnd 9: *K1, 1/1 RC, p1; rep from * to end.
Rnd 10: Rep Rnd 2.
Rnd 11: *1/1 RC, k1, p1; rep from * to end.
Rnd 12: Rep Rnd 2.
Rnds 13–16: Repeat Rnds 9–12.
Repeat Rnds 1–16 for pattern.

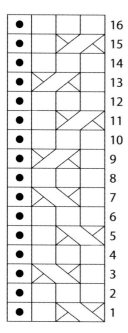

Stitches

- ☐ k
- ☐• p
- ⧄ 1/1 RC
- ⧅ 1/1 LC

Special Stitches:

1/1 RC Slip 1 stitch to cable needle and hold in back; k1, k1 from cable needle.
1/1 LC Slip 1 stitch to cable needle and hold to front; k1, k1 from cable needle.

Column Twist

Flat

Row 1 (RS): *P1, k3; rep from * to end.
Row 2 (WS): *P3, k1; rep from * to end.
Rows 3–4: Repeat Rows 1–2.
Row 5: *P1, 1/2 RC; rep from * to end.
Row 6: *P3, k1; rep from * to end.
Row 7: *P1, k3; rep from * to end.
Row 8: *P3, k1; rep from * to end.
Rows 9–16: Repeat Rows 5–8.
Repeat Rows 1–16 for pattern.

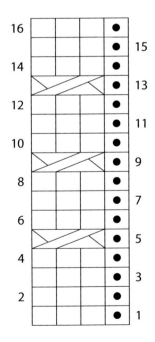

Stitches

☐	k on the RS; p on the WS
⊡	p on the RS; k on the WS
◪	1/2 RC

Round

Rnds 1–4: *P1, k3; rep from * to end.
Rnd 5: *P1, 1/2 RC; rep from * to end.
Rnds 6–8: *P1, k3; rep from * to end.
Rnds 9–16: Repeat Rnds 5–8.
Repeat Rnds 1–16 for pattern.

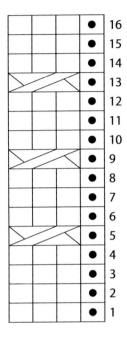

Stitches

☐	k
⊡	p
◪	1/2 RC

*Note: You may optionally change the right-crossing cable to a left-crossing one by changing 1/2 RC to 1/2 LC.

Special Stitches:

1/2 RC Slip 2 stitches to cable needle and hold in back; k1, k2 from cable needle.
1/2 LC Slip 1 stitch to cable needle and hold in front; k2, k1 from cable needle.

Single Twist Rib

Flat

Row 1 (RS): *K3, p1; rep from * to end.
Row 2 (WS): *K1, p3; rep from * to end.
Row 3: *1/2 LC, p1; rep from * to end.
Row 4: *K1, p3; rep from * to end.
Repeat Rows 1–4 for pattern.

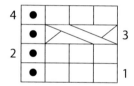

Stitches

☐ k on the RS; p on the WS
● p on the RS; k on the WS
▱ 1/2 LC

Round

Rnds 1–2: *K3, p1; rep from * to end.
Rnd 3: *1/2 LC, p1; rep from * to end.
Rnd 4: *K3, p1; rep from * to end.
Repeat Rnds 1–4 for pattern.

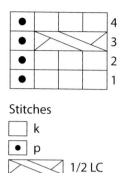

Stitches

☐ k
● p
▱ 1/2 LC

*Note: You may optionally change the left-crossing cable to a right-crossing one by changing 1/2 LC to 1/2 RC.

Special Stitches:

1/2 LC Slip 1 stitch to cable needle and hold in front; k2, k1 from cable needle.
1/2 RC Slip 2 stitches to cable needle and hold in back; k1, k2 from cable needle.

Another Shift

Flat

Rows 1–8: *K2, p2; rep from * to end.
Row 9: *1/1 RC; rep from * to end.
Rows 10–18: *P2, k2; rep from * to end.
Row 19: *1/1 RC; rep from * to end.
Row 20: *K2, p2; rep from * to end.
Repeat Rows 1–20 for pattern.

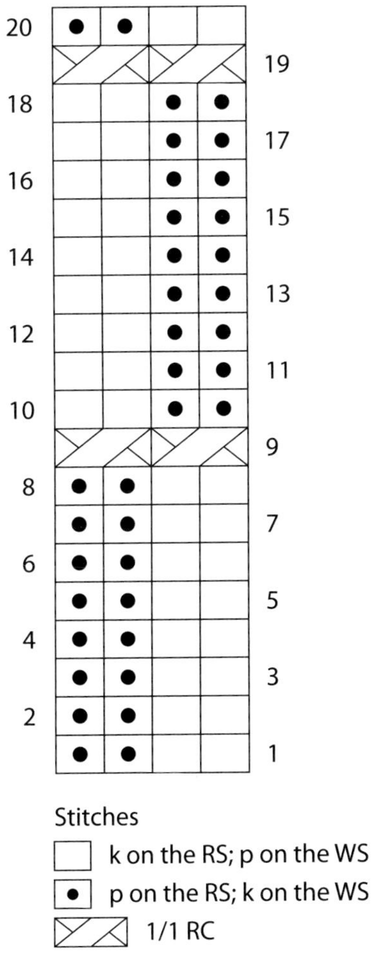

Round

Rnds 1–8: *K2, p2; rep from * to end.
Rnd 9: *1/1 RC; rep from * to end.
Rnds 10–18: *P2, k2; rep from * to end.
Rnd 19: *1/1 RC; rep from * to end.
Rnd 20: *K2, p2; rep from * to end.
Repeat Rnds 1–20 for pattern.

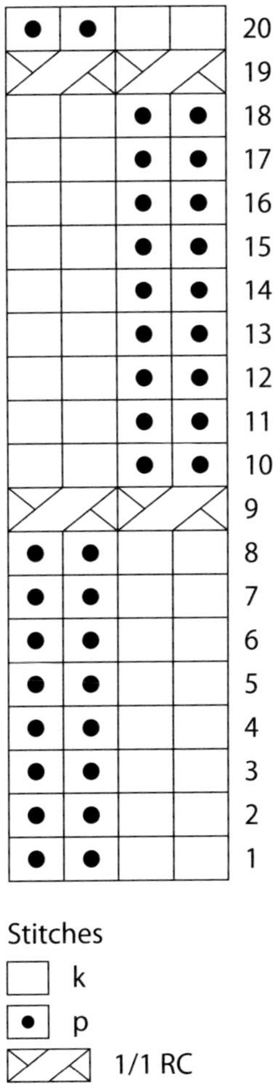

Stitches

☐ k on the RS; p on the WS
⊡ p on the RS; k on the WS
◰◲ 1/1 RC

Stitches

☐ k
⊡ p
◰◲ 1/1 RC

*Note: You may optionally change the right-crossing cable to a left-crossing one by changing 1/1 RC to 1/1 LC.

Special Stitches:

1/1 RC Slip 1 stitch to cable needle and hold in back; k1, k1 from cable needle.
1/1 LC Slip 1 stitch to cable needle and hold to front; k1, k1 from cable needle.

Subtle Lines

Flat

Row 1 (RS): *P2, 1/1 RC; rep from * to end.
Row 2 (WS): Purl.
Row 3: Knit.
Row 4: Purl.
Row 5: *1/1 RC, p2; rep from * to end.
Rows 6-8: Repeat Rows 2-4.
Repeat Rows 1-8 for pattern.

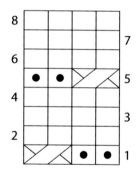

Stitches

	k on the RS; p on the WS
•	p on the RS; k on the WS
⧅	1/1 RC

Round

Rnd 1: *P2, 1/1 RC; rep from * to end.
Rnds 2-4: Knit.
Rnd 5: *1/1 RC, p2; rep from * to end.
Rnds 6-8: Knit.
Repeat Rnds 1-8 for pattern.

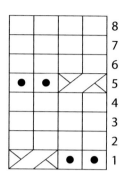

Stitches

	k
•	p
⧅	1/1 RC

*Note: You may optionally change the right-crossing cable to a left-crossing one by changing 1/1 RC to 1/1 LC.

Special Stitches:

1/1 RC Slip 1 stitch to cable needle and hold in back; k1, k1 from cable needle.
1/1 LC Slip 1 stitch to cable needle and hold to front; k1, k1 from cable needle.

Dancing Cables

Flat

Row 1 (RS): *K2, 1/1 LC; rep from * to end.
Row 2 (WS): *P1, 1/1 RC-Rev, p1; rep from * to end.
Repeat Rows 1–2 for pattern.

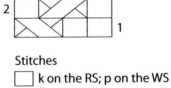

Stitches

☐ k on the RS; p on the WS
⧄ 1/1 RC-Rev
⧄ 1/1 LC

Round

Rnd 1: *K2, 1/1 LC; rep from * to end.
Rnd 2: *K1, 1/1 RC, k1; rep from * to end.
Repeat Rnds 1–2 for pattern.

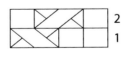

Stitches

☐ k
⧄ 1/1 RC
⧄ 1/1 LC

Special Stitches:

1/1 RC Slip 1 stitch to cable needle and hold in back; k1, k1 from cable needle.
1/1 LC Slip 1 stitch to cable needle and hold to front; k1, k1 from cable needle.
1/1 RC-Rev Slip 1 stitch to cable needle and hold in back; p1, p1 from cable needle.

Tucked In

Flat

Rows 1–2: Purl.
Row 3: *K1, p2, k1; rep from * to end.
Row 4: Purl.
Row 5: *K1, 1/1 LPC, k1; rep from * to end.
Row 6: Purl.
Rows 7–8: Repeat Rows 5–6.
Row 9: Rep Row 3.
Row 10: Purl.
Repeat Rows 1–10 for pattern.

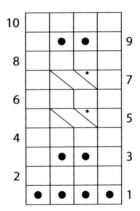

Stitches

☐ k on the RS; p on the WS
⊡ p on the RS; k on the WS
⧄ 1/1 LPC

Round

Rnd 1: Purl.
Rnd 2: Knit.
Rnd 3: *K1, p2, k1; rep from * to end.
Rnd 4: Knit.
Rnd 5: *K1, 1/1 LPC, k1; rep from * to end.
Rnd 6: Knit.
Rnds 7–8: Repeat Rnds 5–6.
Rnd 9: Rep Rnd 3.
Rnd 10: Knit.
Repeat Rnds 1–10 for pattern.

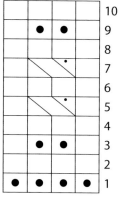

Stitches

☐	k
●	p
◿	1/1 LPC

Special Stitch:

1/1 LPC Slip 1 stitch to cable needle and hold in front; p1, k1 from cable needle.

Split Rib

Flat

Rows 1–2: *K1, p1; rep from * to end.
Row 3: *1/1/1 RPC, p1; rep from * to end.
Row 4: Rep Row 1.
Repeat Rows 1–4 for pattern.

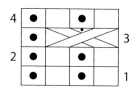

Stitches

☐	k on the RS; p on the WS
●	p on the RS; k on the WS
⨝	1/1/1 RPC

Round

Rnds 1–2: *K1, p1; rep from * to end.
Rnd 3: *1/1/1 RPC, p1; rep from * to end.
Rnd 4: Rep Rnd 1.
Repeat Rnds 1–4 for pattern.

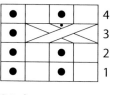

Stitches

☐	k
●	p
⨝	1/1/1 RPC

*This cable utilizes 2 cable needles.

Special Stitch:

1/1/1 RPC Slip 1 stitch to 1st cable needle and hold in back; slip 1 stitch to 2nd cable needle and hold in back; k1, p1 from 2nd cable needle, k1 from 1st cable needle.

Back and Forth

Flat

Rows 1–2: *P2, k2; rep from * to end.
Row 3: 2/2 RPC; rep from * to end.
Rows 4–6: *K2, p2; rep from * to end.
Row 7: 2/2 LPC; rep from * to end.
Row 8: *P2, k2; rep from * to end.
Repeat Rows 1–8 for pattern.

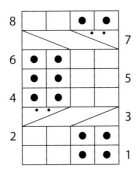

Stitches

☐	k on the RS; p on the WS
⊡	p on the RS; k on the WS
⧄	2/2 RPC
⧄	2/2 LPC

Round

Rnds 1–2: *P2, k2; rep from * to end.
Rnd 3: 2/2 RPC; rep from * to end.
Rnds 4–6: *K2, p2; rep from * to end.
Rnd 7: 2/2 LPC; rep from * to end.
Rnd 8: *P2, k2; rep from * to end.
Repeat Rnds 1–8 for pattern.

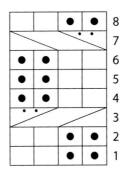

Stitches

☐	k
⊡	p
⧄	2/2 RPC
⧄	2/2 LPC

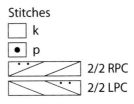

Special Stitches:

2/2 RPC Slip 2 stitches to cable needle and hold in back; k2, p2 from cable needle.
2/2 LPC Slip 2 stitches to cable needle and hold in front; p2, k2 from cable needle.

Skyview Cable

Flat

Row 1 (RS): Purl.
Row 2 (WS): *K1, p3; rep from * to end.
Row 3: 2/1 RC, p1; rep from * to end.
Row 4: *K1, p3; rep from * to end.
Row 5: Purl.
Row 6: Knit.
Row 7: Purl.
Row 8: *P3, k1; rep from * to end.
Row 9: *P1, 2/1 RC; rep from * to end.
Row 10: *P3, k1; rep from * to end.
Row 11: Purl.
Row 12: Knit.
Repeat Rows 1–12 for pattern.

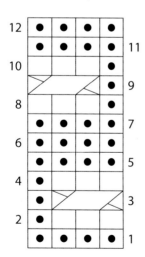

Stitches

☐ k on the RS; p on the WS
⊡ p on the RS; k on the WS
▱ 2/1 RC

* This is worked on a fabric of
Reverse Stockinette st.

Round

Rnd 1: Purl.
Rnd 2: *K3, p1; rep from * to end.
Rnd 3: 2/1 RC, p1; rep from * to end.
Rnd 4: *K3, p1; rep from * to end.
Rnds 5–7: Purl.
Rnd 8: *P1, k3; rep from * to end.
Rnd 9: *P1, 2/1 RC; rep from * to end.
Rnd 10: *P1, k3; rep from * to end.
Rnds 11–12: Purl.
Repeat Rnds 1–12 for pattern.

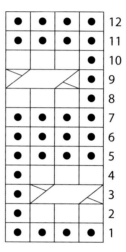

Stitches

☐ k
⊡ p
▱ 2/1 RC

* This is worked on a fabric of
Reverse Stockinette st.

*Note: You may optionally change the right-crossing cable to a left-crossing one by changing 2/1 RC to 2/1 LC.

Special Stitches:

2/1 RC Slip 1 stitch to cable needle and hold in back; k2, k1 from cable needle.
2/1 LC Slip 2 stitches to cable needle and hold in front; k1, k2 from cable needle.

Rib Dips

Flat

Row 1 (RS): *1/1 LC, 1/1 RC; rep from * to end.
Row 2 (WS): *K1, p2, k1; rep from * to end.
Row 3: *P1, k2, p1; rep from * to end.
Rows 4–5: Repeat Rows 2–3.
Row 6: Rep Row 2.
Row 7: *1/1 RC, 1/1 LC; rep from * to end.
Row 8: Rep Row 2.
Row 9: Rep Row 3.
Rows 10–11: Repeat Rows 8–9.
Row 12: *P1, k2, p1; rep from * to end.
Repeat Rows 1–12 for pattern.

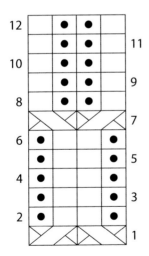

Stitches

⬜ k on the RS; p on the WS
● p on the RS; k on the WS
⬜ 1/1 RC
⬜ 1/1 LC

Round

Rnd 1: *1/1 LC, 1/1 RC; rep from * to end.
Rnds 2–6: *P1, k2, p1; rep from * to end.
Rnd 7: *1/1 RC, 1/1 LC; rep from * to end.
Rnds 8–12: *K1, p2, k1; rep from * to end.
Repeat Rnds 1–12 for pattern.

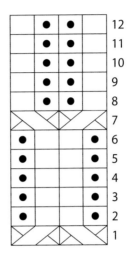

Stitches

⬜ k
● p
⬜ 1/1 RC
⬜ 1/1 LC

Special Stitches:

1/1 RC Slip 1 stitch to cable needle and hold in back; k1, k1 from cable needle.
1/1 LC Slip 1 stitch to cable needle and hold to front; k1, k1 from cable needle.

Woven Cable

Round

Rnd 1: *1/1 LC, p2; rep from * to end.
Rnds 2–3: *K2, p2; rep from * to end.
Rnd 4: *P2, k2; rep from * to end.
Rnd 5: *P2, 1/1 LC; rep from * to end.
Rnds 6–7: *P2, k2; rep from * to end.
Rnd 8: *K2, p2; rep from * to end.
Repeat Rnds 1–8 for pattern.

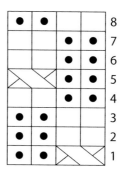

Stitches

□ k

● p

⧄⧅ 1/1 LC

Flat

Row 1 (RS): *1/1 LC, p2; rep from * to end.
Rows 2–3: *K2, p2; rep from * to end.
Row 4: *P2, k2; rep from * to end.
Row 5: *P2, 1/1 LC; rep from * to end.
Rows 6–7: *P2, k2; rep from * to end.
Row 8: *K2, p2; rep from * to end.
Repeat Rows 1–8 for pattern.

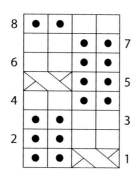

Stitches

□ k on the RS; p on the WS

● p on the RS; k on the WS

⧄⧅ 1/1 LC

*Note: You may optionally change the left-crossing cable to a right-crossing one by changing 1/1 LC to 1/1 RC.

Special Stitches:

1/1 LC Slip 1 stitch to cable needle and hold to front; k1, k1 from cable needle.
1/1 RC Slip 1 stitch to cable needle and hold in back; k1, k1 from cable needle.

CHAPTER 6

TEXTURE

A little twist here, a tweak or a slipped stitch there, and a whole new world of texture opens wide. The patterns presented in this chapter are made with unique stitches, such as working into one stitch a couple of times or fun twists to different decreases, resulting in fabric that captures the vision. Working within a 2- or 4-stitch multiple means learning what can happen on a small scale without overwhelming the novice.

Bubble Stitch

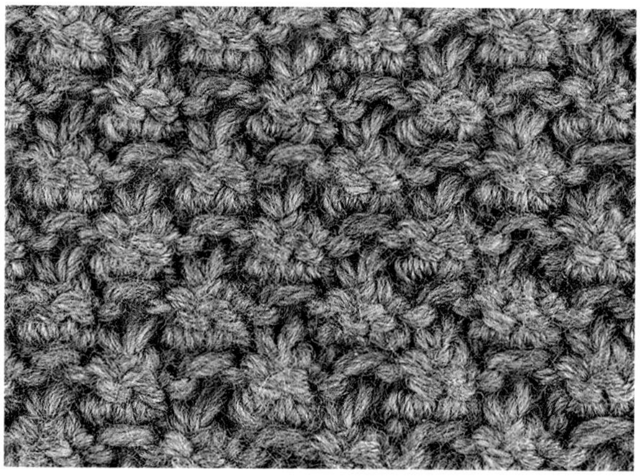

Flat

Row 1 (RS): Knit.
Row 2 (WS): *K3tog, (p1, k1, p1) in 1; rep from * to end.
Row 3: Knit.
Row 4: *(P1, k1, p1) in 1, k3tog; rep from * to end.
Repeat Rows 1–4 for pattern.

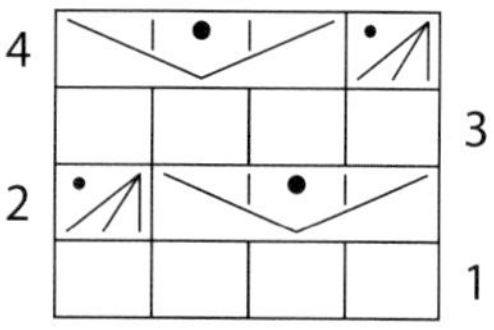

Stitches
k on the RS; p on the WS
(p1, k1, p1) in 1
k3tog

Round

Rnd 1: Knit.
Rnd 2: *(K1, p1, k1) in 1, p3tog; rep from * to end.
Rnd 3: Knit.
Rnd 4: *P3tog, (k1, p1, k1) in 1; rep from * to end.
Repeat Rnds 1–4 for pattern.

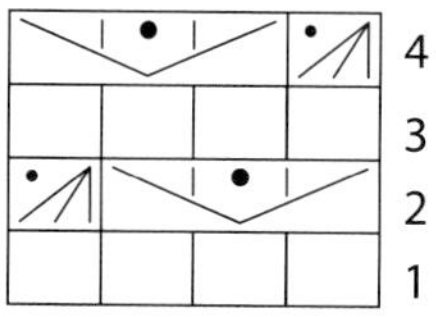

Stitches
k
(k1, p1, k1) in 1
p3tog

Special Stitch:

(K1, p1, k1) in 1 Knit, leaving the stitch on the needle, then purl, and then knit into the same stitch.

Granite Stitch

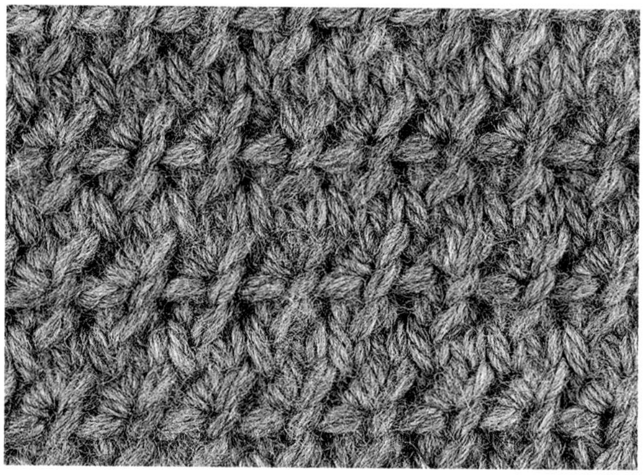

Flat

Row 1 (RS): Knit.
Row 2 (WS): *P2tog; rep from * to end.
Row 3: *(K1, p1) in 1; rep from * to end.
Row 4: Purl.
Repeat Rows 1–4 for pattern.

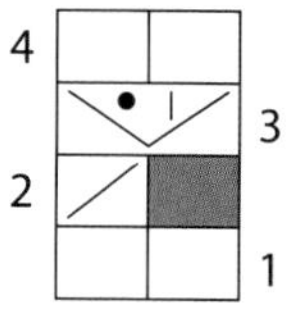

Stitches
No stitch
k on the RS; p on the WS
(k1, p1) in 1
p2tog

* St count is decreased by half on Row 2. The stitch count is increased to the original st count on Row 3.

Round

Rnd 1: Knit.
Rnd 2: *K2tog; rep from * to end.
Rnd 3: *(K1, p1) in 1; rep from * to end.
Rnd 4: Knit.
Repeat Rnds 1–4 for pattern.
*St count is decreased by half in Rnd 2. The stitch count is increased to the original stitch count on Rnd 3.

Stitches

| | No stitch |
| | k |
 (k1, p1) in 1
| | k2tog |

* St count is decreased by half in Rnd 2.
The stitch count is increased to the
original st count on Rnd 3.

Special Stitch:

(K1, p1) in 1 Knit, leaving the stitch on the needle, and then purl into the same stitch.

Woven Columns

Flat

Row 1 (RS): *[Sl 1 wyif] twice, k2; rep from * to end.
Row 2 (WS): *P2, [sl 1 wyib] twice; rep from * to end.
Row 3: Rep Row 1.
Row 4: Purl.
Row 5: *K2, [sl 1 wyif] twice; rep from * to end.
Row 6: *[Sl 1 wyib] twice, p2; rep from * to end.
Row 7: Rep Row 5.
Row 8: Purl.
Repeat Rows 1–8 for pattern.

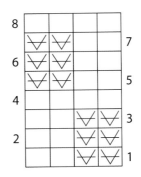

Stitches

| | k on the RS; p on the WS |
| | sl 1 wyif on the RS; sl 1 wyib on the WS |

Round

Rnds 1–3: *[Sl 1 wyif] twice, k2; rep from *
to end.
Rnd 4: Knit.
Rnds 5–7: *K2, [sl 1 wyif] twice; rep from *
to end.
Rnd 8: Knit.
Repeat Rnds 1–8 for pattern.

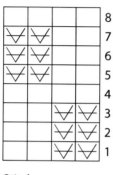

Stitches

☐ k

⊻ sl 1 wyif

Special Stitches:

Sl 1 wyib With the working yarn in back,
insert the right needle into the next stitch as
if to purl and transfer the stitch from the left
needle to the right.
Sl 1 wyif With the working yarn in front,
insert the right needle into the next stitch as
if to purl and transfer the stitch from the left
needle to the right.

Rosette Mesh

Flat

Row 1 (RS): Knit.
Row 2 (WS): *Make Rosette; rep from *
to end.
Row 3: Knit.
Row 4: *P1, *Make Rosette; rep from * to last
st, p1.
Repeat Rows 1–4 for pattern.

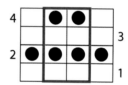

Stitches

☐ k on the RS; p on the WS

⬛ Make Rosette

Borders

— rep

Round

Rnd 1: Knit.
Rnd 2: *Make Rosette; rep from * to end.
Rnd 3: Knit.
Rnd 4: *K1, *Make Rosette; rep from * to last st, k1.
Repeat Rnds 1–4 for pattern.

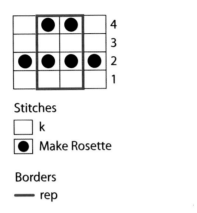

Stitches

☐ k
⬤ Make Rosette

Borders

— rep

Special Stitch:

Make Rosette P2tog, but do not drop the sts from the left-hand needle; k2tog (the same sts), then slip st from left-hand needle.

Woven Herringbone

Flat

Row 1 (RS): *K2, [sl 1 wyif] twice; rep from * to end.
Row 2 (WS): *Sl 1 wyib, p2, sl 1 wyib; rep from * to end.
Row 3: *[S1 wyif] twice, k2; rep from * to end.
Row 4: *P1, [sl 1 wyib] twice, p1; rep from * to end.
Rows 5–12: Repeat Rows 1–4.
Row 13: *[S1 wyif] twice, k2; rep from * to end.

Row 14: *Sl 1 wyib, p2, sl 1 wyib; rep from * to end.
Row 15: *K2, [sl 1 wyif] twice; rep from * to end.
Row 16: *P1, [sl 1 wyib] twice, p1; rep from * to end.
Rows 17–24: Repeat Rows 13–16.
Repeat Rows 1–24 for pattern.

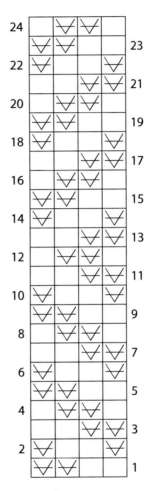

Stitches

☐ k on the RS; p on the WS
⋁ sl 1 wyif on the RS; sl 1 wyib on the WS

Round

Rnd 1: *K2, [sl 1 wyif] twice; rep from * to end.
Rnd 2: *Sl 1 wyif, k2, sl 1 wyif; rep from * to end.
Rnd 3: *[S1 wyif] twice, k2; rep from * to end.
Rnd 4: *K1, [sl 1 wyif] twice, k1; rep from * to end.
Rnd 5–12: Repeat Rnds 1–4.
Rnd 13: *[S1 wyif] twice, k2; rep from * to end.
Rnd 14: *Sl 1 wyif, k2, sl 1 wyif; rep from * to end.
Rnd 15: *K2, [sl 1 wyif] twice; rep from * to end.
Rnd 16: *K1, [sl 1 wyif] twice, k1; rep from * to end.
Rnd 17–24: Repeat Rnds 13–16.
Repeat Rnds 1–24 for pattern.

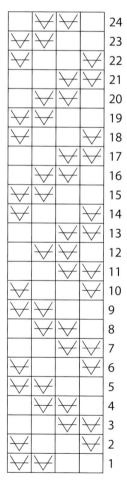

Stitches

☐ k

⋎ sl 1 wyif

Special Stitches:

Sl 1 wyib With the working yarn in back, insert the right needle into the next stitch as if to purl and transfer the stitch from the left needle to the right.
Sl 1 wyif With the working yarn in front, insert the right needle into the next stitch as if to purl and transfer the stitch from the left needle to the right.

Faux Cable

Flat

Row 1 (RS): *P1, k3; rep from * to end.
Row 2 (WS): *P3, k1; rep from * to end.
Row 3: *P1, sl 1, k2, psso; rep from * to end.
Row 4: *P1, yo, p1, k1; rep from * to end.
Repeat Rows 1–4 for pattern.

Stitches

☐ k on the RS; p on the WS

• k on the RS; p on the WS

▨ No stitch

⊠ sl 1, k2, psso

○ yo

Round

Rnds 1–2: *P1, k3; rep from * to end.
Rnd 3: *P1, sl 1, k2, psso; rep from * to end.
Rnd 4: *P1, k1, yo, k1; rep from * to end.
Repeat Rnds 1–4 for pattern.

Stitches

☐	k
●	p
▨	No stitch
▧	sl 1, k2, psso
○	yo

Stitches

☐	k on the RS; p on the WS
⋎	sl 1 wyif

Another Woven Column

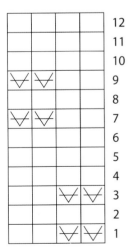

Round

Rnd 1: *[Sl 1 wyif] twice, k2; rep from * to end.
Rnd 2: Knit.
Rnd 3: Rep Rnd 1.
Rnds 4–6: Knit.
Rnd 7: *K2, [sl 1 wyif] twice; rep from * to end.
Rnd 8: Knit.
Rnd 9: Rep Rnd 7.
Rnds 10–12: Knit.
Repeat Rnds 1–12 for pattern.

Flat

Row 1 (RS): *[Sl 1 wyif] twice, k2; rep from * to end.
Row 2 (WS): Purl.
Rows 3–4: Rep Rows 1–2.
Row 5: Knit.
Row 6: Purl.
Row 7: *K2, [sl 1 wyif] twice; rep from * to end.
Row 8: Purl.
Rows 9–10: Rep Rows 7–8.
Row 11: Knit.
Row 12: Purl.
Repeat Rows 1–12 for pattern.

Stitches

☐	k
⋎	sl 1 wyif

Special Stitch:

Sl 1 wyif With the working yarn in front, insert the right needle into the next stitch as if to purl and transfer the stitch from the left needle to the right.

High Lift

Flat

Row 1 (RS): *[Sl 1 wyif] 3 times, k1; rep from * to end.
Row 2 (WS): Purl.
Rows 3–4: Rep Rows 1–2.
Row 5: *K1, k1-us, k2; rep from * to end.
Row 6: Purl.
Repeat Rows 1–6 for pattern.

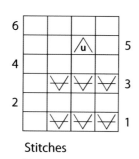

Stitches

☐	k on the RS; p on the WS
⋎	sl 1 wyif
⟋u⟍	k1-us

Round

Rnd 1: *[Sl 1 wyif] 3 times, k1; rep from * to end.
Rnd 2: Knit.
Rnds 3–4: Rep Rnds 1–2.
Rnd 5: *K1, k1-us, k2; rep from * to end.
Rnd 6: Knit.
Repeat Rnds 1–6 for pattern.

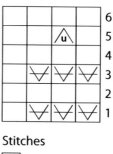

Stitches

☐	k
⋎	sl 1 wyif
⟋u⟍	k1-us

Special Stitches:

K1-us Insert right-hand needle under the 2 slipped stitch strands at the front of the work, to lift them up to the current row; knit into the next stitch as normal, pass 2 slipped strands over the stitch just knit.

Sl 1 wyif With the working yarn in front, insert the right needle into the next stitch as if to purl and transfer the stitch from the left needle to the right.

Short Twisted Zig

Flat

Row 1 (RS): *K2, RT; rep from * to end.
Row 2 (WS): *P1, sl 1 wyif, p2; rep from * to end.
Row 3: *K1, RT, k1; rep from * to end.
Row 4: *P2, sl 1 wyif, p1; rep from * to end.
Row 5: *RT, k2; rep from * to end.
Row 6: P3, sl 1 wyif; rep from * to end.
Row 7: *LT, k2; rep from * to end.
Row 8: *P2, sl 1 wyif, p1; rep from * to end.
Row 9: *K1, LT, k1; rep from * to end.
Row 10: *P1, sl 1 wyif, p2; rep from * to end.
Row 11: *K2, LT; rep from * to end.
Row 12: *Sl 1 wyif, p3; rep from * to end.
Repeat Rows 1–12 for pattern.

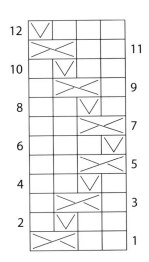

Stitches

⨉	RT
☐	k on the RS; p on the WS
⋁	sl 1 wyif
⨉	LT

Round

Rnd 1: *K2, RT; rep from * to end.
Rnd 2: *K2, sl 1 wyib, k1; rep from * to end.
Rnd 3: *K1, RT, k1; rep from * to end.
Rnd 4: *K1, sl 1 wyib, k2; rep from * to end.
Rnd 5: *RT, k2; rep from * to end.
Rnd 6: *Sl 1 wyib, k3; rep from * to end.
Rnd 7: *LT, k2; rep from * to end.
Rnd 8: *K1, sl 1 wyib, k2; rep from * to end.
Rnd 9: *K1, LT, k1; rep from * to end.
Rnd 10: *K2, sl 1 wyib, k1; rep from * to end.
Rnd 11: *K2, LT; rep from * to end.
Rnd 12: *K3, sl 1 wyib; rep from * to end.
Repeat Rnds 1–12 for pattern.

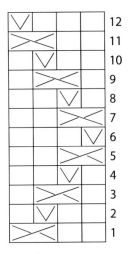

Stitches

⨉	RT
☐	k
⋁	sl 1 wyib
⨉	LT

Special Stitches:

LT Left Twist: Skip the next stitch and knit into the back of the 2nd stitch; leave on the left-hand needle; then knit the skipped stitch; slip both stitches off the left-hand needle together.

Sl 1 wyib With the working yarn in back, insert the right needle into the next stitch as if to purl and transfer the stitch from the left needle to the right.

Sl 1 wyif With the working yarn in front, insert the right needle into the next stitch as if to purl and transfer the stitch from the left needle to the right.

RT Right Twist: Skip the next stitch and knit into the 2nd stitch; leave on the left-hand needle; then knit the skipped stitch; slip both stitches off the left-hand needle together.

Cartridge Rib

Row 1 (RS): *K2, sl 1 wyif, k1; rep from * to end.
Row 2 (WS): *K3, sl 1 wyif; rep from * to end.
Repeat Rows 1–2 for pattern.

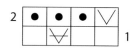

Stitches

☐ k on the RS; p on the WS

⊻ sl 1 wyif on the RS

⦿ p on the RS; k on the WS

⊽ sl 1 wyif on the WS

Round

Rnd 1: *K2, sl 1 wyif, k1; rep from * to end.
Rnd 2: *Sl 1 wyib, p3; rep from * to end.
Repeat Rnds 1–2 for pattern.

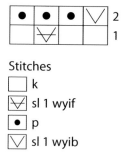

Stitches

☐ k

⊻ sl 1 wyif

⦿ p

⊽ sl 1 wyib

Special Stitches:

Sl 1 wyib With the working yarn in back, insert the right needle into the next stitch as if to purl and transfer the stitch from the left needle to the right.

Sl 1 wyif With the working yarn in front, insert the right needle into the next stitch as if to purl and transfer the stitch from the left needle to the right.

Purl Twist

Flat

Row 1 (RS): Knit.
Row 2 (WS): *PT; rep from * to end.
Row 3: Knit.
Row 4: *P1, *PT; rep from * to last st, p1.
Repeat Rows 1–4 for pattern.

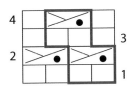

Stitches

 k on the RS; p on the WS

[⊠•] PT

Borders

— rep

Round

Rnd 1: Knit.
Rnd 2: *RT; rep from * to end.
Rnd 3: Knit.
Rnd 4: *K1, *RT; rep from * to last st, k1.
Repeat Rnds 1–4 for pattern.

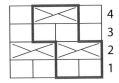

Stitches

 k

[⊠] RT

Borders

— rep

Special Stitches:

PT Purl Twist: Purl 2 stitches together, but do not drop from needle; purl the first stitch again and then slip both stitches from the needle together.

RT Right Twist: Skip the next stitch and knit into the 2nd stitch; leave on the left-hand needle; then knit the skipped stitch; slip both stitches off the left-hand needle together.

Fisherman's Rib

Flat

Row 1 (RS): Knit.
Row 2 (WS): *K1, k1b; rep from * to end.
Row 3: *K1, k1b; rep from * to end.
Repeat Rows 2–3 for pattern.

Stitches

☐ k on the RS; p on the WS

[•] p on the RS; k on the WS

[⋔] k1b on WS

[⋔] k1b on RS

Borders

— rep

Rnd 1: Knit.
Rnd 2: *P1b, p1; rep from * to end.
Rnd 3: *K1, k1b; rep from * to end.
Repeat Rnds 2–3 for pattern.

Stitches

	k
•	p
⋔	p1b
⋔	k1b

Borders

— rep

Special Stitches:
K1b Knit into stitch 1 row below.
P1b Purl into stitch 1 row below.

Bee Stitch

Flat

Row 1 (RS): Knit.
Row 2 (WS): *K1b, k1; rep from * to end.
Row 3: Knit.
Row 4: *K1, k1b; rep from * to end.
Row 5: Knit.
Repeat Rows 2–5 for pattern.

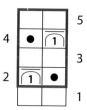

Stitches

⋔	k1b
	k on the RS; p on the WS
•	p on the RS; k on the WS

Borders

— rep

Round

Rnd 1: Purl.
Rnd 2: *K1, k1b; rep from * to end.
Rnd 3: Purl.
Rnd 4: *K1b, k1; rep from * to end.
Rnd 5: Purl.
Repeat Rnds 2–5 for pattern.

Stitches

	k
•	p
⋔	k1b

Borders

— rep

Special Stitches:
K1b Knit into stitch 1 row below.
P1b Purl into stitch 1 row below.

Slipped Comb

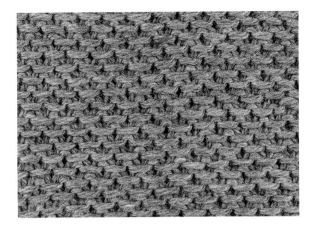

Flat

Row 1 (RS): Knit.
Row 2 (WS): *K1, sl 1 wyib; rep from * to end.
Row 3: Knit.
Row 4: *Sl 1 wyib, k1; rep from * to end.
Repeat Rows 1–4 for pattern.

Stitches

☐	k on the RS; p on the WS
☐•	k on the RS; p on the WS
☒	sl 1 wyib

Round

Rnd 1: Knit.
Rnd 2: *Sl 1 wyif, p1; rep from * to end.
Rnd 3: Knit.
Rnd 4: *P1, sl 1 wyif; rep from * to end.
Repeat Rnds 1–4 for pattern.

Stitches

☐	k
☐•	p
☒	sl 1 wyif

Special Stitches:

Sl 1 wyib With the working yarn in back, insert the right needle into the next stitch as if to purl and transfer the stitch from the left needle to the right.
Sl 1 wyif With the working yarn in front, insert the right needle into the next stitch as if to purl and transfer the stitch from the left needle to the right.

Long Zags

Flat

Row 1 (RS): *K3, k-w2; rep from * to end.
Row 2 (WS): *S1 wyif, k3; rep from * to end.
Row 3: *K3, sl 1 wyib; rep from * to end.
Row 4: *S1 wyif, k3; rep from * to end.
Row 5: *RC-w2; rep from * to end.
Row 6: *K3, sl 1 wyif; rep from * to end.
Row 7: *S1, k3; rep from * to end.
Row 8: *K3, sl 1 wyif; rep from * to end.
Row 9: *LC-w2; rep from * to end.
Repeat Rows 2–9 for pattern.

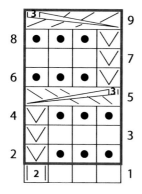

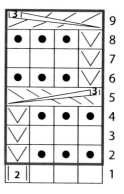

Stitches

 k-w2

☐ k on the RS; p on the WS

▽ sl 1 wyib on the RS; sl 1 wyif on the WS

• p on the RS; k on the WS

RC-w2

LC-w2

Borders

— rep

Stitches

k-w2

☐ k

▽ sl 1 wyib

• p

RC-w2

LC-w2

Borders

— rep

Round

Rnd 1: *K3, k-w2; rep from * to end.
Rnd 2: *P3, sl 1 wyib; rep from * to end.
Rnd 3: *K3, sl 1 wyib; rep from * to end.
Rnd 4: Rep Rnd 2.
Rnd 5: *RC-w2; rep from * to end.
Rnd 6: *Sl 1 wyib, p3; rep from * to end.
Rnd 7: *S1, k3; rep from * to end.
Rnd 8: Rep Rnd 6.
Rnd 9: *LC-w2; rep from * to end.
Repeat Rnds 2–9 for pattern.

Special Stitches:

K-w2 Knit, wrapping yarn 2 times around the needle and dropping the extra wrap on the next row.

LC-w2 Left Cross with 2 Wraps: Slip the next stitch onto a cable needle and hold to front; k3, k-w2 into stitch on cable needle.

Sl 1 wyib With the working yarn in back, insert the right needle into the next stitch as if to purl and transfer the stitch from the left needle to the right.

Sl 1 wyif With the working yarn in front, insert the right needle into the next stitch as if to purl and transfer the stitch from the left needle to the right.

RC-w2 Right Cross with 2 Wraps: Slip the next 3 stitches onto a cable needle and hold to back; k-w2 into next stitch, k3 from cable needle.

Portcullis

Flat

Row 1 (RS): *Kyok in 1, sk2p; rep from * to end.
Row 2 (WS): Purl.
Repeat Rows 1–2 for pattern.

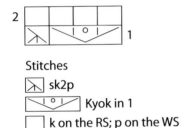

Stitches

⧄	sk2p
⌄◦	Kyok in 1
☐	k on the RS; p on the WS

Round

Rnd 1: *Kyok in 1, sk2p; rep from * to end.
Rnd 2: Knit.
Repeat Rnds 1–2 for pattern.

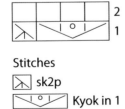

Stitches

⧄	sk2p
⌄◦	Kyok in 1
☐	k

Special Stitches:

Kyok in 1 Knit, leaving the stitch on the needle, then yarn over, and then knit into the same stitch.
Sk2p Slip one stitch knitwise and then knit 2 stitches together and pass the slipped stitch over.

Linen Ridge

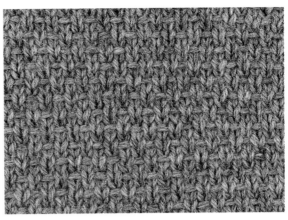

Flat

Row 1 (RS): Knit.
Row 2 (WS): *Sl 1 wyib, p1; rep from * to end.
Row 3: Knit.
Row 4: *P1, sl 1 wyib; rep from * to end.
Repeat Rows 1–4 for pattern.

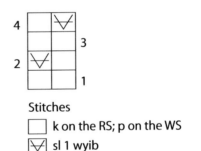

Stitches

☐	k on the RS; p on the WS
⩔	sl 1 wyib

Round

Rnd 1: Knit.
Rnd 2: *K1, sl 1 wyif; rep from * to end.
Rnd 3: Knit.
Rnd 4: *Sl 1 wyif, k1; rep from * to end.
Repeat Rnds 1–4 for pattern.

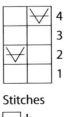

Stitches

☐	k
⩔	sl 1 wyif

Special Stitches:

Sl 1 wyib With the working yarn in back, insert the right needle into the next stitch as if to purl and transfer the stitch from the left needle to the right.

Sl 1 wyif With the working yarn in front, insert the right needle into the next stitch as if to purl and transfer the stitch from the left needle to the right.

Tuck Stitch

Flat

Row 1 (RS): Knit.
Row 2 (WS): Purl.
Rows 3–4: Rep Rows 1–2.
Row 5: *K4b, k3; rep from * to end.
Row 6: Purl.
Row 7: Knit.
Rows 8–9: Rep Rows 6–7.
Row 10: Purl.
Row 11: *K2, k4b, k1; rep from * to end.
Row 12: Purl.
Repeat Rows 1–12 for pattern.

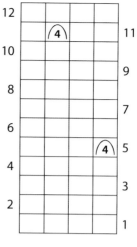

Stitches

☐ k on the RS; p on the WS

④ k4b

Round

Rnds 1–4: Knit.
Rnd 5: *K4b, k3; rep from * to end.
Rnds 6–10: Knit.
Rnd 11: *K2, k4b, k1; rep from * to end.
Rnd 12: Knit.
Repeat Rnds 1–12 for pattern.

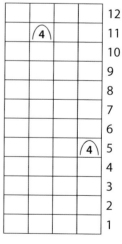

Stitches

☐ k

④ k4b

Special Stitch:

K4b Knit into the stitch 4 rows below.

Double Rice Stitch

Flat

Row 1 (RS): Knit.
Row 2 (WS): *K-tbl, p1; rep from * to end.
Row 3: Knit.
Row 4: *P1, k-tbl; rep from * to end.
Repeat Rows 1–4 for pattern.

Stitches

☐ k on the RS; p on the WS
⟨⟩ k-tbl

Round

Rnd 1: Knit.
Rnd 2: *K1, p-tbl; rep from * to end.
Rnd 3: Knit.
Rnd 4: *P-tbl, k1; rep from * to end.
Repeat Rnds 1–4 for pattern.

Stitches

☐ k
⟨⟩ p-tbl

Special Stitches:

K-tbl Knit through the back loop.
P-tbl Purl through the back loop.

CHAPTER 7

A FAB FINISH

Blocking

Washing and blocking your pieces, especially for those that will be seamed, is essential for a beautiful fabric. The chemistry of water and/or heat plus drying teaches the stitches to hold hands nicely, lining everything up and smoothing out the lumps. It neatens the edging, opens up lace, and helps cables pop up.

TOOLS FOR BLOCKING

Iron or steamer. I have a Conair Garment Steamer that emits continuous steam.

Rust-proof pins.

Lace wires: a good option for shawl or scarf knitters. I have them but rarely use them.

Surface. You can use pre-marked blocking boards, an ironing board or table, a rug covered with a sheet, a mattress, or even a dressmaker's form.

STEAMING

Steaming is my personal favorite method because it is quick. However, it doesn't work quite as well for synthetics, and I definitely do not recommend it for metal, bamboo, or most cellulose fibers.

Begin by pinning the edges down, matching the measurements to the schematic measurements, and gently steam your piece. If you are using an iron, do not press it to the fabric—keep the steam about an inch above the fabric.

While the piece is still damp, use your fingers to pinch any cables or pull open any eyelets. I typically pin my edges down to smooth them out for an easier seaming process.

When it comes to ribbing, don't pin it out. Instead, pat it down to condense and then permeate with steam. Let it dry and then give a few quick pulls widthwise, followed by a few quick pulls lengthwise. This process really makes it fluffier and more pronounced.

WET BLOCKING

Wet blocking isn't hard, but it can be time-consuming and a space hog. Wet blocking is necessary for most fine-gauge lace (lace weight), for blooming certain wools, or for metal, bamboo, and other fibers not recommended for steam.

Soak the pieces in a sink full of lukewarm or cool water. I often drop in a bit of no-rinse wool wash to help reduce some of the "wooly" odor or vinegar smell that hand-dyed yarns can initially have.

Lift the wet pieces out without stretching them, roll them up, and squeeze out the excess

water. Then lay them on a towel, roll them up again, and step on the towel to remove the last bit of water.

Lay out your pieces on a safe surface, such as a mattress or blocking boards, and pin to shape. This is where you can have a lot of fun by creating fun points and scallops with your pins.

Seaming

SEAMING BOUND-OFF EDGES

This often includes shoulder seams and arm-hole bind-off sections in sweaters and sleeves. There isn't much guesswork—just connect "V" stitch to "V" stitch.

Begin by placing your pieces, RS facing, next to each other, bound-off edge to bound-off edge.

1. From beneath the piece on the left, insert your needle into the visible gap between the selvedge edge and the first stitch, just below the bind-off.

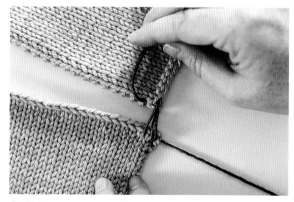

2. Bring your needle to the other piece and, from beneath, bring it up between the selvedge edge and first stitch.

3. Bring your needle back to the first piece; insert it into the very hole you came out of with your yarn. Push the needle through and out the other side of the entire "V" stitch just below the bind-off.

4. Move to the other piece; insert your needle into the very same hole that your yarn came out of before. Push the needle all the way through and out the other side of the entire "V" stitch just below that bind-off.

Repeat Steps 3–4 for a couple of stitches (about 4–6 depending on weight of yarn).

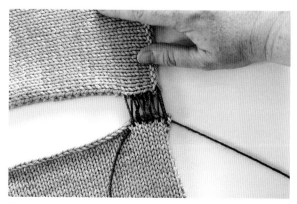

5. Grab the 2 ends of the sewing yarn and pull snug (don't yank).

Repeat Steps 3–5 until you have seamed the length. Weave in your ends and voilà!

SEAMING SELVEDGE EDGES

Note: Picking up two bars makes for a more elastic seam, but I prefer to pick up one bar in the set-up phase.

Begin by placing your pieces, RS facing, next to each other, selvedge edge to selvedge edge.

SET-UP PHASE

1. From beneath the piece on the left, insert your needle into the top strand of the cast-on edge, between the selvedge edge and the first stitch.

2. Bring your needle to the other piece and, from beneath, pick up the top cast-on strand, between the selvedge edge and first stitch.

3. Bring your needle back to the first piece, and insert it into the very hole you came out of with your yarn. Angle your needle under the Garter stitch bar and up through the hole on the other side of the bar.

4. Move to the other piece; insert your needle into the very same hole that your yarn came out of before. Angle your needle under the Garter stitch bar and up through the hole on the other side of the bar.

REGULAR SEAMING PHASE

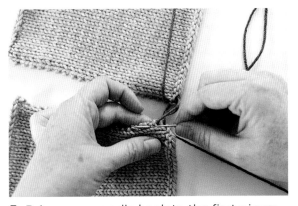

5. Bring your needle back to the first piece; insert it into the very hole you came out of with your yarn. Angle your needle under the next 2 bars. Push your needle out the hole on the other side of the second bar.

6. Move to the other piece; insert your needle into the very same hole that your yarn came out of before. Angle your needle under 2 Garter stitch bars and out through the hole.

Repeat Steps 5–6 for a couple of stitches (about 4–6 depending on weight of yarn).

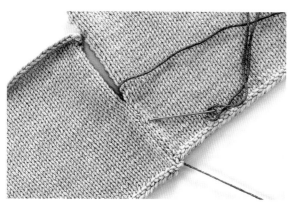

7. Grab the two ends of your seaming yarn and give a gentle pull (don't yank!) to tighten up the stitches.

Repeat Steps 5–7 until you have seamed the length. Weave in your ends.

SEAMING SELVEDGE EDGES TO BOUND-OFF OR CAST-ON EDGES

This little area can be tricky because selvedge edges aren't the same width as regular stitches. Don't be afraid to experiment with the number of bars you pick up per stitch. I generally pick up 1 bar, then 2, then 1, then 2, and so on.

1. Starting out as indicated in the above tutorials, insert your needle into the "V" stitch right under the bind-off edge.

2. Bring your needle up and insert it into 2 bars of the selvedge edge.

3. Insert your needle into where it came out from before, and bring it out the other side of the "V" stitch.

4. Insert your needle into the spot it came out from before and go under 1 bar of the selvedge edge.

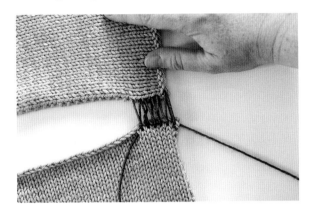

Repeat Steps 1–4 until you are done.

Picking Up Stitches

PICKING UP STITCHES FROM A BIND-OFF OR CAST-ON EDGE

For every bound-off or cast-on stitch, you'll pick up one stitch.

1. Insert the tip of your right-hand needle underneath the sideways "V" of the bind-off/cast-on stitch all the way through to the other side.

2. Wrap your yarn around, just as you normally would when knitting.

3. Using your needle, pull that wrapped yarn back through where you came from, to the front. You've picked up one stitch.

Repeat Steps 1–3 until you have picked up the specified number of stitches. When finished, you'll turn your work so that the wrong side is facing, to begin working the pattern.

PICKING UP STITCHES FROM A SIDE OR SELVEDGE EDGE

1. Insert the tip of your right-hand needle through the selvedge hole all the way through to the other side.

2. Wrap your yarn around, just as you normally would when knitting.

3. Using your needle, pull that wrapped yarn back through the hole to the front. You've picked up one stitch.

Repeat Steps 1–3 until you have picked up the specified number of stitches. When finished, you'll turn your work so that the wrong side is facing, to begin working the pattern.

CHAPTER 8

SPECIAL TECHNIQUES

CABLE CAST-ON

1. Insert the tip of the right-hand needle between the first and second stitch on the left-hand needle.

2. Wrap your yarn around the right tip just as if you were knitting a regular stitch. Pull that loop through between the two stitches to the front.

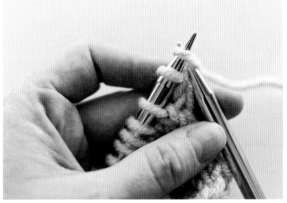

3. Place that loop onto the left needle in front of the first stitch. You've now cast-on one stitch.

Repeat Steps 1–3 until you have cast on all the stitches required.

KITCHENER STITCH

You'll need 2 needles and a tapestry needle to work this grafting stitch.

1. Make sure your stitches are divided evenly between 2 needles and hold them parallel to each other with the right sides of the fabric facing out and the wrong side of the fabric facing in. Thread your tapestry needle with yarn twice the length of the piece you are seaming. Imagine your tapestry needle is like a knitting needle and insert it into the first stitch on the front needle as if to purl. Pull the yarn all the way through, leaving the stitch on the needle.

2. Next, insert the tapestry needle through the first stitch on the back needle as if to knit. Pull the yarn through, leaving the stitch on the needle and being careful that it doesn't wrap around the front needle in the process.

3. Insert the tapestry needle through the first stitch on the front needle as if to knit.

4. Pull the yarn all the way through and drop the stitch off the front needle.

5. Insert the tapestry needle into the next stitch on the front needle and pull the yarn through, leaving the stitch on the needle.

6. Moving to the back needle, insert the tapestry needle into the first stitch as if to purl.

8. Insert the tapestry needle into the next stitch on the back needle as if to knit.

7. Pull the yarn all the way through and drop the stitch from the needle.

Repeat Steps 3–8 until all stitches have been worked.

S2k1p (slip 2, knit 1, psso)

1. Insert your right-hand needle into the next 2 stitches as if to knit, but . . .

4. Insert the tip of the left-hand needle into the slipped stitches and . . .

2. . . . slip them over, together, unworked to the right-hand needle.

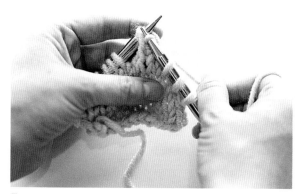

5. . . . lift them up and over the stitch just knit, right off the needle.

3. Knit the next stitch like normal.

You've decreased 2 stitches.

Sk2p (slip 1, ktog, psso)

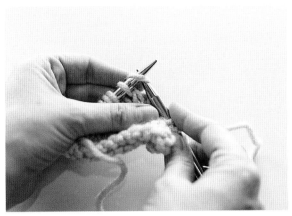

1. Insert your right-hand needle into the next stitch as if to knit, and . . .

4. Insert the tip of the left-hand needle into the slipped stitch and lift it up and over the 2 stitches you knit together and off the right-hand needle.

2. . . . slip it over unworked to the right-hand needle.

You've decreased 2 stitches.

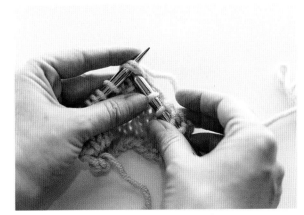

3. Knit the next 2 stitches together.

M1 (Make 1)

1. With your left needle tip, lift up the horizontal bar between the stitches, from front to back.

2. Knit it through the back loop. You've increased 1 stitch.

Kfb (knit front and back)

1. Knit into the next stitch like normal and . . .

2. . . . pull your new loop through to the front.

3. Before dropping that old stitch from the left-hand needle, take the tip of your right-hand needle and insert it into the back loop of the same stitch you just knit and . . .

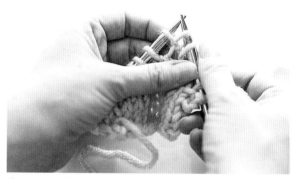

4. . . . pull your yarn through to the front.

5. Now you can drop that old stitch from the left-hand needle. You've increased 1 stitch.

K1b (knit one below)

1. Insert right-hand needle into the hole 1 stitch below the stitch on the needle.

2. Wrap yarn around like a normal knit stitch and pull through to the front. Drop the old stitch.

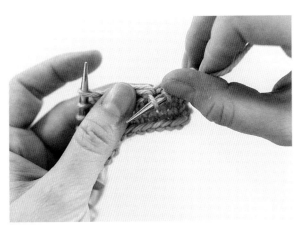

3. You'll find 2 bars wrapped around the new stitch on the back.

K4b (knit four below)

1. Insert right-hand needle into the 4th hole, 4 rows below the stitch on the needle.

2. Wrap yarn around like a normal knit stitch and pull through to the front. Drop the old stitch.

3. You'll find 5 bars wrapped around the new stitch on the back (they will be loose).

(K1, p1, k1) in 1 (knit 1, purl 1, knit 1 in same stitch)

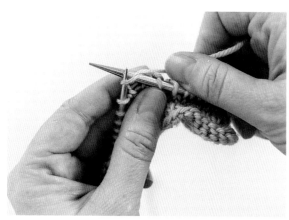

1. Knit, leaving the old stitch on the left-hand needle.

2. Bring yarn to the front and purl into the same stitch.

3. Bring yarn to the back and knit again into the same stitch.

4. Drop the old stitch from the left-hand needle. 2 stitches have been increased.

Wrap KYOK (wrap, knit, yarn over, knit)

1. Slip the next 3 sts, as if to purl, to the right-hand needle.

2. Lift the 1st slipped st up and over the last 2 sts, off the needle.

3. Slide the 2 wrapped sts back to the left-hand needle and then k1, yo, k1.

1/1 RC (1 over 1 right cross)

1. Slip 1 stitch to cable needle and hold in back.

2. Knit the next stitch on the left-hand needle.

3. Knit the stitch from cable needle.

Other cabled variations are worked similarly. Follow the instructions for how many stitches to place on cable needles and how to work the stitches (whether knit or purl).

3. Knit the stitch from the cable needle.

1/1 LC (1 over 1 left cross)

1. Slip 1 stitch to cable needle and hold in front of knitting.

Other cabled variations are worked similarly. Follow the instructions for how many stitches to place on cable needles and how to work the stitches (whether knit or purl).

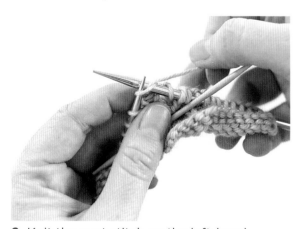

2. Knit the next stitch on the left-hand needle.

MAKE ROSETTE

LT (left twist)

1. P2tog, but do not drop the sts from the left-hand needle.

2. K2tog in the same sts.

1. Skip the next stitch and knit into the back of the 2nd stitch, leaving it on the left-hand needle.

3. Then slip sts from left-hand needle.

2. Then knit the skipped stitch.

3. Slip both stitches off the left-hand needle together.

2. Then knit the skipped stitch.

RT (right twist)

3. Slip both stitches off the left-hand needle together.

1. Skip the next stitch and knit into the 2nd stitch, leaving it on the left-hand needle.

K-w2 (knit, wrap 2)

1. Knit, wrapping yarn 2 times around the needle.

2. Then drop the extra wrap on the next row.

LC-w2 (left cross with 2 wraps)

1. Slip the next stitch onto a cable needle and hold to front.

2. Knit 3 stitches.

3. K-w2 into stitch on cable needle (and drop the extra wrap on next row).

RC-w2 (right cross with 2 wraps)

1. Slip the next 3 stitches onto a cable needle and hold to back.

2. K-w2 into next stitch.

3. Knit 3 from cable needle.

Kyok in 1 (knit, yarn over, knit in same stitch)

1. Knit, leaving the stitch on the needle.

2. Yarn over.

3. And then knit into the same stitch again.

4. Drop the old stitch from the left-hand needle.

Abbreviations

The pattern recipes utilize these standard abbreviations.

Approx.	Approximately	**P2tog**	Purl two stitches together
Beg	Begin(ing)	**Rem**	Remain(ing)
BO	Bind off	**Rep(s)**	Repeat(s)
BOR	Beginning of round	**RH**	Right-hand
CO	Cast on	**Rnd(s)**	Round(s)
Cont	Continue	**RS**	Right side
Dec(s)	Decrease(s)	**Sl**	Slip
Dpn(s)	Double-pointed needles	**Ssk**	Slip, slip, knit: Sl next st as if to knit, the next stitch as if to purl, and then insert the left-hand needle into the front of both stitches and knit together through the back loop
Est	Establish(ed)		
Foll	Following		
Inc(s)	Increase(s)		
K	Knit		
K2tog	Knit two stitches together	**sssk**	Sl next 2 sts as if to knit, the next st as if to purl, and then insert the left hand needle into the front of both sts and knit together through the back loops
K3tog	Knit three stitches together		
Kfb	Knit front and back		
LH	Left-hand	**St(s)**	Stitch(es)
M	Marker	**St st**	Stockinette st
M1	Make 1	**Tbl**	Through the back loop(s)
P	Purl	**Tog**	Together
Patt	Pattern	**WS**	Wrong side
Pm	Place marker	**Wyib**	With yarn in back
Psso	Pass the slipped stitch over	**Wyif**	With yarn in front
Pwise	Purlwise	**Yo**	Yarn over

Material Resources and Credits

Overwhelming thanks to the companies who provided yarn and resources to make this book possible! Their beautiful fibers are truly the star of the show.

SweetGeorgia Yarns
www.sweetgeorgiayarns.com

Lion Brand Yarn Company
www.lionbrandyarn.com

Knit One, Crochet Too, Inc.
www.knitonecrochettoo.com

Plymouth Yarn Company, Inc.
www.plymouthyarn.com

Anzula
www.anzula.com

Red Heart
www.redheart.com

Premier Yarns
www.premieryarns.com

Knit Picks
www.knitpicks.com

Patons and Bernat from Yarnspirations
www.yarnspirations.com

Akerworks, Inc. (gauge tool)
www.akerworks.com

Knitter's Pride (knit blockers)
www.knitterspride.com

Acknowledgments

I am incredibly blessed to have such a huge support network in my life through my family and friends. Their encouragement, hugs, laughter, late-night texts, uplifting emails, and, dare I say, even eye-rolling at my dramatic moments have helped my confidence as I step closer to the person, designer, and author I strive to be one day.

I especially could not do any part of my job (or most aspects of life) without my husband, Jeremy, by my side. He and my girls, Ayla and Sophie, are my biggest cheerleaders, making me feel as if I can take on the world. They are the inspiration that lights everything I do.

My deepest love and gratitude to my mom, Cynthia, for the laughs but even more for the advice and support that help me think through the puzzles.

SO many thanks to my co-workers and friends at SweetGeorgia Yarns: Felicia, Teresa, Hubert, Brigid, Leah, Charlotte, Jessica, Yammie, David, Heather, Hoi, Eugene, Deborah, and Allison. I literally could not have taken on a book without their unending reassurance and creative energy (and yarn support). Being on this team is one of the most amazing things I could ask for.

My sample knitters for this book are the biggest blessings on this planet: Rose Tussing, Danielle Cohen, Abby Martin, Jessica Parker, Jessica Anderson, and Elke at Knit-Smile-Enjoy. You guys are invaluable!

To my dearest friends who have been by my side mentally and emotionally throughout this whole project—Cat Whitlock, Mary Beth Temple, Lindsey Stephens, Rose Tussing, Jen Cook, Corrina Ferguson, Kara Gott Warner, Amy Alcorn, Jill Wright, and Adam and Julia Wilson—go my unending love, raised glasses, and plentiful "I owe you one's."

And finally, many thanks to my editor, Candi Derr, for her encouragement from the beginning. I couldn't ask for a better one.